Wild Orchids of the Northeast

UNIVERSITY PRESS OF FLORIDA

Florida A&M University, Tallahassee
Florida Atlantic University, Boca Raton
Florida Gulf Coast University, Ft. Myers
Florida International University, Miami
Florida State University, Tallahassee
University of Central Florida, Orlando
University of Florida, Gainesville
University of North Florida, Jacksonville
University of South Florida, Tampa
University of West Florida, Pensacola

*Platanthera pallida*, pale fringed orchis

# *Wild Orchids of the Northeast*

New England, New York, Pennsylvania, and New Jersey

**Paul Martin Brown**

*with original artwork by Stan Folsom*

University Press of Florida
Gainesville
Tallahassee
Tampa
Boca Raton
Pensacola
Orlando
Miami
Jacksonville
Ft. Myers

12 11 10 09 08 07 6 5 4 3 2 1

Library of Congress Cataloging-in-Publication Data
Brown, Paul Martin.
Wild orchids of the Northeast: New England, New York, Pennsylvania, and New Jersey / Paul Martin Brown; drawings by Stan Folsom.
p. cm.
Includes bibliographical references and index.
ISBN-13: 978-0-8130-3034-0 (alk. paper)
1. Orchids—Northeastern States—Identification. I. Title.
QK495.O64B7389 2006
584'.40974—dc22
2006023038

The University Press of Florida is the scholarly publishing agency for the State University System of Florida, comprising Florida A&M University, Florida Atlantic University, Florida Gulf Coast University, Florida International University, Florida State University, University of Central Florida, University of Florida, University of North Florida, University of South Florida, and University of West Florida.

University Press of Florida
15 Northwest 15th Street
Gainesville, FL 32611-2079
http://www.upf.com

To Charles J. Sheviak, Ph.D.

Thank you, Chuck, for all of the help and encouragement you have given to so many over the years!

## *A Reminder*

Our wild orchids are a precious resource. For that reason they should never be collected from their native habitats, either for ornament or for home gardens. All orchids grow in association with specific fungi and these fungi are rarely present out of the orchids' original home. Searching for and finding many of these choice botanical treasures is one of the greatest pleasures for both professional and amateur botanists. Please leave them for others to enjoy.

# Contents

# *Foreword*

If we exclude those species found in Florida, the northeastern area of the United States covered by this book contains nearly one-half of all the orchid species found in this country. In terms of knowledge of these approximately sixty wild orchid species, including their variations, color phases and forms, distribution, rarity, and current taxonomic status, Paul Martin Brown is uniquely qualified to guide readers of this work through their fascinating world. The text you now hold in your hands will answer all your orchid questions, so this foreword will be employed to cast some illumination on the author of this guide, Paul Martin Brown.

My lovely wife Valerie first met Paul Martin Brown on a dismal rainy day in August of 1995 when she accompanied me to a "secret location" near the base of Cape Cod. The purpose of our meeting was to find and photograph *Spiranthes vernalis*, and whatever other orchid species we might encounter. Immediately after I provided the requisite social introductions, Paul's first comment to Valerie was something to the effect that he was pleasantly surprised she was even willing to speak with him. We all smiled or laughed at Paul's candor, for we all understood that for the last year my wonderful wife of less than five years had been too frequent1y abandoned—temporarily widowed at home while a disproportionately large amount of my life was consumed by an "orchid addiction," a botanical obsession that Paul was cheerfully aiding and abetting. Part of the intensity of my orchid obsession sprang from the fact that I was preparing a manuscript on the orchids of the Northeast for Syracuse University Press. The final deadline for submission was quickly closing in, hence my nonstop travels around the Northeast capturing as many orchid images on film as time, weather, luck, and nature would allow.

I originally met Paul Martin Brown in August of 1994, precisely one year before my wife first made his acquaintance. I had been making innumerable telephone calls around the Northeast pursuing various aspects of orchid information, and Shirley Curtis, an avid orchid enthusiast, asked me if I knew of Paul Martin Brown. I did not, but following her informative leads less than twenty-four hours later I had met and was accompanying Paul Martin Brown and his orchid associates on an outing to eastern Long Island. That day, in their company, I studied and photographed the orange fringed orchis, *Platanthera ciliaris*, the orange crested orchis, *P. cristata*, and the endemic pale fringed orchis, *P. pallida*, plus the very rare (in the Northeast) crane-fly orchis, *Tipularia discolor*. On the way home, courtesy of additional advice Paul provided, I added the elusive three birds orchid, *Triphora trianthophora* to the weekend's successes.

That first meeting and field trip became an often repeated ritual. I would mentally zero in on a different species of orchid or other wildflower on which I wished to set my photographic sights. (My orchid manuscript was an outgrowth of a series of general wildflower guides I was simultaneously preparing for Syracuse University Press.) I would make the call, and Paul would respond with informative advice, remarkably accurate verbal maps, or even guided field trips to locate my latest green grail. What is most noteworthy of all his assistance, and what I did not learn until some time later, was that during this same period Paul was also preparing a manuscript on the orchids of the Northeast, his for Cornell University Press. Rather than conceptualizing my work as competition, he later expressed the opinion and hope that the two works would be complementary (we ended up reviewing each other's books for the same publication). Paul continued to support my studies and efforts right up to the time both guides were released, coincidentally within a few weeks of each other in 1997. For his many assistances, I owe Paul Martin Brown a large debt and offer this foreword in recognition of that fact.

After 1997, to my wife's delight, my life slowed down. Now at a very leisurely pace, we finally completed our quest to photograph every species of orchid found in the Northeast. The intensity with which I had obsessed about orchids in the mid-90s was delineated by publishing deadlines and the geographic scope of my manuscript. Paul Martin Brown's obsessions are both grander and more constant in nature and the pace with which he continues to pursue wild orchids has remained undiminished. In this guide Paul shares his latest insights and information with all of us. This book will take the reader as far as possible without actually accompanying them on a guided field trip, but if this were possible I imagine Paul would agree to provide that service as well.

*William Kent Chapman*

# *Preface*

While I was teaching for the New England Wildflower Society from 1982 to 1994 it became apparent that the field trips and courses on native orchids were very popular, but there was no single reference that applied to the orchids found in the northeastern United States. *Stalking the Wild Orchids* (Brown, 1988) soon grew into *A Field and Study Guide to the Wild Orchids of New England and New York* (Brown, 1993). In 1997 we were fortunate to have Cornell University Press publish a complete reworking of the latter as *Wild Orchids of the Northeastern United States*. In both its original conception and later reworking, the line drawings of each species were the work of Stan Folsom. The last volume treated the orchids found throughout all of New England, New York, adjacent Pennsylvania, and New Jersey. A great deal has transpired since then and we have learned a considerable amount, both about the wild orchids and about field guides.

*Wild Orchids of the Northeast: New England, New York, Pennsylvania, and New Jersey* is not an attempt at a revision of the 1997 book but an entirely new work with many added features, facts, and photographs as well as numerous new drawings and paintings.

## A Note About Field Guides

The primary purpose of a field guide is to assist the user in identifying, in this case, the wild orchids of much of the northeastern United States. It is not intended to be either an exhaustive treatise on those species or the ultimate reference for that area. It is intended to be used primarily in the field and is designed for locating information easily while one foot is in the proverbial bog. The photographs have been taken in the field and are intended to illustrate the species as the user will see them. They are neither studio shots nor great works of art, just good diagnostic photos that portray the plants in their habitats. The line drawings also have the same goal, that of assisting the user in identifying the orchids. Many times line drawings can communicate different aspects of the plants that photographs cannot. The user is always encouraged to consult additional references for more detailed descriptions and regional accounts for individual species. It is always possible to write more on any subject and more certainly could be said for each species. But first and foremost this is a field guide. By combining the resources of the keys, descriptions, photographs, and line drawings, the user should be able, with relative simplicity, to identify all the orchids within the range of this book.

A work such as this, with such a large geographic scope, has involved the advice and counsel of many people. Those who facilitated the research and made major contributions to the information gathered here include Norris Williams, keeper, and Kent Perkins, manager, of the University of Florida Herbarium, Florida Museum of Natural History, Gainesville; Gustavo Romero, Orchid Herbarium of Oakes Ames, Judith Warnement, Botany Libraries, Harvard University Herbaria; Chuck Sheviak, Paul Catling; Shirley Curtis, Sally Puth, Anne Wagner, Scott Stewart, Ann Malmquist, Mark Larocque, Bill Chapman, Scott Shriver, John Carmody, Francis Underwood, Roger Bradley, Frank Di Stefano, and the late Philip Keenan.

The staff at University Press of Florida has continued its usual support, especially John Byram, editor in chief, and Gillian Hillis, managing editor, without whom this book would never have been completed. And, again, my partner Stan Folsom, whose paintings and drawings grace the pages of this book, has been a source of support and inspiration through the entire project. For that I am most grateful.

# *Abbreviations and Symbols*

ca. = about or approximate, in reference to measurements
cm = centimeter
*f.* = *filius*; son of, or the younger
m = meter
mm = millimeter
nm = nothomorph or nothovariety, indicating an intraspecific hybrid
subsp. = subspecies
var. = variety
× between or preceding a name denotes a hybrid or hybrid combination
* = naturalized
≠ = misapplied name

## Publications

AOS = American Orchid Society
*FNA* = *Flora of North America, North of Mexico* (volume 26, including the *Orchidaceae*)
INPI = International Plant Names Index
*NANOJ* = *North American Native Orchid Journal*

# *Part 1*

## Orchids and the Northeast

# The Northeast

For the purpose of this field guide the geographic area of the northeastern United States includes all of Maine, New Hampshire, Vermont, Massachusetts, Connecticut, Rhode Island, New York, Pennsylvania, and New Jersey, as shown in the map below.

## Orchids and the Northeast

Apart from the more comprehensive regional floras of the nineteenth and early twentieth centuries, the earliest publication that detailed what was known at that time concerning the wild orchids of New England was by Baldwin (1884). Deane, in 1891, published a brief but detailed and personal account of the New England species as an article in a larger periodical. The next two books devoted to orchids of the Northeast appeared almost simultaneously in the early years of the twentieth century—Grace Greylock Niles' classic *Bog Trotting for Orchids* (1904) and William Hamilton Gibson's *Our Native Orchids* (1905). Niles' work is packed full of personal anecdotes and frequently spotlights many other flowering plants and ferns, primarily from western New England. Her information was often so complete that it is still possible to follow her narrative and walk within her footsteps to the very same places she visited more than a century ago! Niles' work also contains some of the first published color photographs of wild orchids.

Gibson's book was an expansion of his field notes and written primarily to accompany his meticulous drawings. This work contained the first illustrated keys to the orchid species of the Northeast.

Although it would be more than twenty years before the next publication of native orchids of eastern North America, the work was well under way by two diverse gentlemen and their wives. Henry Morris and Edward Eames met on a regular basis with the goal to locate, document, and photograph all the wild orchids in the Gray's Manual range—eastern North America south to the Virginia/North Carolina line and west to the Mississippi Valley. With their wives to haul and tote the bulky cameras and equipment they traveled from their homes in Peterborough, Ontario, and Buffalo, New York, to search for and find all of these species and, along the way, several new color and growth forms. Working with information from M. L. Fernald at Harvard University, they sought out local orchid experts and enthusiasts who would help guide them down muddy roads and waist-deep bogs and fens in search of their quarries. The result, in 1929, was perhaps the greatest publication of its time on wild orchids of northeastern North America—titled simply *Our Wild Orchids*, with extensive *in situ* photographs and endless personal anecdotes.

Although Fernald's work at Harvard always featured the Orchidaceae he was at this point consumed with the new edition of *Gray's Manual of Botany* (1950) and his numerous expeditions to Newfoundland and Nova Scotia. During this period surrounding the Second World War, Donovan Stewart Correll was assembling data for the first book to be published covering all the native orchids found in North America north of Mexico. Illustrated with line drawings by Blanche Ames Ames and, eventually, Gordon Dillon, *The Native Orchids of North America, north of Mexico* (1950) soon became the premier reference for both professional and amateur native orchidophiles.

Although Correll's work covered much of the continent, his work in the Northeast is evident as many of those species are treated in greater depth. It was this work that inspired and guided Carlyle Luer in his quest for the North American orchids and resulted in his two monumental works, *The Native Orchids of Florida* (1972) and *The Native Orchids of the United States and Canada excluding Florida* (1975).

As Luer's works were disseminated, the last quarter of the twentieth century was bringing forth such researchers in the Northeast (and elsewhere) as Chuck Sheviak, Paul Catling, Frankie Brackley, Bill Chapman, Philip Keenan, Eric Lamont, and Paul Martin Brown. Published works, especially concerning new species, started appearing in rapid succession and by 1997 books by Chapman and Brown covered the wild orchids of New England and New York. In the interim Brackley's thesis on the orchids of New Hampshire appeared in *Rhodora* (1985) and Philip Keenan's series of copiously illustrated articles appeared in the *American Orchid Society Bulletin* and *Orchids* (1985–2001; see appendix 3, p. 337). Again, most of these articles concerned those orchids found in the Northeast.

Regional organizations devoted to native flora often featured orchids and the production of the New York Flora Association's atlas of flowering plants of New

York detailed county records. Natural Heritage Programs and their like in all the northeastern states were now tracking many of the rarest of the orchids and some form of protection was given to most of the orchids in the Northeast. The past ten years (1995–2005) have seen the publication of more than fifteen new works devoted to specific regions or states in North America, including many in the greater Northeast.

Although the history of orchid research and publication in New Jersey and Pennsylvania is not nearly as plentiful as that in New England and New York, the lure of the Pine Barrens of New Jersey, now more appropriately known as the Pinelands, was a magnet that drew botanists from Boston, New York, and Philadelphia on annual trips to the bogs and savannas for more than a century and a half. Fernald, Long, and compatriots gravitated to this region in the early years of the twentieth century and many initial discoveries were made on these forays. Access was primarily by train as the roads were few and difficult to negotiate. Although much of the orchid news from these early years may be found in publications of the New England Botanical Club (*Rhodora*), Philadelphia Botanical Club, and Torrey Botanical Club (*Torreya, Bulletin of the Torrey Botanical Club*) it is in Witmer Stone's *The Plants of Southern New Jersey* (1910, 1911, 1973) that one finds almost all of these explorations detailed as well as an abundance of information on the orchids found in southern New Jersey and in areas apart from the Pine Barrens, particularly the Cape May area.

Although the aforementioned botanical clubs, especially the Philadelphia Botanical Club, still make forays into southern New Jersey, it is the amateur photographers and botanists like Rick Radke, the scientists of the New Jersey Natural Heritage Program, field trip leaders of organizations such as the New England Wild Flower Society and New Jersey Audubon Society, and researchers such as Bob Yanettii who have been able to keep detailed records of the wild orchids in this fragile environment.

Seminal work on the orchids of western Pennsylvania by Henry and Buker (1955, 1962) and Henry, Buker, and Pearth (1975) laid the foundation for continued research in that portion of the state and it continues today primarily by Albert Shriver, Clete Smith, and J. Scott Shriver of Pittsburgh. Their work on the orchids of the Upper Ohio River Basin will eventually culminate in a detailed publication that will cover the western half of Pennsylvania, eastern half of Ohio, the whole of West Virginia, and the westernmost counties of Maryland and New York—146 counties in all. Mark Larocque has made several excellent discoveries in southeastern Pennsylvania and has kept careful tabs on that part of the state while other active members of the various botanical clubs that center in Pennsylvania continue to make both discoveries and rediscoveries.

In all genera found in this region the work in volume 26 of *Flora of North*

*America* (2002) has greatly fine-tuned the identification and distribution of these orchids. The generic treatments in the *Flora* were authored by individuals and teams considered to be authorities on these genera. Although there are some variations in the treatments, specific guidelines were followed by the authors and, in respect to distribution, the authors verified each state with an herbarium specimen or substantiated record. The orchids were treated at the species, subspecies, and varietal levels; forma, in general, were not discussed, but some authors treated hybrids. This compendium brings together information that has been fragmented, at best, for many years, necessitating the completion of many species treatments that had been in progress. Each author or team of authors set its own parameters for delimitation of species; several new species were described and new, or possibly older, names were used in the *Flora*.

# *An Introduction to Orchids*

Orchids hold a special fascination for many people, perhaps because of their perceived extreme beauty, rarity, and mystery. In actuality, orchids are the largest family of flowering plants on earth, with nearly 30,000 species. Although many are exceedingly beautiful, many more are small and dull colored, barely 2 or 3 mm across! There is hardly any place on this planet, other than Antarctica, that does not have some species of orchid growing within its native flora. Even the oases within the great deserts of the world harbor a few species. In the more northerly climes orchids can be found well above the Arctic Circle. Orchids grow at elevations greater than 15,000 feet as well as within highly developed urban areas of the globe. In this region, the northeastern part of the United States, orchids abound throughout. Some of the rarest species globally are found here. Because of their milder climate, Cape Cod, Long Island, and southern New Jersey have become the northernmost limit for many southern species.

Because of the sheer number of orchids in the world there is an enormous amount of morphological diversity among them. Although orchids all possess certain qualifying characteristics, their general morphology can be as variable as the imagination. But viewed closely under a lens, even the tiniest of orchids has the distinctive features that make it an orchid!

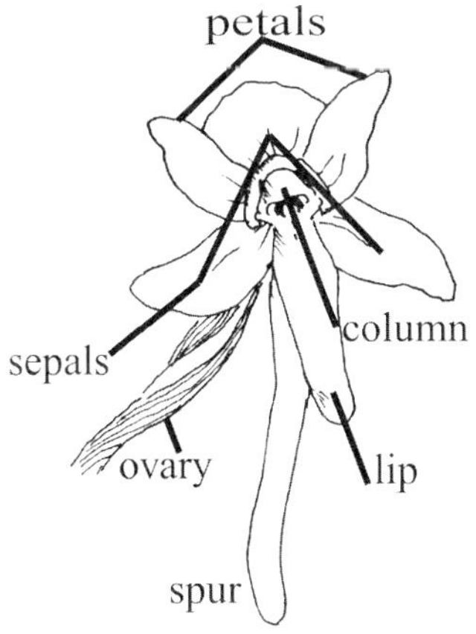

Characteristics of the orchid family, the Orchidaceae, are quite simple, despite their diversity. First, they are monocotyledons, or monocots—a major class of the plant kingdom that has a single emerging leaf-like structure when the seed germinates (as opposed to dicotyledons, or dicots, which have two leaf-like structures). Grasses, lilies, and palms are also monocots. Second, orchids have three *sepals*, two *petals*, and a third petal that is modified into a *lip*. This prominent structure is actually a guide for the pollinator—sort of a landing platform that directs the agent of pollination toward the nectary. Third, the stamens and pistil are united into a *column*, a structure unique to the orchids that effects fertilization when the agent of pollination passes by on its way to the nectary. Again, because of the size of the family, there are many pollinators, not just insects. Orchids have been documented to be pollinated by the usual bees, butterflies, wasps, and flies, as well as by hummingbirds, and a few are even rain-assisted in their pollination. Many orchids emit a fragrance at a certain time of day, or night, to attract their specific pollinator. Beyond that there are those species that, by various means, are self-pollinating.

Because of the great number of genera and species, occasionally there are what appear to be exceptions. A few genera have monoecious or dioecious flowers—male and female flowers on separate inflorescences or separate plants. In others, the petals and/or lip may be so modified that they are barely recognizable; in yet others, the flowers never open: they are cleistogamous and self-fertilized in the bud. But all of these exceptions aside, the vast majority of orchid flowers look like orchids!

Within the northeastern United States as defined in this field guide, all of the orchids are terrestrial, growing with the roots in the ground and taking in water and nutrients through root hairs and/or swollen stems that are tuber-, bulb-, or corm-like.

In nature, all orchids consume fungi as a food (carbon) source. Each wild orchid has this unique relationship with naturally occurring fungi. While nearly impossible to see with the naked eye, these fungi are essential to the growth and development of any wild orchid. In this relationship, a fungus infects the orchid roots and the fungus is then consumed as a food source, initially prompting seed germination and then sustaining seedling development. As a mature plant, the orchid is capable of producing food via both photosynthesis and the consumption of its root fungi. A number of different fungi may contribute nutrients, growth regulators, vitamins, and moisture at various levels and at different times throughout the orchid's life cycle. It is this special relationship between orchid and fungus that makes native orchids extremely difficult to transplant. In most cases, native orchids that have been moved from their natural location will die within a few years as a result of this disruption of the orchid-fungal association.

The leaves of orchids are nearly as diverse as the flowers. As is characteristic of all monocots, they have parallel primary veins. They may be long and slender, or grass-like, or round and fat, or hard and leathery, or soft and hairy—just about any configuration. If you are a novice, before you start to use this book take a few moments to look through the photographs and drawings and see the typical floral parts. Try to get a better feeling for what an orchid is and then go out and find some!

# *Which Orchid Is It?*

A key is a written means for identifying an unknown species. The principles used in keying are very simple. A series of questions is asked in the form of couplets, or paired questions; the user needs to determine a positive or negative response to each half of the pair. Be sure to read both halves of the couplet before deciding on your answer. The half of the couplet that matches your observation of the orchid in question directs you to the next set of couplets and eventually to the genus and/or species name. As you progress through the key, the illustrations may help you in making your determinations.

Choose the specimen you wish to identify carefully. Look for a typical, average plant—neither the largest nor the smallest. **This key is designed so you should be able to use it without picking any of the orchids**. Only in the case of a few similar species will detailed examinations be necessary. The use of measurements has been kept to a minimum, as has the use of color. Be aware that white-flowered forms exist in many of the species and they usually occur with the typical color form.

Before you start to use the key you should always mentally note the following:

placement and quantity of leaves, i.e., basal vs. cauline; opposite vs. alternate; 1, 2, or more
placement and quantity of flowers, i.e., terminal vs. axillary; single vs. multiple
geographic location and habitat

Three vocabulary words that will help in your understanding of the key:

**pseudobulb**—the swollen storage organ at the base of the leaves, found occasionally in these terrestrial orchids but usually in epiphytes, which grow with roots exposed, usually in tree bark and in tropical and subtropical climates
**bract**—a small, reduced leaf that usually is found on the flowering stem and/or within the inflorescence
**spur/mentum**—a projection at the base of the lip; it may be variously shaped from slender and pointed (spur) to short and rounded (mentum)

Other terms are illustrated within the key or can be found in the glossary on page 343.

## Using the Key

If you are using the key for the first time, start with a species with which you are familiar—perhaps the **common grass-pink**, *Calopogon tuberosus.*

Starting with couplet 1
1a lip inflated or sac shaped . . . 2
1b lip otherwise . . . 5
which takes us to couplet 5

5a (green) leaves (apparently) lacking at flowering time; stem bracts may be present . . . 6
5b (green) leaves present at flowering time . . . 10
which takes us to couplet 10

10a spur or mentum present . . . 11
10b spur or mentum lacking . . . 15
which takes us to couplet 15

10b

15a pseudobulbs present, although they may be well hidden in the leaf bases . . . 16
15b pseudobulbs lacking . . . 17
which takes us to couplet 17

17a leaves essentially basal or extending up the lower 1/4 of the stem and rapidly reduced to leafy bracts . . . . . . ***Spiranthes***
17b leaves essentially cauline . . . 19
which takes us to couplet 19

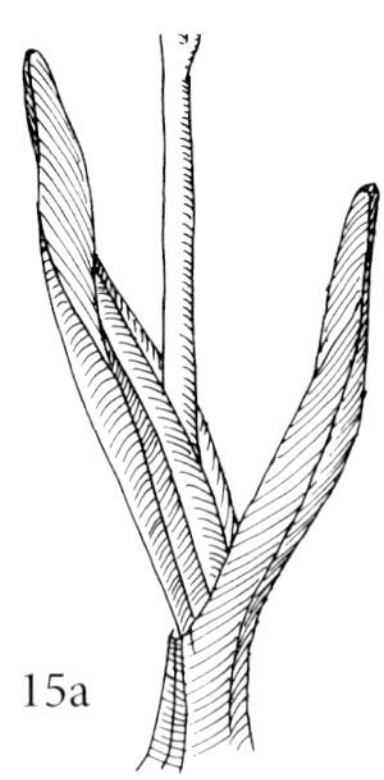
15a

19a flowers non-resupinate
(lip uppermost . . . . . ***Calopogon***, p. 35
19b flowers resupinate (lip lowermost) . . . 20

19a
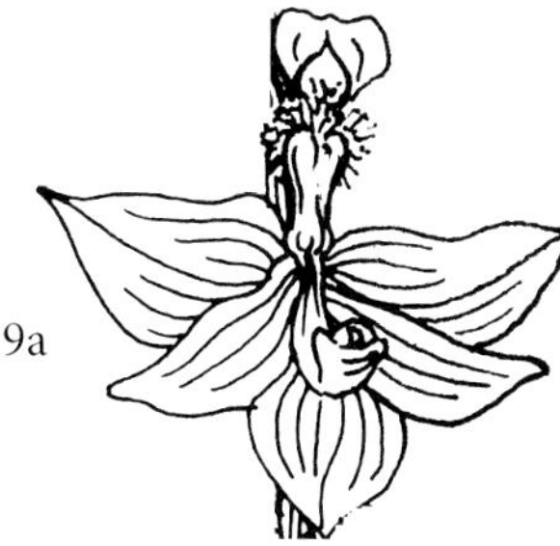

To continue to species, turn to the entry for *Calopogon* on page 35 and, if there is more than one species in the genus, follow the same procedure with the key to the species.

This key is constructed for use in the field or with live specimens and is based on characters that are readily seen. It is not a technical key in the strictest sense, but intended simply to aid in field identification.

Keys are not difficult if you take your time, learn the vocabulary, and hone your observational skills. Like any skills, the more you use them the easier it becomes.

### Key to the Genera

1a lip inflated, cup, or sac shaped . . . 2
1b lip otherwise . . . 5

2a
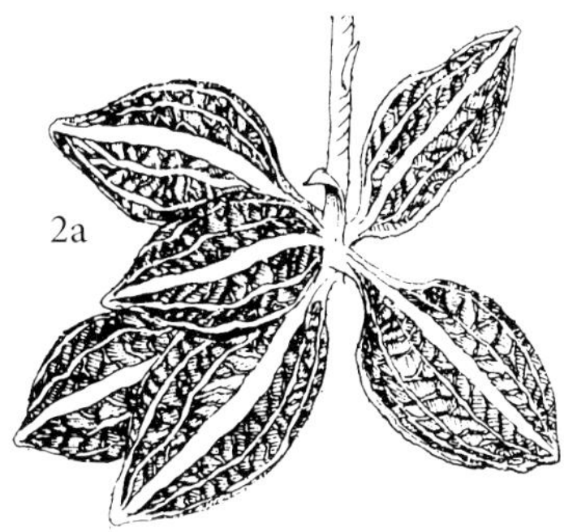

2a flowers in spikes; small, whitish in color; leaves in a basal rosette . . . . . ***Goodyera***, p. 95
2b flowers otherwise . . . 3

3a lip an inflated slipper . . . . . ***Cypripedium***, p. 67
3b lip spade or boat-shaped . . . 4

3a
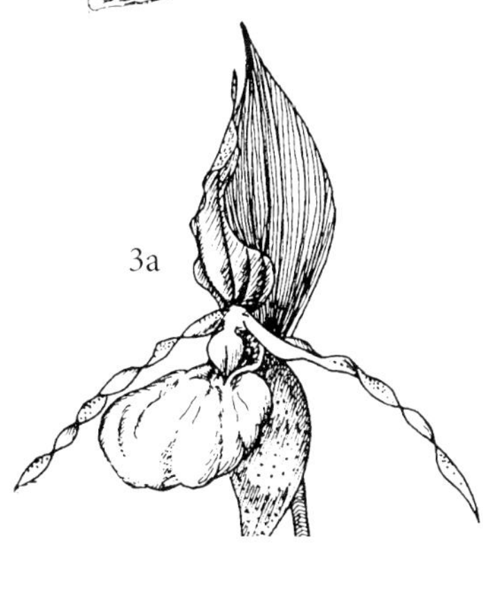

4a flowers and leaves several . . . . . ***Epipactis***, p. 85
4b flower and leaf single . . . . . ***Calypso***, p. 39

LEAVES LACKING AT FLOWERING TIME

5a (green) leaves (apparently) lacking at flowering time; stem bracts may be present . . . 6

5b (green) leaves present at flowering time . . . 10

6a plants lacking chlorophyll (no green stems or leaves evident) . . . . . ***Corallorhiza***, p. 51

6b plants with chlorophyll (green stems or leaves evident) . . . 7

7a spur or mentum present; flowers brown; asymmetrical . . . . . ***Tipularia***, p. 221

7b spur or mentum lacking . . . 8

8a flower bright pink, rarely white or lilac-blue; usually 1, rarely 2 or 3 . . . . . ***Arethusa***, p. 31

8b flowers white or brown in a few to many-flowered spike . . . 9

9a inflorescence a spike, often with many (20–60) small, tubular, white or cream-colored flowers with delicately frilled lips, usually in a loose to dense spiral . . . . . ***Spiranthes***, p. 194

9b inflorescence a raceme with fewer flowers (±10), not white in color . . . . . ***Aplectrum***, p. 27

9a

LEAVES PRESENT AT FLOWERING TIME

## Spur or Mentum Present

10a spur or mentum present . . . 11

10b spur or mentum lacking . . . 15

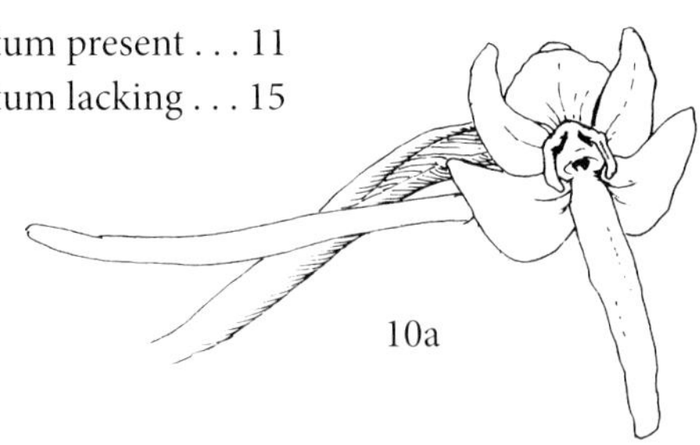

10a

11a

11a inflorescence terminal on a leafy stem . . . 13

11b inflorescence terminal on a scape (leafless stem) . . . 12

12a plants with a single basal leaf; lip of flowers spotted . . . . . ***Amerorchis***, p. 23
12b plants with several basal leaves; flowers pink, purple and/or white; lip unspotted . . . . . ***Galearis***, p. 91

13a lip oblong and notched at tip . . . . . ***Coeloglossum***, p. 47
13b lip otherwise; **never** notched at the tip . . . 14

14a lip entire (not divided), or with 3 teeth . . . . . ***Gymnadeniopsis***, p. 105
14b lip entire, divided, or fringed, but the margin **never** notched or toothed, petals erose or toothed but not fringed . . . . . ***Platanthera***, p. 147

14a

14b

## Spur or Mentum Lacking

15a pseudobulbs present, although they may be well hidden in the leaf bases . . . 16
15b pseudobulbs lacking . . . 18

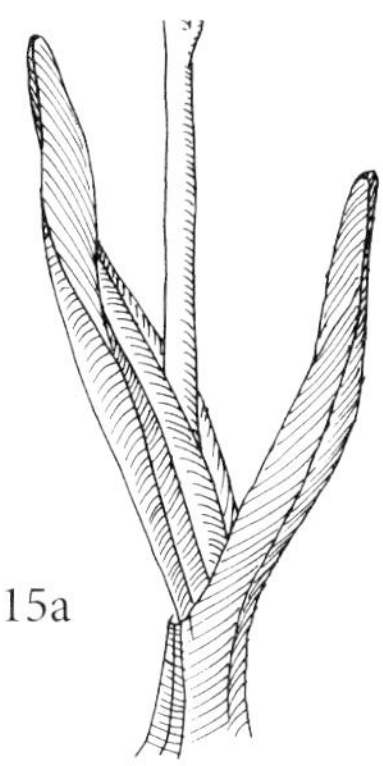
15a

16a petals and sepals similar; inflorescence a (flat-topped) corymb . . . . . ***Malaxis***, p. 139
16b petals and sepals dissimilar; petals filiform, thread-like; inflorescence a raceme . . . . . ***Liparis***, p. 121

16a

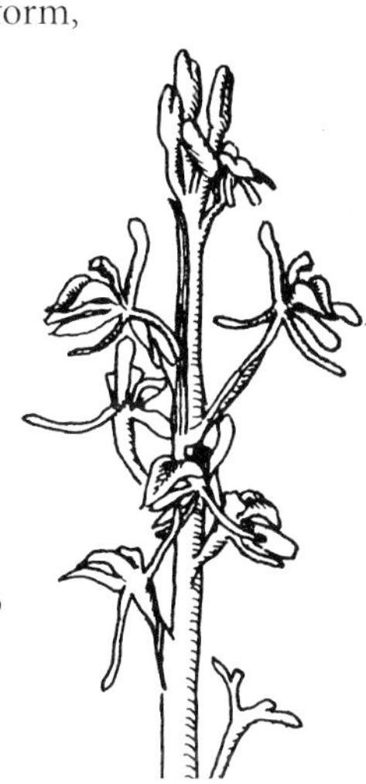
16b

### Leaves Basal

17a leaves essentially basal or extending up the lower 1/4 of the stem and rapidly reduced to leafy bracts . . . 18
17b leaves essentially cauline . . . 19

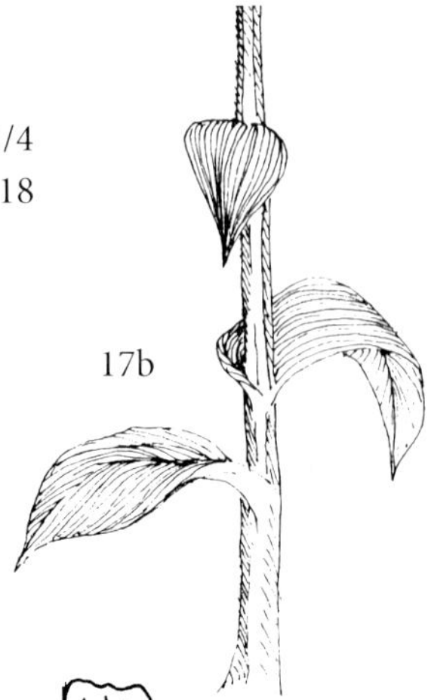

17b

18a flowers large and bright pink, usually solitary, rarely 2 or 3 . . . . . ***Arethusa***, p. 31
18b inflorescence a many-flowered spike (usually twisted) of small white or cream flowers . . . . . ***Spiranthes***, p. 194

### Leaves Cauline

19a flowers non-resupinate, lip uppermost . . . . . ***Calopogon***, p. 35
19b flowers resupinate, lip lowermost . . . 20

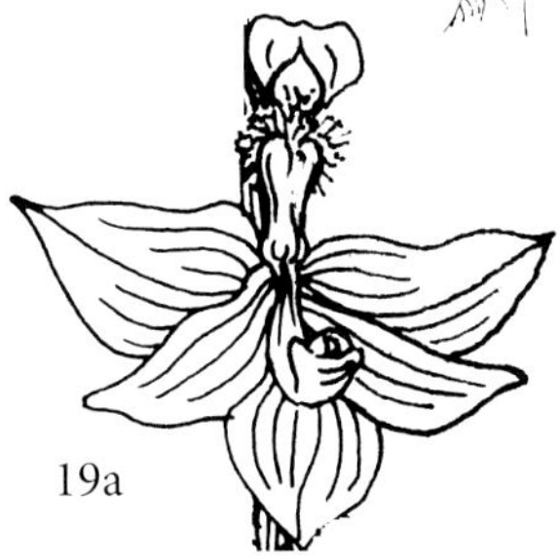

19a

20a leaves opposite or whorled . . . 21
20b leaves solitary or alternate (except in rare individuals) . . . 22

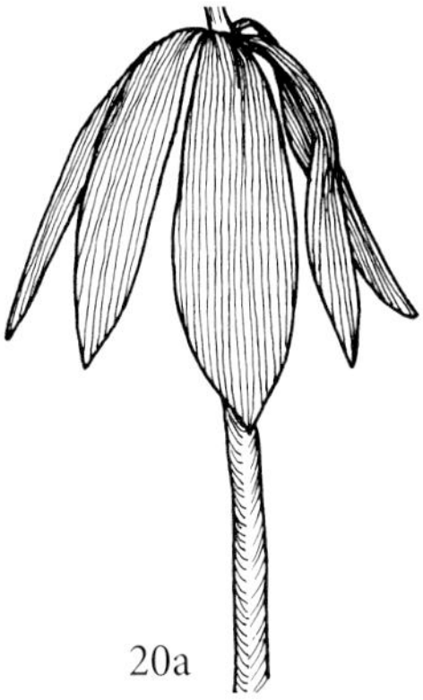

20a

21a leaves 2, opposite . . . . . ***Listera***, p. 127
21b leaves 5–7, whorled . . . . . ***Isotria***, p. 115

22a leaf solitary, bracts may be present . . . 23
22b leaves several, alternate . . . . . ***Triphora***, p. 225

23a inflorescence a raceme of very small, innumerable, inconspicuous green flowers . . . . . ***Malaxis***, p. 139
23b inflorescence otherwise; flowers larger and showy, pink, lavender, or white; usually 1 (rarely 2–4) . . . 24

24a lip with a distinct, knobby beard
..... ***Pogonia***, p. 191
24b lip delicately veined but lacking a beard
..... ***Cleistes***, p. 43

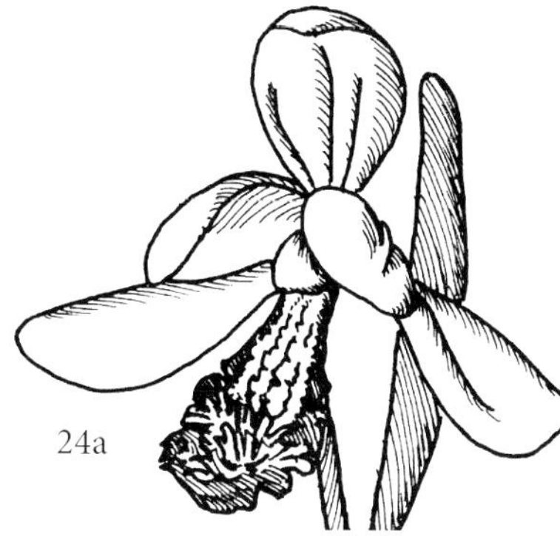
24a

## Some Important Notes About . . .

### PLANT NAMES

Example: *Platanthera hookeri* (Torrey) Lindley, Hooker's orchis

The Latin name consists of a genus and a species. The genus (*Platanthera*) is the broader group to which the plant belongs and the specific epithet (*hookeri*) is the plant being treated. After the two Latin names is the name or names of the people who first described the plant. The example above illustrates two different author citations. In the example, Torrey originally described and named the species, but as *Habenaria hookeri*, therefore his name appears immediately after the genus and species. Subsequently Lindley transferred it to the genus *Platanthera*; Torrey's name was then placed in parentheses to distinguish him as the original authority, and Lindley's name was added after Torrey's.

Other ranks may occur, such as subspecies, variety, and forma. Subspecies and variety usually designate a variation that has a significant difference from the species and a definite geographic range, such as *Platanthera flava* var. *herbiola*. Varieties and subspecies should always breed true, i.e., offspring will resemble the parents. There can always be a bit of disagreement over the rank of variety versus subspecies and which term is better used. Color variations, which occur throughout the range of the species, are best treated as forma, as in the white-flowered form of the large purple fringed orchis, *Platanthera grandiflora* forma *albiflora* (Rand & Redfield) Catling. These forms can, and do, occur randomly and rarely breed true. All forma that have received names among the species occurring within the range of this work are listed in this book, although several have yet to be documented for this region. Orchid enthusiasts and botanists alike will note several new forms as well as a number of "old" forms that have been resurrected. The new combinations were necessary to recognize certain taxa at the forma level and recent research has uncovered a number of forms previously published many years ago that, although plants corresponding to these forms are easily found, have been abandoned. They are presented here for the first time in many years.

### COMMON NAMES

Common names are never as consistent throughout the range of the plants as we would like. The most frequently used common names are listed here.

Orchid or Orchis? For common names either *orchid* or *orchis* may be used, but traditionally *orchis* has been used for certain genera and that has been maintained here.

### SIZE

Average height of the plants, floral size, and number of flowers are given, with extremes in parentheses. The relative scale of each line drawing is for an average plant and is based on the flower size.

### COLOR

The color of the flowers as it normally occurs is given. Remember to check to see if color variants such as white-flowered forms occur. In some genera the overall color of the petals and sepals, the perianth, is given and the lip color follows.

### FORMS AND HYBRIDS

The diversity of forms, randomly occurring variations such as color and habit, and hybrids are what can take hunting for native orchids to another level. After mastering many of the species one can be challenged to search for all the variations. It would be unrealistic to think that all of these forms occur within the range of this work, but many of them do. To better understand these forms, note that each is annotated with the original publication and the geographic type locality of the taxon, the geographic location where the form was originally described. Those that have been documented within the northeastern United States are often noted within the text and it is expected that several of the other forms will also be found.

Hybrids present a very different situation. Whereas forms are the result of genetic diversity within a species, hybrids rely on an outside element, that of the pollinator, to create the resulting hybrid as a cross between two species. In certain parental combinations hybrids are very predictable, but in other situations they are very rare. Most are obvious intermediates between the putative parents, and when both parental species are present the hybrids should be carefully sought.

### FLOWERING PERIODS

Flowering periods are not as easy to isolate for this entire region. Latitude, exposure, and elevation play a major role in flowering times. Typically plants flower earlier in the spring in the more temperate coastal areas and much later further north and in the mountains, whereas autumn-flowering species tend to flower earlier in the north and later southward.

### RANGE MAPS

Both the continental range and the local range are given for each species. State names enclosed in brackets indicate literature reports that cannot be verified. The range maps are intended to illustrate the general range of a given species and are based on verifiable specimens in herbarium records, normally housed in herbaria at any number of colleges and universities. A photograph from a reliable source, documented with date and place, will, upon rare occasion, be allowed as a verifiable report. Literature reports are noted in the text and are just that: a report in any one of a number of publications that cannot be backed up by either a specimen or a verifiable record.

The red dots represent areas of local distribution and the green dots, areas of widespread distribution. In neither situation are relative rarity or size of populations implied, simply frequency of populations. With few exceptions, the range maps do not attempt to differentiate between extant and extirpated populations, nor do they convey how many populations are known from a given area; if a population is well documented to be extirpated it is shown as a red dot with a black border. When the range of a species or variety extends beyond the boundaries of states or areas defined in this field guide, an arrow is used to indicate such.

# *Part 2*

## The Wild Orchids of New England, New York, Pennsylvania, and New Jersey

## *Amerorchis*

*Amerorchis* is a monotypic genus proposed in 1968 to accommodate this species, formerly included within the widespread and variable genus *Orchis*. It is variable in its coloration with five color forms noted. Often abundant in the northern portions of its range it is exceedingly rare and local in the southern reaches of its haunts.

## *Amerorchis rotundifolia* (Banks *ex* Pursh) Hultén

**small round-leaf orchis**

forma *angustifolia* (Rousseau) P.M. Brown—narrow-leafed form
*Bulletin Jardin du Botanical Etat* 27: 371, fig. 35. 1957, as *Orchis rotundifolia* Banks ex Pursh forma *angustifolia* J. Rousseau, type: Quebec

forma *beckettiae* (Boivin) Hultén—white-flowered form
*Naturaliste Canadien* 87: 42. 1960, as *Orchis rotundifolia* forma *beckettiae* Boivin, type: Manitoba

forma *immaculata* Mazurski & L.P. Johnson—white-lipped form
*Lindleyana*, 10(1): 1. 1995, type: Ontario.

forma *lineata* (Mousley) Hultén—lined-lip form
*Canadian Field-Naturalist* 55: 65. 1941, as *Orchis rotundifolia* Banks *ex* Pursh var. *lineata* Mousley, type: Quebec.

forma *rosea* P.M. Brown—pink-flowered form
*North American Native Orchid Journal* 10: 34. 2004, type: Manitoba

forma *wardii* P.M. Brown—pink/white/green-flowered form
*North American Native Orchid Journal* 10: 34. 2004, type: Manitoba

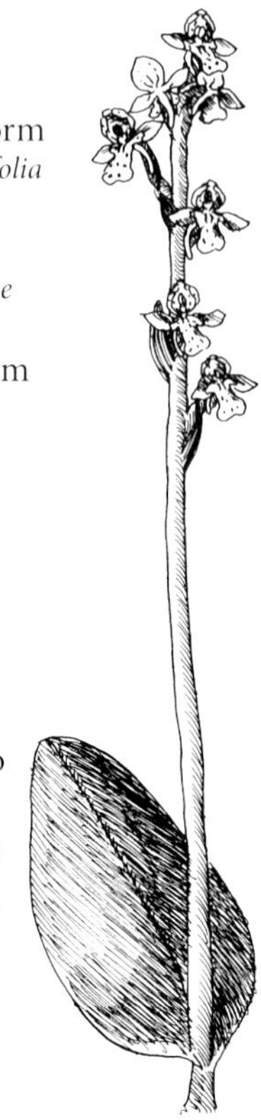

**Range:** Alaska east to Newfoundland and Greenland, south to Montana and Wyoming, Minnesota east to Maine
**In the Northeast: Maine, New Hampshire, Vermont, New York**: rare and local in northern Maine; extirpated in New Hampshire, Vermont, New York
**Plant:** terrestrial, 4–15 (20) cm tall
**Leaves:** 1; ovate, to 7 cm wide × 10 cm long or, in the forma *angustifolia*, only 3–4 cm wide; the short petiole close to the ground
**Flowers**: 4–15; the sepals white to pale pink; the three-lobed lip spotted with darker pink or purple or, in the forma *lineata*, the lip with broad pink to purple lines replacing the spots or, in the forma *immaculata*, the lip pure white or, in the forma *rosea*, the entire flower suffused with rosy-pink or, in the forma *wardii*, the flower pink and white and green or, in the forma *beckettiae*, the entire flower pure white; individual flower size 0.75–1.5 cm; spur slender, ca. 5 mm long
**Habitat:** calcareous woodlands usually with arborvitae, *Thuja occidentalis*, and other conifers
**Flowering period:** mid-June to early July

The **small round-leaf orchis**, *Amerorchis rotundifolia*, a much sought-after gem of the northern woodlands, has always been one of the rarest orchids in the northeastern United States. Growing in moist, mossy coniferous woodlands, plants can often reach 35 cm in height and hold their speckled flowers well above the surrounding forest floor vegetation. Although it is highly variable in floral coloring throughout its continental range, in the few extant sites in Maine plants are surprisingly uniform. The various leaf and color forms are very rare and known only from a few scattered locales, primarily in Canada and Alaska (Brown and Folsom, 2006, 2006a). Plants of *Amerorchis rotundifolia* have not been seen in the other northeastern states for many years.

forma *beckettiae*

Above, top: forma *lineata*; forma *wardii*; bottom forma *immaculata*, forma *rosea*

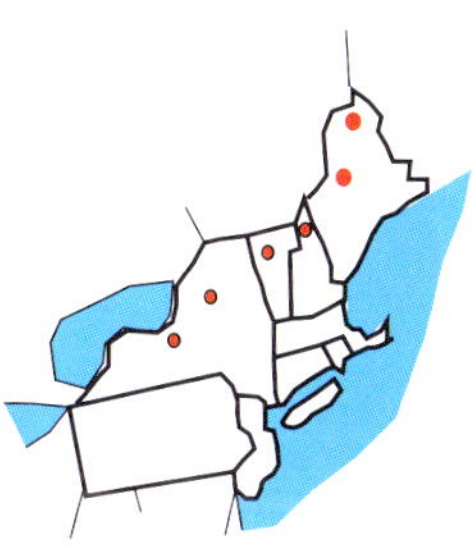

## *Aplectrum*

A small genus consisting of only two species, one found in North America, the other in Japan. It is one of several genera found in eastern North America with analogs in Japan.

## *Aplectrum hyemale* (Mühlenberg *ex* Willdenow) Nuttall

**putty-root; Adam-and-Eve**

forma *pallidum* House—yellow-flowered form

*Torreya* 3: 54. 1903, as *Aplectrum spicatum* var. *pallidum* House, type: New York

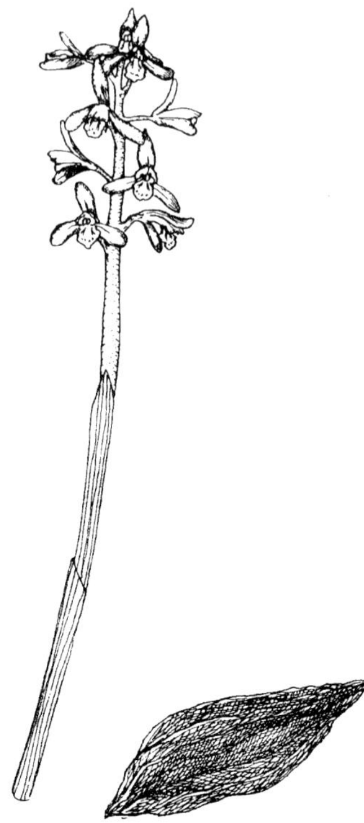

**Range**: Minnesota east to southern Quebec and Vermont, south to northern South Carolina and west to eastern Oklahoma

**In the Northeast: [New Hampshire], Vermont, Massachusetts, Connecticut, New York, Pennsylvania, New Jersey**: rare to occasional, more frequent southward; found primarily in the hills and mountains

**Plant:** terrestrial, 18–50 cm tall

**Leaves:** 1; ovate, plicate, 3–8 cm wide × 10–20 cm long; appearing in the autumn and withering at flowering time in the spring

**Flowers:** 3–20, greenish-yellow suffused with brown and purple, the white lip three-lobed, prominently ridged, and with magenta spots or, in the forma *pallidum*, the stem and flowers yellow and the lip unspotted; individual flower size 1.5–2.0 cm

**Habitat:** rich, moist woodlands, bottomlands, and deciduous slopes

**Flowering period:** April to mid-May

*Aplectrum hyemale*, **putty-root,** a not uncommon orchid of the central and southern Appalachian Mountains and foothills, reaches the northern limit of its range in western Vermont with disjunct populations in southern Quebec. It is nowhere frequent in the Northeast and, although the flowers are prominent, the coloring renders them almost inconspicuous in the similarly colored forest surroundings. The distinctive leaf is much easier to find in the late autumn of the year when it is nearly erect. By spring it has reclined and is usually withering when the flower spike starts to emerge. The large, pendant seed capsules also are diagnostic on the fruiting stems later in the season. Occasional reports from New Hampshire have never been substantiated.

forma *pallidum*

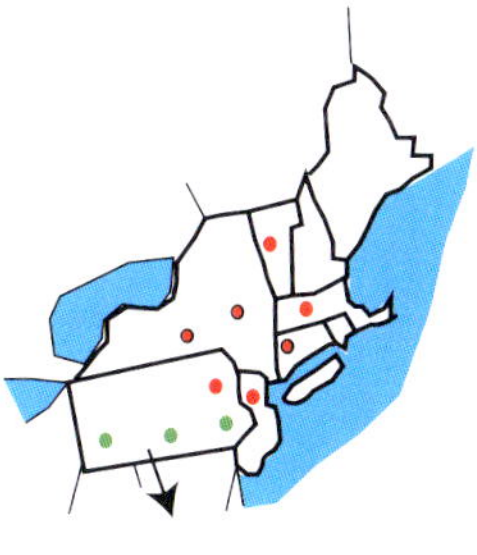

## *Arethusa*

*Arethusa* is a monotypic genus found in eastern North America and Japan. The brilliantly colored flowers are a feature of many of the bogs and fens of northeastern North America.

## *Arethusa bulbosa* Linnaeus

### dragon's-mouth

forma *albiflora* Rand & Redfield—white-flowered form
*Flora of Mt. Desert Island* 152. 1894, type: Maine
forma *subcaerulea* Rand & Redfield—lilac-blue flowered form
*Flora of Mt. Desert Island* 152. 1894, type: Maine

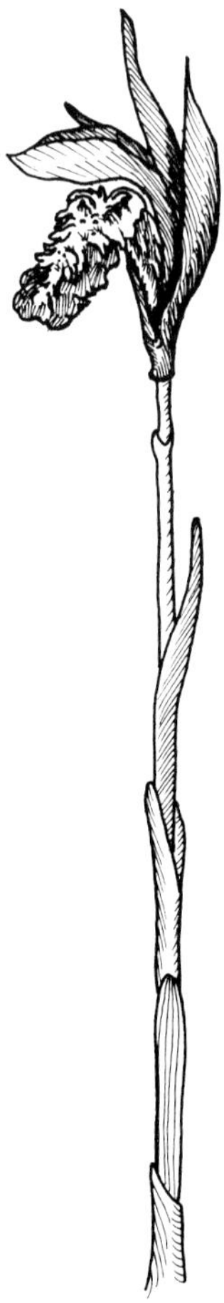

**Range:** southern Manitoba east to Newfoundland, south to northern South Carolina, west to northern Indiana and central Minnesota
**In the Northeast: Maine, New Hampshire, Vermont, Massachusetts, Connecticut, Rhode Island, New York, Pennsylvania, New Jersey:** locally common in bogs and raised heaths throughout in the north and becoming increasingly rare southward
**Plant:** terrestrial, 4–15 (20) cm tall
**Leaves:** 1; linear, 0.3–1.2 cm wide × 5.0–23.0 cm long; appressed to the flowering stem when young and continuing to develop as the plant matures
**Flowers:** usually 1, occasionally 2–4; rose, rich pink, or magenta or, in the forma *albiflora*, flowers pure white or, in the forma *subcaerulea*, lilac-blue; individual flower size 1–3 cm; miniature individuals, with flowers no more than 5 mm tall, rarely occur
**Habitat:** sphagnum bogs, fens, and seeps
**Flowering period:** late spring
To many native orchid enthusiasts *Arethusa* is the ultimate gem of the northern affinity bogs and fens. Fortunately it is one of the commonest orchids in the northern portion of its range and one of the first of the showy 'bog pinks' to flower each spring. Plants often appear leafless at flowering time, as the emerging grass-like leaf is nearly appressed to the flower stalk, although it will elongate later in the season. The beautiful pink flowers are distinctive and could be confused (at a distance) only with the rose pogonia, *Pogonia ophioglossoides*, with which it frequently grows.

forma *albiflora*

forma *subcaerulea*

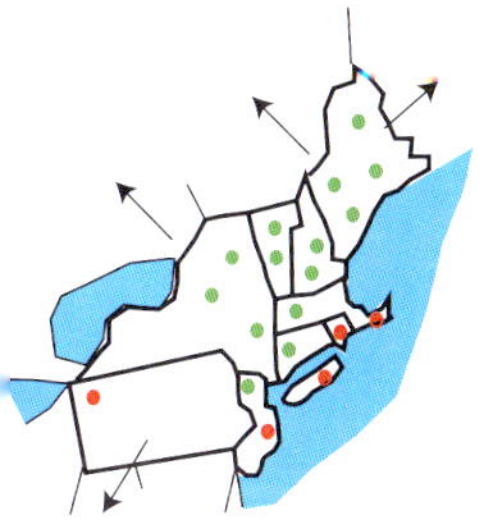

## *Calopogon*

The genus *Calopogon* is a New World genus comprising five species, with only one also occuring outside of the United States and Canada. The non-resupinate (uppermost) lip is distinctive and easily identifies the genus. A single species occurs in the northeastern United States.

## *Calopogon tuberosus* (Linnaeus) Britton, Sterns, & Poggenberg var. *tuberosus*

**common grass-pink**

forma *albiflorus* Britton—white-flowered form
*Bulletin of the Torrey Botanical Club* 17: 125. 1890, type: New Jersey

**Range**: Minnesota east to Newfoundland, south to Florida, and west to Texas
**In the Northeast: Maine, New Hampshire, Vermont, Massachusetts, Connecticut, Rhode Island, New York, Pennsylvania, New Jersey**: locally common throughout
**Plant:** terrestrial, 25–115 cm tall, although much shorter in open, northern bogs and heaths
**Leaves:** 1–2(3); slender, ribbed, up to 0.3–4.0 cm wide × 3.0–45.0 cm long and less than the height of the plant
**Flowers:** 3–17, non-resupinate, opening in slow succession; deep to pale pink or, in the forma *albiflorus*, white, with a golden crest on the lip; individual flower size 2.5–3.5 cm
**Habitat:** bogs, seeps, sphagnous roadsides, raised heaths
**Flowering period:** late June to July

One of the most frequent orchids found in the eastern and central United States and Canada, the **grass-pink** is a brilliant, showy plant that prefers open sphagnum bogs, heaths, damp gravel pits, and seeps. Plants of *Calopogon tuberosus* flower over a long period of time, with only a few flowers open at once. It is not unusual to find local stands of several hundred plants. Like all grass-pinks, the flowers have the lip uppermost, non-resupinate, and this feature easily separates the genus from any other with a similar morphology. The var. *simpsonii* is confined to the rocky marls of the southernmost counties of Florida. Two dwarfed forms—var. *nanum* Nieuwland, from exposed tundra-like sites and var. *latifolius* (H. St. John) B. Boivin, plants with a broad leaf taller than the short spike, common in the open heaths of the Maine and the Canadian Maritimes, have proven to be environmental morphs; when grown in other conditions, these plants revert to typical size and leaf shape (Catling and Lucas, 1987).

forma *albiflorum*

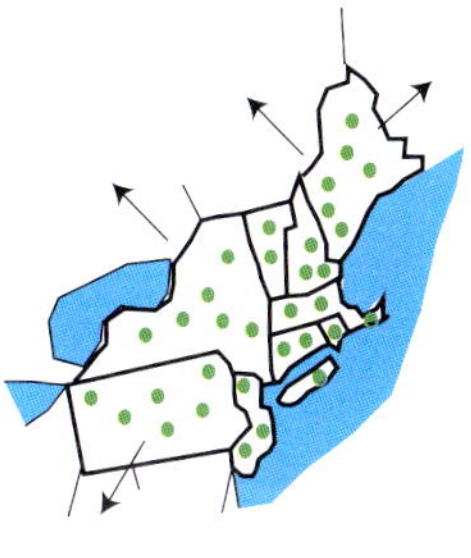

## *Calypso*

The fairy-slipper is one of the most sought-after and delightful of all native orchids found in the northern hemisphere. Four varieties are known, each from its own geographic niche. Plants are usually found in dark, rich coniferous forests or, in the far north, in open tundra and barrens. The small white bulbs are nestled in the mosses and the single leaf, which appears in the autumn, is winter green and withers shortly after the plant flowers.

forma *bulbosa*

forma *americana*

forma *occidentalis*

forma *speciosa*

The variety *bulbosa* occurs in northern Eurasia, variety *speciosa* in Japan, and variety *occidentalis* in western North America. All differ slightly from each other and are defined geographically. The varieties *bulbosa* and *americana* are most similar as are the varieties *occidentalis* and *speciosa* (Brown and Folsom, 2005a).

*Calypso bulbosa* (Linnaeus) Oakes var. *americana* (R.Brown) Luer

**eastern fairy-slipper**

forma *albiflora* P.M. Brown—white-flowered form
*North American Native Orchid Journal,* 1(1): 17. 1995, type: Vermont

forma *biflora* P.M. Brown—two-flowered form
*North American Native Orchid Journal* 10: 35. 2004, type: Maine

forma *rosea* P.M. Brown—pink-flowered form
*North American Native Orchid Journal* 1(1): 17. 1995, type: Newfoundland

**Range:** Alaska east to Newfoundland, south in the Rocky Mountains; south to the upper Great Lakes region and northern New England
**In the Northeast: Maine, New Hampshire, Vermont, New York**: rare and local in northern Maine and Vermont; extirpated in New Hampshire and New York
**Plant:** terrestrial, 4–22 cm tall
**Leaves:** 1; strongly ribbed, ovate to cordate, 12–62 cm wide × 10–54(62) cm long
**Flowers**: 1, or in the forma *biflora*, 2; the petals and sepals erect to spreading pink; the lip saccate, ovate, white with dark maroon markings, or, in the forma *albiflora*, the entire flower pure white or, in the forma *rosea*, entirely pink, all with a prominent golden beard; individual flower size 2–4 cm
**Habitat:** calcareous woodlands usually with arborvitae, *Thuja occidentalis*, and other conifers or in open barrens in Newfoundland and Labrador
**Flowering period:** late May to early July

The undisputed gem of the northern woodlands and barrens, the **eastern fairy-slipper** is a widespread though local orchid that often deserves its ancient name of Hider-of-the-North! Whether it is growing in the deep, dark arborvitae swamps within the woodlands or nestled in the open tundra of Newfoundland, the delicate, captivating flowers demand attention. This is one species that always makes the wish list of new native orchid enthusiasts but, alas, is often one of the last to be seen. Unless growing in very old cedar swamps the plants are vulnerable to succession and local stands may decline each year.

forma *biflora*

forma *rosea*

forma *albiflora*

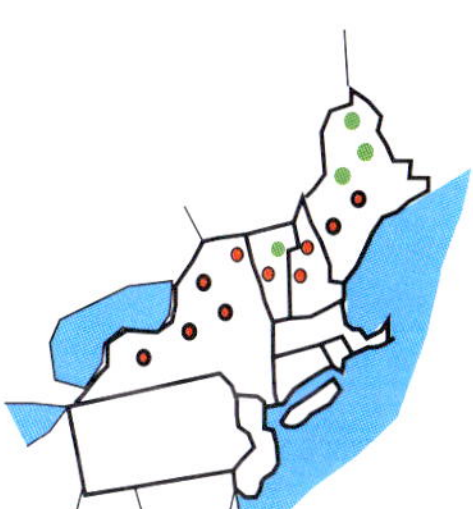

## *Cleistes*

The genus *Cleistes* comprises about 25 species in the Western Hemisphere, including many that grow in wet savannas in northern South America. Most of the species have, at one time, been classified as *Pogonia*, a very closely related genus, and some current authors treat them that way today. Based on recent DNA analyses, the two species in the United States may properly belong in a new genus.

## *Cleistes divaricata* (Linnaeus) Ames

### large spreading pogonia

forma *leucantha* P.M. Brown—white-flowered form
*North American Native Orchid Journal* 1(1): 8. 1995, type: Florida

**Range:** New Jersey south to Florida, primarily along the Coastal Plain
**In the Northeast: New Jersey:** very rare and local with few plants in the Pinelands of New Jersey and (historically) Cape May
**Plant:** terrestrial, 30–70 cm tall
**Leaves:** 1; narrowly lanceolate, glaucous, to 2.5 cm wide × 20.0 cm long; a smaller floral bract, 1.5 × 8.0 cm and resembling a leaf, subtends the flower
**Flowers:** 1, rarely 2; sepals purple, petals deep pink; lip pink veined in darker pink with a yellow crest or, in the forma *leucantha*, the sepals apple green and the petals white; lip to 34–56 mm long, appearing to taper to a point; individual flower size 7 × 7 cm
**Habitat:** open pinelands and damp meadows
**Flowering period:** June to early July

The **large spreading pogonia**, *Cleistes divaricata*, is unquestionably one of the most striking native orchids found on the southeastern Coastal Plain. The large, showy, rosy-pink flowers hold their heads high among the vegetation. Plants seem to flower best two–three years following a burn. Subsequently the competition becomes too dense and only sterile leaves can be found. Although abundant habitat exists in the Pinelands savannas of southern New Jersey, few plants have ever been found and currently even fewer are present. When not flowering it could easily be mistaken for a large plant of the **rose pogonia**, *Pogonia ophioglossoides*, but in flower it would not be misidentified. At various times plants have been seen in Bulltown, Lower Forge, Martha, and the orchid-rich savannas upstream of Quaker Bridge. Stone (1911) notes that it was also found at the Bennett Bogs in Cape May County.

## *Coeloglossum*

*Coeloglossum* is a monotypic circumpolar genus. The plants occur in a variety of habitats in boreal and mountainous areas throughout much of the northern hemisphere. Two varieties are known and a third, var. *interjecta*, intermediate between both the predominately Eurasian var. *viride* and the widespread North American var. *virescens*, was described by Fernald but appears to be based upon plants with the leaves appressed to the stem rather than wide-spreading. Recent molecular studies (Pridgeon et al., 1997; Bateman, 1997) have placed this genus within the genus *Dactylorhiza*, but Sheviak and Catling (FNA, 2002) have chosen to recognize the two genera as separate but closely related.

*Coeloglossum viride* (Linnaeus) Hartman var. *virescens* (Mühlenberg) Luer

**long-bracted green orchis**

**Range**: Alaska east to Newfoundland, south to Washington, New Mexico, Iowa, and North Carolina
**In the Northeast: Maine, New Hampshire, Vermont, Massachusetts, Connecticut, Rhode Island, New York, Pennsylvania, New Jersey:** rare to occasional throughout; more frequent in calcareous woodlands
**Plant:** terrestrial, 20–80 cm tall
**Leaves:** 3–5; 2 cm wide × up to 30 cm long passing into slender floral bracts
**Flowers**: 8–35; the linear petals and ovate sepals forming a hood; the lip oblong and notched at the tip; flowers subtended by bracts distinctly exceeding the flowers; petals and sepals green, the 1 cm lip often suffused with purple; spur minute and inconspicuous
**Habitat:** deciduous mesic woodlands, open coniferous forests, often along roadsides and trails
**Flowering period:** June to August

The **long-bracted green orchis**, despite its coloration, is a conspicuous and distinctive member of the woodland orchid flora of eastern North America. The long, slender bracts subtending each flower give rise to the common name, and upon close examination reveal the distinctive notched lip. After pollination the floral parts remain on the plant so as to appear still in flower many weeks after anthesis.

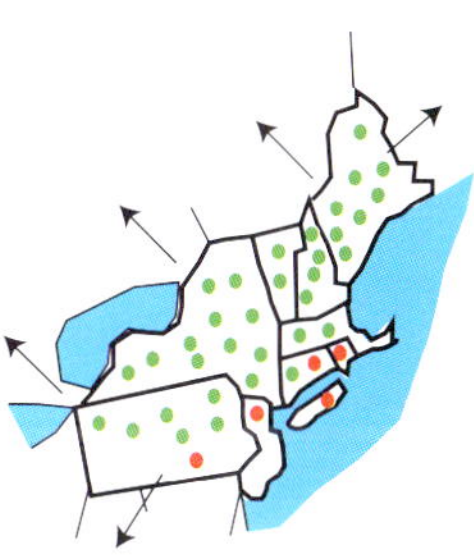

## *Corallorhiza*

The genus *Corallorhiza* has 13 species throughout North America and Hispaniola. One species, *C. trifida*, is widespread across Eurasia. The plants are entirely mycotrophic and some are thought to be saprophytes. They arise from a coralloid rhizome, hence the name. The entire genus is easily recognizable by its leafless stems, although they may be variously colored, and by their small flowers. Five species and two varieties are found within northeastern North America.

### Key to the coralroots, *Corallorhiza*

1a flowers cleistogamous, flower very small, less than 3 mm, autumn flowering . . . . . **autumn coralroot**, *Corallorhiza odontorhiza* var. *odontorhiza*, p. 56
1b flowers chasmogamous . . . 2

2a spring flowering . . . 3
2b summer and autumn flowering . . . 6

3a lip white; plain or more often with dark spots . . . 4
3b lip red or tan, solid or faintly striped; flowers red to orange, tepals striped, wide-spreading . . . . . **striped coralroot**, *Corallorhiza striata* var. *striata*, p. 60

4a stems slender; yellow, chartreuse, or tan; early spring flowering . . . 5
4b stems slender, brownish; petals and sepals indistinct, autumn flowering . . . . . **Pringle's autumn coralroot**, *Corallorhiza odontorhiza* var. *pringlei*, p. 58

5a lip unlobed, spade-shaped, spotted . . . . . **Wister's coralroot**, *Corallorhiza wisteriana*, p. 64
5b lip with 2 lateral lobes or teeth; plain or spotted . . . . . **early coralroot**, *Corallorhiza trifida*, p. 62

6a stems stout; variously colored; petals and sepals distinct; sides of lip broadened, flowers open wide; late spring–summer flowering . . . . . **western spotted coralroot**, *Corallorhiza maculata* var. *occidentalis*, p. 54
6b sides of lip parallel; summer-flowering . . . . . **spotted coralroot,** *Corallorhiza maculata* var. *maculata*, p. 52

## *Corallorhiza maculata* (Rafinesque) Rafinesque var. *maculata*

### spotted coralroot

forma *flavida* (Peck) Farwell—yellow-stemmed form
*Report (Annual) of the Regents University of the State of New York.* New York State Museum 50: 126. 1897, as *Corallorhiza multiflora* var. *flavida* Peck, type: New York

forma *rubra* P.M. Brown—red-stemmed form
*North American Native Orchid Journal* 1(1): 8–9. 1995, type: Vermont

**Range:** British Columbia east to Newfoundland, south to California, Arizona, and New Mexico; in the Appalachian Mountains south to northern Georgia and South Carolina
**In the Northeast: Maine, New Hampshire, Vermont, Massachusetts, Connecticut, Rhode Island, New York, Pennsylvania, New Jersey**: occasional throughout, usually in open woodlands
**Plant:** terrestrial, mycotrophic, 20–50 cm tall; stems bronzy-tan or, in the forma *flavida*, bright yellow or, in the forma *rubra*, red
**Leaves:** none
**Flowers:** 5–20; tepals typically brownish or, in the forma *flavida*, bright yellow or, in the forma *rubra*, red; lip white, spotted with madder purple or, in the forma *flavida*, unspotted or, in the forma *rubra*, spotted with bright red; lip with the middle lobe not expanded, the sides obviously parallel; individual flowers 5.0–7.5 mm, the floral parts not wide-spreading and appearing somewhat cupped; individual flowers 5.0–7.5 mm, mentum obscure
**Habitat:** rich mesic and mixed forests
**Flowering period**: late June to August, rarely into September

The **spotted coralroot** is the most frequently encountered species of coralroot found within eastern North America and widespread and relatively common throughout much of the Northeast. The variation in the stem color is usually evident in even small populations. Annual populations vary greatly and often colonize disturbed areas.

*Corallorhiza maculata* var. *occidentalis*, the **western spotted coralroot**, occurs primarily in the western and northern portions of North America and *C. maculata* var. *mexicana* in southwestern Arizona and Mexico.

forma *rubra*

forma *flavida*

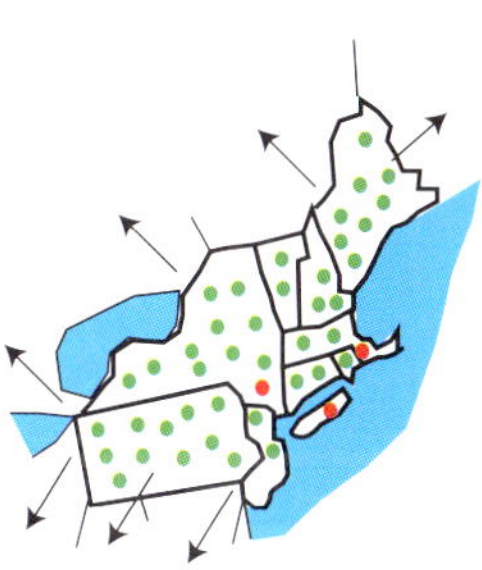

## *Corallorhiza maculata* (Rafinesque) Rafinesque var. *occidentalis* (Lindley) Ames

### western spotted coralroot

forma *aurea* P.M. Brown—golden yellow/spotted form
*North American Native Orchid Journal* 1: 195. 1995, type: Washington

forma *immaculata* (Peck) Howell—yellow spotless form
*Marin Flora*, ed. 2: 363. 1970, as *Corallorhiza maculata* Rafinesque var. *immaculata* M.E. Peck, type: California

forma *intermedia* Farwell—brown-stemmed form
*Report (Annual) of the Michigan Academy of Sciences* 19: 247. 1917, as *Corallorhiza maculata* var. *intermedia* Farwell, type: Michigan

forma *punicea* (Bartholomew) Weatherby & Adams—red-stemmed form
*Rhodora* 24: 147. 1922, as *Corallorrhiza maculata* var. *punicea*, type: Michigan

**Range:** British Columbia east to Newfoundland, south to California, Arizona, New Mexico, Minnesota, New England and Virginia
**In the Northeast: Maine, New Hampshire, Vermont, Massachusetts, Connecticut, Rhode Island, New York, Pennsylvania, New Jersey**: rare to occasional throughout, usually in open mixed woodlands
**Plant:** terrestrial, mycotrophic, 20–50 cm tall; stems bronzy-tan or, in the forma *immaculata*, yellow or, in the forma *intermedia*, brown or, in the forma *punicea*, strikingly deep red
**Leaves:** none
**Flowers:** 5–20+; tepals typically colored bronzy-tan as the stems or, in the forma *intermedia*, the stems' brown or, in the forma *punicea*, the stems' deep red with the lip spotted in purple or dark red or, in the forma *immaculata*, yellow to white, the lip lacking all spotting; lip with the middle lobe expanded, the sides obviously broadened; individual flowers 5.0–7.5 mm, the floral parts widespreading, mentum obscure
**Habitat:** rich mesic and mixed forests
**Flowering period:** late May to July

The common name **western spotted coralroot** is somewhat misleading as this variety extends eastward through the Great Lakes region to Newfoundland and south, sparingly, to West Virginia. Northward both the nominate variety and var. *occidentalis* may occur in the same woodlands and are usually well separated in flowering time. The broadened lip easily separates var. *occidentalis* from the straight-sided lip of var. *maculata*.

forma *immaculata*

forma *aurea*

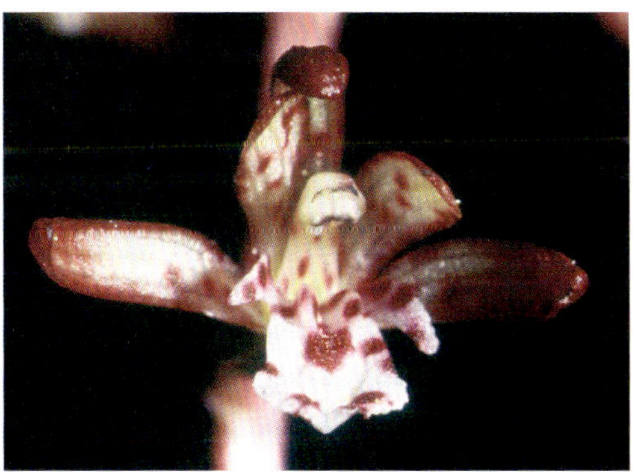

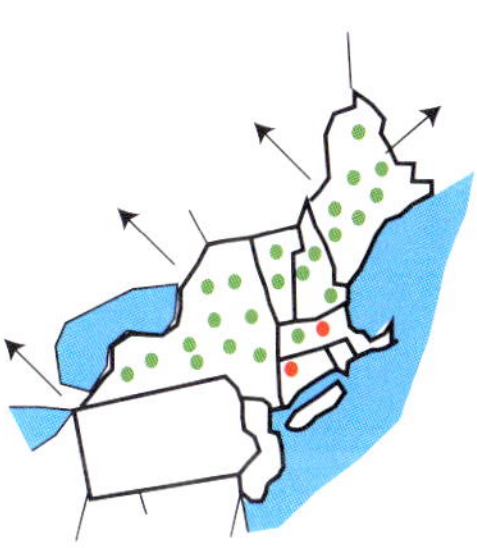

## *Corallorhiza odontorhiza* (Willdenow) Poiret var. *odontorhiza*

**autumn coralroot**

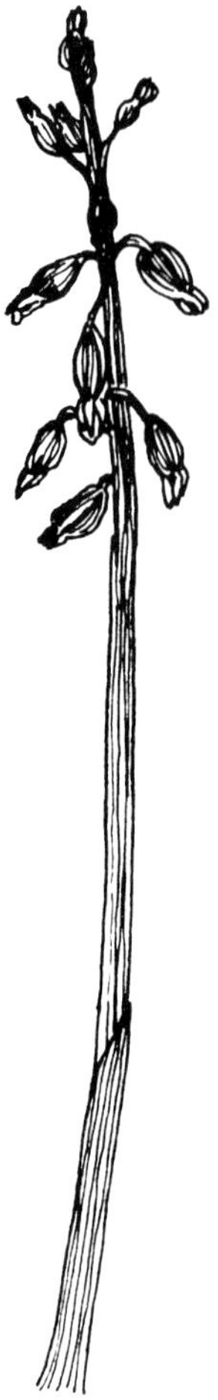

forma *flavida* Wherry—yellow-stemmed form
*Journal of the Washington Academy of Science* 17: 36. 1927, type: Washington, D.C.

**Range:** South Dakota east to Maine, south to Oklahoma and northern Florida
**In the Northeast: Maine, New Hampshire, Vermont, Massachusetts, Connecticut, Rhode Island, New York, Pennsylvania, New Jersey**: widespread, but never common
**Plant:** terrestrial, mycotrophic, 5–10 cm tall; stems bronzy-green or, in the forma *flavida*, yellow
**Leaves:** lacking
**Flowers:** 5–12; cleistogamous; sepals green suffused with purple, covering the petals; lip, rarely evident in this variety, white spotted with purple or, in the forma *flavida*, unspotted; individual flower size 3–4 mm
**Habitat:** rich, calcareous woodlands
**Flowering period:** September to October

The fact that this inconspicuous little orchid is rarely found may be attributed more to its size and habit than necessarily to its rarity. The **autumn coralroot** appears to be never common anywhere and is usually found by accident. Although easily overlooked this plant is rare in the north and becomes more frequent in calcareous woodlands and disturbed areas southward.

The short stems often flower among the fallen leaves in the autumn months and the coloration, *sans* chlorophyll, makes them even harder to see. Woodlands near or among old limestone and marble quarrying activities are often a good place to search for this species.

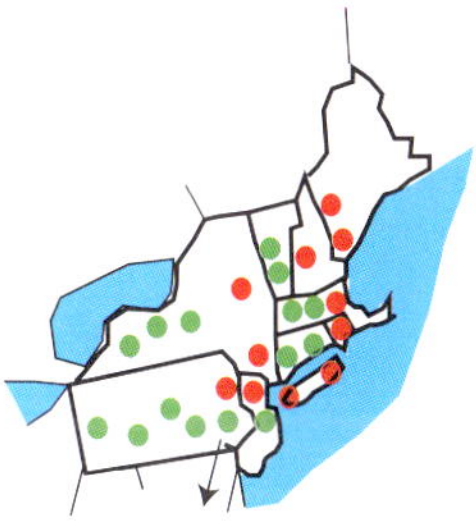

## *Corallorhiza odontorhiza* (Willdenow) Poiret var. *pringlei* (Greenman) Freudenstein

### Pringle's autumn coralroot

**Range**: Wisconsin and Ontario east to Maine, south to Iowa, Tennessee, and Georgia; Mexico, Central America
**In the Northeast: Maine, Vermont, Massachusetts, Connecticut, Pennsylvania, New York**: rare and scattered distribution
**Plant:** terrestrial, mycotrophic, 5–15 cm tall; stems bronzy-green
**Leaves:** lacking
**Flowers:** 5–12; chasmogamous; the sepals green suffused with purple, spreading and revealing the petals; lip broad, white, spotted with purple; individual flower size 5–10 mm
**Habitat:** rich, mesic forests and calcareous woodlands
**Flowering period:** September to October

**Pringle's autumn coralroot** is an extremely rare variety with its center of distribution in the lower Great Lakes. This variety has been only recently described; although plants with showy, chasmogamous, wide-spreading flowers and well-developed lips have been known for some time, this may be an extreme expression of the nominate variety.

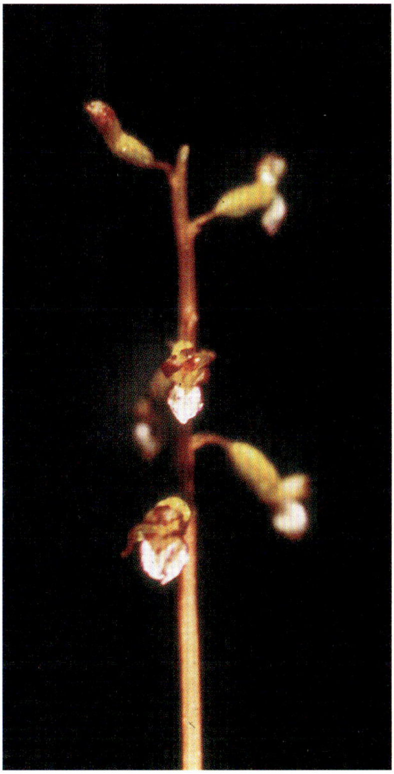

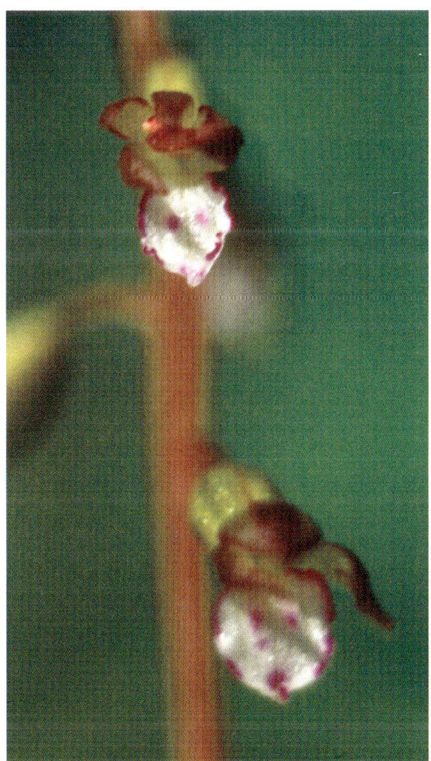

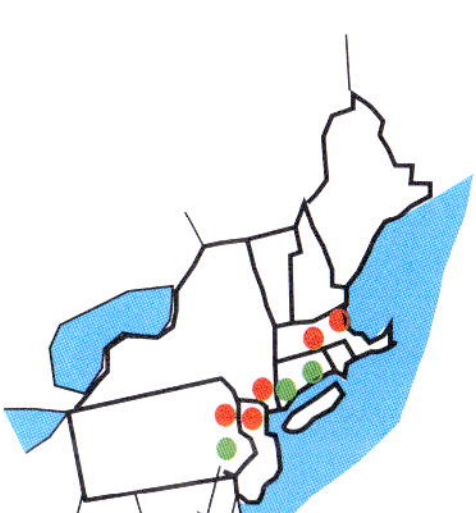

## *Corallorhiza striata* Lindley var. *striata*

### striped coralroot

forma *eburnea* P.M. Brown—yellow/white form
*North American Native Orchid Journal* 1(1): 9. 1995, type: New Mexico

forma *fulva* Fernald—dusky tan-colored form
*Rhodora* 48: 197. 1946, type: Quebec

**Range:** British Columbia east to Newfoundland, south to California, Texas, and New York
**In the Northeast: New York, [Vermont]:** very rare in cold swamps near Syracuse
**Plant:** terrestrial, mycotrophic, 20–50 cm tall; stems golden-pink with reddish-purple lines or, in the forma *eburnea*, the stems yellow or, in the forma *fulva*, the stems tawny
**Leaves:** none
**Flowers:** 8–35; tepals yellowish-pink with reddish-purple lines; lip white but striped purple-red with confluent lines and appearing solid or, in the forma *eburnea*, flowers yellow to white or, in the forma *fulva*, the flowers tawny; individual flowers ca. 0.75–1.5 cm
**Habitat:** rich mesic and mixed forests
**Flowering period**: late May to July

The **striped coralroot** is the largest and certainly the showiest of all the coralroots in North America. A common orchid of the upper Great Lakes area, this striking species has long been known from Cazenovia, New York. Plants there are sporadic in their appearance and often grow in the company of yellow lady's-slippers. The Vermont report is that of Dole in *Flora of Vermont* (1936). Although abundant habitat exists in the northern portions of the state the species has never been vouchered.

forma *eburnea*

## *Corallorhiza trifida* Chatelain

### early coralroot

forma *verna* (Nuttall) P.M. Brown—yellow stemmed/white lipped form

*Journal of the Academy of Natural Sciences*, Philadelphia 3: 136. 1823 as *Corallorhiza verna* Nuttall, type: Massachussetts

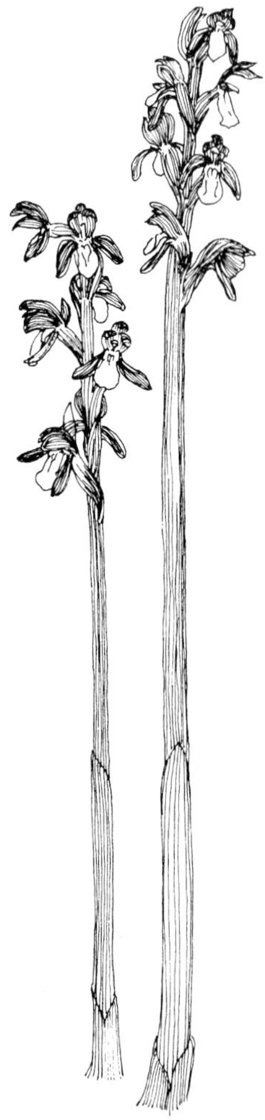

**Range:** Alaska east to Newfoundland, south to California, northern New Mexico, and in scattered localities to West Virginia

**In the Northeast: Maine, New Hampshire, Vermont, Massachusetts, Connecticut, Rhode Island, New York, Pennsylvania, New Jersey**: occasional to local, especially northward

**Plant:** terrestrial, mycotrophic, 5–30 cm tall; stems yellow to yellow-green in the south to bronze in the far north

**Leaves:** none

**Flowers:** 8–15; tepals yellow-green to bronze, occasionally spotted with purple, wide-spreading; lip white, often spotted with purple, especially in highly colored northern individuals; mentum inconspicuous; individual flowers 0.5–1.0 cm

**Habitat:** rich mesic and mixed forests, open tundra and barrens

**Flowering period**: late May to July

Although smaller than many of the other coralroots in our area, the bright greenish-yellow stems of **early coralroot** stand out among their forest companions. In the northernmost areas plants grow out in the open barrens and tundra and tend to blend in a bit more. Coloration can vary somewhat in that the plants of open exposed areas are often suffused with bronze and the floral parts with purple spots. The plants more common in the southern portion of the range with pure white lips were designated as variety *verna* by Nuttall nearly 200 years ago, but that variation is better treated as a form.

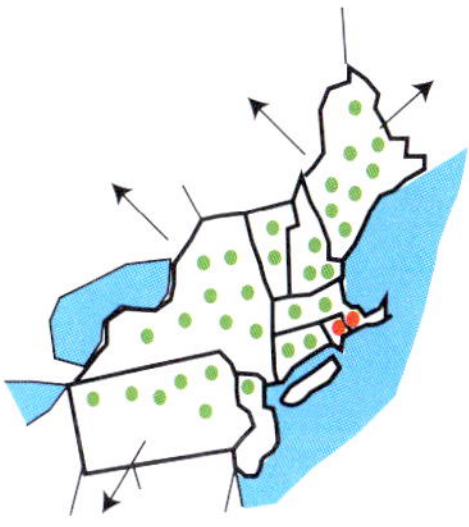

## *Corallorhiza wisteriana* Conrad

### Wister's coralroot

forma *albolabia* P.M. Brown—white-lipped form
*North American Native Orchid Journal* 1(1): 9–10. 1995, type: Florida

forma *cooperi* P.M. Brown—cranberry-pink colored form
*North American Native Orchid Journal* 10: 22. 2004, type: Florida

forma *rubra* P.M. Brown—red-stemmed form
*North American Native Orchid Journal* 1(1): 62 (pl. 4). 2000, type: Florida

**Range:** Washington east to New Jersey, south to Arizona and Florida; Mexico
**In the Northeast**: **Pennsylvania, New Jersey**: very rare and not reliable
**Plant:** terrestrial, mycotrophic, 5–30 cm tall; stem brownish-yellow or, in the forma *albolabia*, yellow or, in the forma *rubra*, red or, in the forma *cooperi*, cranberry-pink
**Leaves:** lacking
**Flowers:** 5–25; sepals green, petals yellow suffused and mottled with purple; lip white spotted with purple or, in the forma *albolabia*, yellow-stemmed, sepals and petals yellow with a pure white lip or, in the forma *cooperi*, the stems, petals, and sepals cranberry-pink, the lip white with dark pink markings or, in the forma *rubra*, red-stemmed, sepals and petals red, with flowers marked red; individual flower size 5–7 mm
**Habitat:** rich, often calcareous woodlands, pine flatwoods, occasionally in lawns and foundation plantings
**Flowering period:** early spring

One of the first orchids to flower in the spring, **Wister's coralroot**, *Corallorhiza wisteriana*, is a great rarity in the Northeast. Just southeast and south of the range of this book plants are more plentiful. There are several records for southeastern Pennsylvania but only one, presumed extirpated, for New Jersey. The pale brown stems and small, spotted, white flowers can often be found as individual plants, but some disturbed sites may have several hundred plants in large clustered colonies. The three color forms are exceedingly rare and known from very few sites.

forma *albolabia*

forma *cooperi*

forma *rubra*

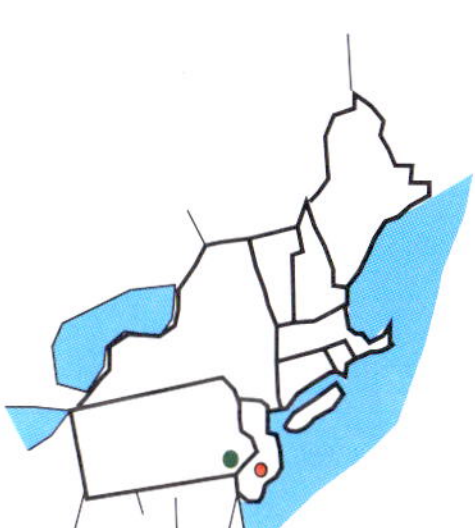

## *Cypripedium*

*Cypripedium* is a distinctive genus of about 45 species, with 12 occurring in North America north of Mexico. Although the leaf arrangement is variable, the lip, an unmistakable pouch-shaped slipper, is always diagnostic. This is often the genus that is first recognized by orchid enthusiasts. There are five species of lady's-slipper found within northeastern North America. The foliage of several species often causes an itching dermatitis, often helpful in catching poachers!

### Key to the lady's-slippers

1a leaves basal . . . . . **pink lady's-slipper**, *Cypripedium acaule*, p. 68
1b leaves cauline . . . 2

2a sepals and petals white, lip shades of pink . . . . . **showy lady's-slipper**, *Cypripedium reginae*, p. 80
2b sepals and petals otherwise . . . 3

3a lip white, veined and spotted with purple; sepals 3 . . . . . **ram's-head lady's-slipper**, *Cypripedium arietinum*, p. 70
3b lip yellow . . . 4

4a flowers commonly large, lip to 5.4 cm long; sepals and petals unmarked to spotted, striped, or reticulately marked with reddish-brown or madder; plants of a variety of habitats, usually mesic to calcareous woodlands or open sites in limestone prairies . . . . . **large yellow lady's-slipper**, *Cypripedium parviflorum* var. *pubescens*, p. 78
4b flowers small, lip 1.5–2.9 cm long . . . 5

5a lip white, petals marked with purple, lip white, often streaked with lavender . . . . . **small white lady's-slipper**, *Cypripedium candidum*, p. 72
5b lip yellow . . . 6

6a flowers small, lip 2.2–3.4 cm long; sepals and petals usually densely spotted with dark reddish-brown appearing as a uniformly dark wash; plants of dry, deciduous, more acidic sites than *C. parviflorum* var. *pubescens* . . . . . **southern small yellow lady's-slipper**, *Cypripedium parviflorum* var. *parviflorum*, p. 74
6b sepals and petals usually suffused with dark reddish-brown or madder; scent intensely sweet; plants of calcareous fens and other mesic to limy wetlands . . . . . **northern small yellow lady's-slipper**, *Cypripedium parviflorum* var. *makasin*, p. 76

## *Cypripedium acaule* Aiton

### pink lady's-slipper, moccasin flower

forma *albiflorum* Rand & Redfield—white-flowered form
*Flora of Mt. Desert Island* 154. 1894, type: Maine

forma *biflorum* P.M. Brown—two-flowered form
*North American Native Orchid Journal* 1: 197. 1995, type: New Hampshire

forma *lancifolium* House—narrow-leaved form
*New York State Museum Bulletin* 254: 236. 1924, type: New York

**Range:** Northwest Territories east to Newfoundland, south to Minnesota, Mississippi, and Georgia
**In the Northeast: Maine, New Hampshire, Vermont, Massachusetts, Connecticut, Rhode Island, New York, Pennsylvania, New Jersey**: occasional throughout, usually in open woodlands, rarely in sphagnum bogs and heaths
**Plant:** terrestrial, 10–55 cm tall
**Leaves:** 2; oblong-obovate, 5–13 cm wide × 10–30 cm long or, in the forma *lancifolium*, 3–5 cm wide; pubescent
**Flowers:** 1, rarely 2 in the forma *biflorum*; sepals green to reddish-brown, petals bronze; lip pale rosy-pink to deep raspberry or, in the forma *albiflorum*, white with pale green petals and sepals; individual flower size ca. 4 × 4 cm; lip 3–6 cm long with a longitudinal fissure
**Habitat:** mixed hardwood and coniferous forest; usually in highly acidic soils
**Flowering period:** late May–July

Perhaps one of the most familiar orchids in eastern North America, *Cypripedium acaule*, the **pink lady's-slipper** or **moccasin flower,** is variable in color and presents itself in just about every shade of pink, some actually tending toward peach. The white-flowered forma *albiflorum* is more frequent northward. Although it is the common lady's-slipper of New England, as one proceeds northward or into limestone areas it becomes one of the rare species of the genus. Occasionally plants are found in sphagnum bogs where they are often dwarfed. Plants are notoriously difficult to transplant and re-establish, although they may persist for a few years. Resist the temptation to move plants, unless they are to be destroyed. It is far better to just admire them in their natural surroundings.

forma *biflorum*

forma *albiflorum*

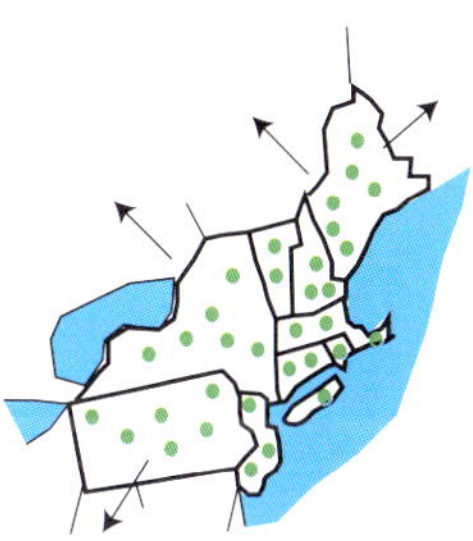

## *Cypripedium arietinum* R. Brown

### ram's-head lady's-slipper

forma *albiflorum* House—white-flowered form
*New York State Museum Bulletin* 243–244: 48. 1923, type: New York

forma *biflorum* P.M. Brown—two-flowered form
*North American Native Orchid Journal* 1(3): 198. 1995, type: Vermont

**Range:** Minnesota east to Nova Scotia, south to Massachusetts
**In the Northeast: Maine, New Hampshire, Vermont, Massachusetts, Connecticut, New York**: rare and local
**Plant:** terrestrial, 10–33 cm tall
**Leaves:** 3–4; elliptic-lanceolate, bluish-green; 1.5–3.0 cm wide × 5–10 cm long
**Flowers:** 1, rarely 2 in the forma *biflorum*; dorsal sepal ovate-lanceolate, greenish with purple-brown veining, lateral sepals separate, slender, slightly twisted, bronzy-green to purplish; petals similar to lateral sepals; lip funnel-shaped, broadened above; white with pink to deep raspberry veining or, in the forma *albiflorum*, white with pale green petals and sepals; individual flower size ca. 1.5 × 2.0 cm; lip 1 cm long with an oval fissure densely pubescent on the margin
**Habitat:** mixed hardwood and coniferous forest; usually in circumneutral to calcareous soils; also found in areas of gypsum
**Flowering period:** late May though June

The **ram's-head lady's-slipper,** *Cypripedium arietinum*, is the smallest flowered and most inconspicuous of all of our species of lady's-slippers. The flowers are about the size of the tip of your finger and are held aloft at the top of the stem. In northern New England it is nowhere common, and southward it is exceedingly rare. Plants are usually confined to calcareous woodlands. The shape of the lip is unique among our North American species and is found again only in the Asian analog, *Cypripedium plectrochilum*. This species is of conservation concern in every state and province in which it occurs.

forma *albolabium*

forma *biflorum*

## *Cypripedium candidum* Mühlenberg *ex* Willdenow

### small white lady's-slipper

**Range:** Saskatchewan south to Nebraska, east to western New York, south to Missouri, Kentucky, and New Jersey; Alabama

**In the Northeast: New York, Pennsylvania, New Jersey**: very rare with few remaining populations

**NATIONALLY SIGNIFICANT SPECIES**

**Globally Threatened**

**Plant:** terrestrial, 11–30 cm tall

**Leaves:** 3–5; alternate, ascending, elliptic to oblanceolate, 2–5 cm wide × 10–20 cm long

**Flowers:** 1–3; sepals and petals green to ochre striped with magenta, lateral sepals united; petals undulate and spiraled; lip white with delicate lavender striping beneath; individual flower size ca. 4 × 3 cm; lip 1.5–2.6 cm, the opening ovate at the base of the lip

**Habitat:** calcareous fens and prairies

**Flowering period:** early spring; late May to early June in our area

The **small white lady's-slipper**, *Cypripedium candidum*, is one of the most imperiled of all the lady's-slippers in North America. Remnant populations may still be found in both New York and New Jersey. Although plants were once known within sight of the city of Syracuse, New York, remaining populations are all in the Rochester vicinity, with the primary populations in Bergen Swamp. When in flower this is the shortest in stature of the eastern lady's-slippers and one of the most highly scented. A delicate, but distinct sweet odor can be detected from as far away as a meter. When the plants emerge the flower bud(s) are tightly enclosed within the unfolding leaves and then pop out to open while the leaves are still usually clasping. After flowering the leaves then fully expand, although they still remain erect. Deep fens in northern New Jersey harbor the few remaining plants in that state and the Pennsylvania plants are presumed extirpated.

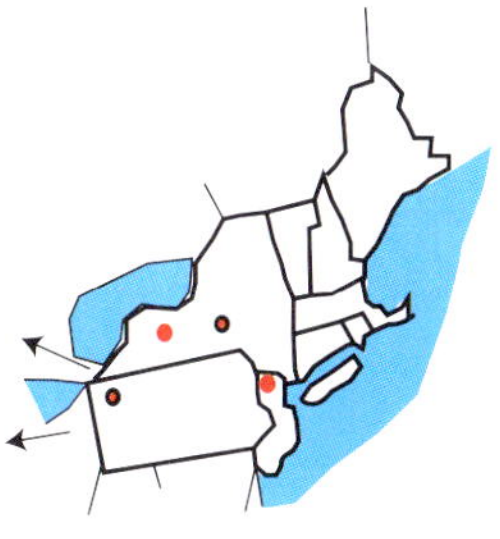

## *Cypripedium parviflorum* Salisbury var. *parviflorum*

### southern small yellow lady's-slipper

forma *albolabium* Magrath & Norman—white-lipped form
*Sida* 13: 372. 1989, type: Oklahoma

**Range:** Kansas east to Massachusetts, south to Arkansas and Georgia
**In the Northeast: Massachusetts, Rhode Island, Connecticut, New York, Pennsylvania, New Jersey**: rare and local in the temperate deciduous forests
**Plant:** terrestrial, 10–60 cm tall
**Leaves:** 4–5; alternate, evenly spaced along the stem, spreading; ovate to ovate-elliptic to lance-elliptic, 2.5–8.0 cm wide × 10–18 long
**Flowers:** 1–2 (3); sepals and petals uniformly dark with dense, minute dark chestnut or reddish-brown spots, often appearing a uniform color; lateral sepals united; petals undulate and spiraled to 10 cm long; lip slipper-shaped, deep, rich yellow, often with scarlet marking within the lip or, in the forma *albolabium*, white; individual flower size ca. 4.5 × 10.0 cm; lip 2.2–3.4 cm, the opening ovate-oblong at the base of the lip
**Habitat:** decidedly acid, deciduous, dry to mesic wooded slopes
**Flowering period:** late spring; early to late May in our area

The recent separation of the two small yellow lady's-slippers has solved an often confusing question. How can small-flowered, dark-petalled yellow lady's-slippers that occur in dry, acid woods be the same as the similar plants in typical calcareous woodlands and wetlands? The answer is that they are not the same; nor are they gradations of the large yellow. The habitat, range, and delicate roselike fragrance should be more than sufficient to identify this uncommon variety. Plants of *Cypripedium parviflorum* var. *pubescens* occurring in acid woodlands should be carefully examined for the possibility of *C. parviflorum* var. *parviflorum*.

forma *albolabium*

Var. *pubescens* and var. *parviflorum*

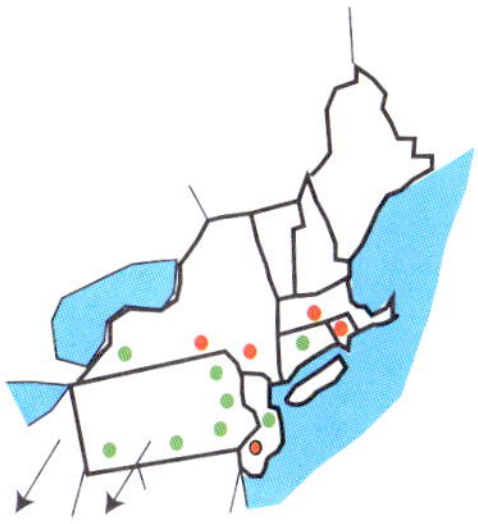

*Cypripedium parviflorum* Salisbury var. *makasin* (Farwell) Sheviak

**northern small yellow lady's-slipper**

**Range:** British Columbia south to northern California, east to Newfoundland, south to Illinois and Pennsylvania

**In the Northeast: Maine, New Hampshire, Vermont, Massachusetts, Pennsylvania, New York**: locally scattered in calcareous wetlands; usually in small populations

**Plant:** terrestrial, 15–35 cm tall

**Leaves:** 3–5; alternate, spreading; ovate to ovate-elliptic to lance-elliptic, 1.6–12.0 cm wide × 5.0–20 cm long; the outer surface of the lowermost sheathing bract sparsely pubescent to glabrous when young

**Flowers:** 1–2(3); sepals and petals suffused with a dark reddish-brown or madder, often appearing as a uniform color; lateral sepals united; petals undulate and spiraled to 10 cm long; lip ovoid, slipper-shaped, usually a deep, rich yellow, with scarlet to purple markings within the lip; individual flower size ca. 2.0 × 3.0 cm; lip 1.5–2.9 cm long, the opening ovate-oblong at the base of the lip; intensely sweetly scented

**Habitat:** mesic to calcareous, moist woodlands, streamsides, bogs, fens, and, to a lesser degree, open heaths

**Flowering period:** late May and on into July northward

The small, richly colored and intensely fragrant flowers of the **northern small yellow lady's-slipper** are in most instances easily distinguished from those of the **large yellow lady's-slipper**. Where the confusion occurs is in finding plants of *Cypripedium parviflorum* var. *pubescens* that have rich, dark petals. Usually these plants also have large lips. Habitat is often a help but it is important to check out all the criteria. In northern Newfoundland it becomes more of a problem as both species grow in the open heaths. The intense fragrance of var. *makasin* is a great help. In all areas of the northeast var. *pubescens* is more frequent than var. *makasin*.

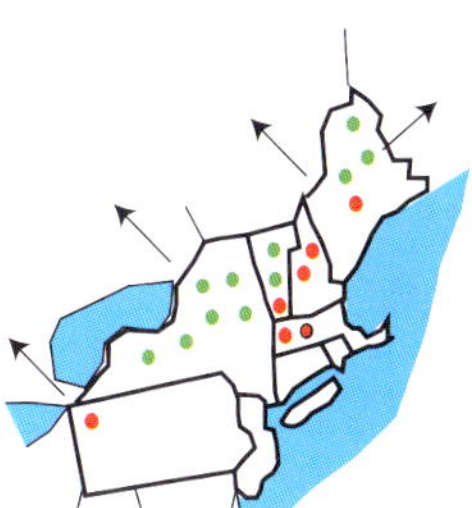

## *Cypripedium parviflorum* Salisbury var. *pubescens* (Willdenow) Knight

### large yellow lady's-slipper

**Range:** Alaska east to Newfoundland, south to Arizona and Georgia
**In the Northeast: Maine, New Hampshire, Vermont, Massachusetts, Connecticut, Rhode Island, New York, Pennsylvania, New Jersey:** locally scattered in neutral to calcareous woodlands; more frequent northward
**Plant:** terrestrial, 15–60 cm tall
**Leaves:** 3–5; alternate, somewhat evenly spaced along the stem, spreading; ovate to ovate-elliptic to lance-elliptic, 2.5–12.0 cm wide × 8.0–20.0 cm long; the outer surface of the lowermost sheathing bract densely pubescent with short, silvery hairs when young
**Flowers:** 1–3(4); sepals and petals spotted, splotched, or marked with brown, chestnut, or reddish-brown spots, rarely appearing as a uniform color; lateral sepals united; petals undulate and spiraled to 10 cm long; lip slipper-shaped, from pale to a deep, rich yellow, less often with scarlet markings within the lip; individual flower size ca. 4.5 × 12.0 cm; lip 2.5–5.4 cm, the opening ovate-oblong at the base of the lip; scent moderate to faint, reminiscent of old roses
**Habitat:** a wide variety of mesic to calcareous, wet to dry woodlands, streamsides, bogs, and fens
**Flowering period:** mid-May, into June through July in the far north

*Cypripedium parviflorum* var. *pubescens* is the classic yellow lady's-slipper so familiar to many wildflower lovers and gardeners. Although it has declined dramatically in some areas in the past twenty-five years, it still can be found in rich forests and swamps throughout much of the mesic and calcareous woodlands of our region. The fact that this is one of the few native orchids than can be cultivated in the garden has led to its decline in the wild. It is not that unusual to come upon sites where in past years there have been many plants, only to find many holes where they have been dug. Because the plants do grow well under cultivation they can be purchased as propagated plants so there is no need for stealing them from the wild! In Aroostook County, Maine, central and northern Vermont, and northern New York this is the most frequently encountered lady's-slipper.

## *Cypripedium reginae* Walter

### showy lady's-slipper

forma *albolabium* Fernald & Schubert—white-flowered form
*Rhodora* 50: 230. 1948, type: hort.

**Range:** Saskatchewan east to Newfoundland, south to Arkansas and southern North Carolina
**In the Northeast: Maine, New Hampshire, Vermont, Massachusetts, Connecticut, New York, Pennsylvania, New Jersey:** locally common in calcareous swamps and fens
**Plant:** robust, to 90 cm tall, often forming large clumps
**Leaves:** 3–5; alternate, somewhat evenly spaced along the stem, spreading; ovate to ovate-elliptic, densely pubescent with distinctive hairs throughout, 6.5–16.0 cm wide × 10.0–25.0 cm long
**Flowers:** 1–3(4); sepals and petals white; dorsal sepal arching or erect, lateral sepals united and cupped under the lip; petals oblong, wide-spreading to 4.7 cm long; lip slipper-shaped, from pale to deep, rich red or maroon or, in the forma *albolabium*, white; the staminode white with contrasting yellow markings; individual flower size ca. 8 × 12 cm; lip globose, 2.5–5.4 cm, the opening ovate
**Habitat:** wet swamps, seeps, calcareous meadows, and open woodlands
**Flowering period:** June into July

*Cypripedium reginae*, the queen of the lady's-slippers, is one of the showiest and most dramatic of all our native orchids. It is not unusual to find swamps with several thousand plants in flower and clumps of many dozen stems. The plants have a preference for calcareous areas and are happy in standing water. In Aroostook County, Maine, and northern Vermont it is not unusual to be able to see plants from the side of the roadway! Some swamps have been known to support upward of 10,000 flowering plants! The stiff hairs on the leaves and stems are an infamous source of dermatitis and more than once have helped to identify a local poacher!

forma *albolabium*

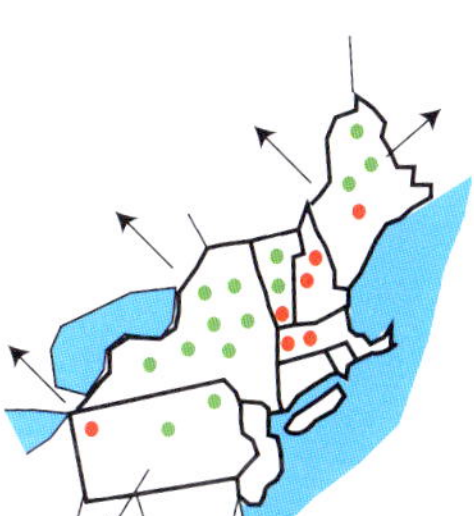

**Hybrids**:

Three interesting hybrids have often been noted from areas where *Cypripedium parviflorum*, in variety, and *C. candidum* are sympatric.

*Cypripedium* ×*andrewsii* Fuller nm *andrewsii*

**Andrews' hybrid lady's-slipper**

(*C. candidum* × *C. parviflorum* var. *makasin*)

*Rhodora* 34: 242. 1932, as *Cypripedium* ×*andrewsii*, type: Wisconsin

*Cypripedium* ×*andrewsii* Fuller nm *favillianum* (Curtis) Boivin

**Faville's hybrid lady's-slipper**

(*C. candidum* × *C. parviflorum* var. *pubescens*)

*Rhodora* 34: 100. 1932, as *Cypripedium* ×*favillianum*, type: Wisconsin

*Cypripedium ×andrewsii* nm *landonii* (Garay) Boivin

**Landon's hybrid lady's-slipper**

(*C. candidum × C. ×andrewsii* nm *favillianum*)

*Canadian Journal of Botany* 31: 660. 1953, as *Cypripedium ×landonii*, type: Ontario

Occasionally hybrids persist when either or both parents are no longer found in the vicinity. This is especially true of *C. candidum*.

*Cypripedium ×herae* Ewacha & Sheviak

**Queen Hera's hybrid lady's-slipper**

*Orchids* 73(4): 296–299. 2004.

This is a curious hybrid between *Cypripedium parviflorum* var. *pubescens* and *C. reginae* that was recently described from near Winnipeg, Manitoba. Although the two parents may often grow nearby throughout much of the range, they flower together only in the far northern portion of their ranges and until now have not been documented to hybridize. The hybrid should be actively sought throughout the sympatric range of the two species. Artificial hybrids of this cross have been made. They are named *Cypripedium* 'Genesis,' and are available commercially.

## *Epipactis*

*Epipactis* is a cosmopolitan genus of about 25 species, with only one, *E. gigantea*, native in (western) North America. Two Eurasian species can also be found in eastern North America.

### Key to the helleborines, *Epipactis*

1a lip a saccate pouch, flowers varying from green to white to reddish, widespread throughout the Northeast . . . . . **broad-leaved helleborine**, *Epipactis helleborine*, p. 87

1b lip spade-shaped, flowers red; very rare in northern Vermont . . . . . **red helleborine**, *Epipactis atrorubens*, p. 85

## *Epipactis atrorubens* (Hoffman *ex* Bernhardii) Besser

### red helleborine*

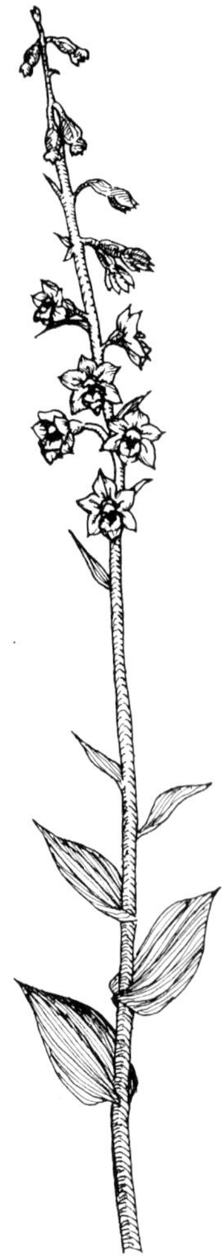

**Range:** Europe
**In the Northeast: Vermont:** in an abandoned asbestos quarry
**Plant:** terrestrial, 10–40 cm tall
**Leaves:** 3–7; alternate, spreading; lance-elliptic, 2.5–4.0 cm wide × 10.0–18.0 cm long
**Flowers:** 15–50; deep red, individual flowers 1–2 cm across
**Habitat:** rocky woodlands; in Vermont they are found in an abandoned asbestos quarry accompanied by several other very unusual plants including the firmoss, *Huperzia selago*, and Green Mountain maidenhair fern, *Adiantum viridi-montanum*.
**Flowering period:** July to August

Although *Epipactis atrorubens*, the **red helleborine**, has occasionally been erroneously reported in North America (Montreal; Scoggin, 1978), the first confirmed site for this European species was in northern Vermont in an abandoned asbestos quarry. The previous reports have proven to be red-flowered plants of the **broad-leaved helleborine**, *Epipactis helleborine*.

## *Epipactis helleborine* (Linnaeus) Cranz

**broad-leaved helleborine***

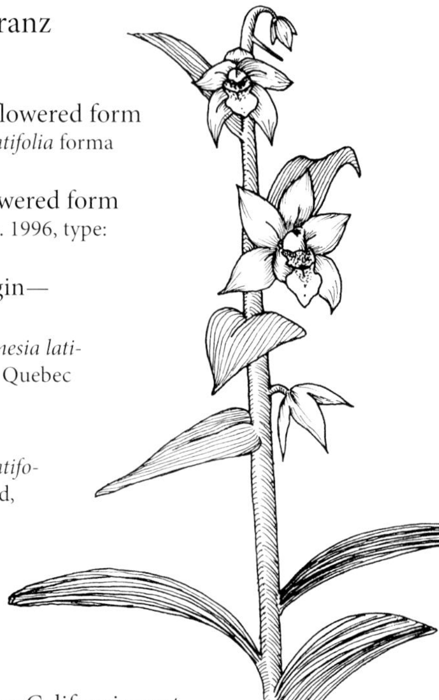

forma *alba* (Webster) Boivin—white-flowered form
*British Orchids*, ed. 2: 21. 1898, as *Epipactis latifolia* forma *alba*, type: Wales

forma *luteola* P.M. Brown—yellow-flowered form
*North American Native Orchid Journal* 4: 318. 1996, type: New Hampshire

forma *monotropoides* (Mousley) Scoggin—albino form
*Canadian Field-Naturalist* 41: 30. 1927, as *Amesia latifolia* forma *monotropoides* Mousley, type: Quebec

forma *variegata* (Webster) Boivin—variegated form
*British Orchids*, ed. 2: 22. 1898, as *Epipactis latifolia* forma *variegata* Webster, type: England, Wales

forma *viridens* A. Gray—green-flowered form
*Botanical Gazette* 4: 202. 1879, type: New York

**Range:** eastern North America; southeastern California; scattered in western North America; Europe
**In the Northeast: Maine, New Hampshire, Vermont, Massachusetts, Connecticut, Rhode Island, New York, Pennsylvania, New Jersey**: becoming locally common in restricted, usually calcareous, areas
**Plant:** terrestrial, 10–80 cm tall, entirely white in the forma *monotropoides*
**Leaves:** 3–7; alternate, spreading; lance-elliptic, 2.5–4.0 cm wide × 10.0–18.0 cm long, green or, in the forma *variegata*, with white markings or, in the forma *monotropoides*, white
**Flowers:** 15–50; yellow-green usually suffused with rosy-pink or, in the forma *alba*, white or, in the forma *luteola*, yellow or, in the forma *viridens*, green; individual flowers 1–3 cm across
**Habitat:** highly variable, from shaded calcareous woodlands to front lawns and garden beds and even the crack in a concrete sidewalk; typically a lime-lover
**Flowering period:** July to August

The widespread European **broad-leaved helleborine**, *Epipactis helleborine*, was first found in North America near Syracuse, New York, in 1878. In the ensuing century-plus it has spread throughout the region and can now be found all the way eastward to downtown Boston, Massachusetts, northward to Nova Scotia and Newfoundland, and, in recent years, westward to California. Plants appear to pop up here and there, usually in the vicinity of calcareous soils or debris. It can be equally happy in woodland and exposed situations. With the exception of forma *viridens*, the various forms are exceedingly rare and are represented by very few collections.

forma *alba*

forma *luteola*

forma *monotropoides*

## *Galearis*

*Galearis* is a small genus of two species with bractless, angled stems and two or three succulent, basal leaves. One species occurs in North America, the other in Asia. Both have showy flowers and have formerly been treated in the genus *Orchis*.

## *Galearis spectabilis* (Linnaeus) Rafinesque

### showy orchis

forma *gordinierii* (House) Whiting & Catling—white-flowered form
*Bulletin of the State Museum of New York* 50: 243–244. 1923, as *Galeorchis spectabilis* forma *gordinierii* House, type: New York

forma *willeyi* (Seymour) P.M. Brown—pink-flowered form
*Rhodora* 72: 48. 1970, as *Orchis spectabilis* forma *willeyi* Seymour, type: Vermont

**Range:** Minnesota east to New Brunswick, south to eastern Oklahoma and Georgia
**In the Northeast: Maine, New Hampshire, Vermont, Massachusetts, Connecticut, Rhode Island, New York, Pennsylvania, New Jersey:** local in mesic or calcareous, deciduous woodlands
**Plant:** terrestrial, 10–15 cm tall
**Leaves:** 2(4); essentially basal, ovate to oblanceolate, 5–10 cm wide × 6–21 cm long
**Flowers:** 3–17; in a loose, terminal spike; floral bract conspicuous and often exceeding the flowers; petals and sepals lavender-purple, lip white; in the forma *gordinierii* the flowers entirely white or, in the forma *willeyi,* the flowers entirely purple; individual flower size ca. 3.5 × 4.5 cm
**Habitat:** rich mesic or calcareous woodlands, often on slopes and streamsides
**Flowering period:** June

**Showy orchis,** *Galearis spectabilis,* is an orchid that is typical of the rich, mesic forest of the Appalachians. It has a preference for neutral to calcareous soils. The fleshy, almost succulent, leaves are distinctive and the plants are often the favorite rooting area for skunks that like to feast on the tasty roots. Many a time it has been assumed that orchid thieves have dug the plants when it has been our striped friends!

forma *gordinierii*

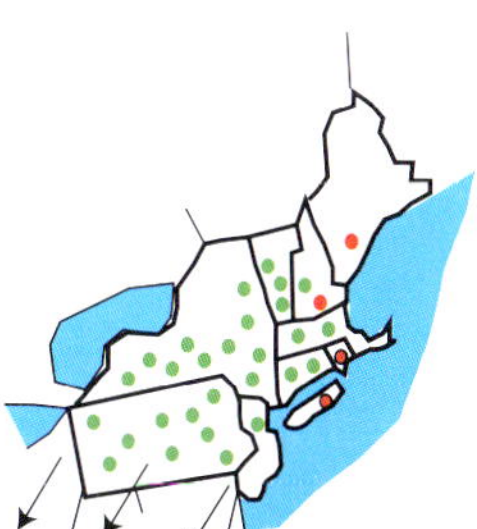

forma *willeyi*

## *Goodyera*

A large genus that is widespread throughout the world, *Goodyera* is known for its beautifully marked and reticulated leaves that often earn the group the name of "jewel orchids." The degree of leaf marking varies greatly even within a species. In the United States and Canada we have four species, all primarily northern or higher elevation in distribution. All four occur within the range of this book.

### Key to the rattlesnake orchises

1a flowers in a dense spike . . . 2
1b flowers in a lax spike . . . 3

2a flowers off-white, dull-colored; leaves dull green . . . . . **giant rattlesnake orchis**, *Goodyera oblongifolia*, p. 96
2b flowers milk white; leaves dark green with prominent markings . . . . . **downy rattlesnake orchis**, *Goodyera pubescens*, p. 98

3a flowers arranged in a one-sided spike; leaves dark green with silver marbling . . . . . **lesser rattlesnake orchis**, *Goodyera repens*, p. 100
3b flowers arranged around the spike; leaves dull green with paler green markings . . . . . **checkered rattlesnake orchis**, *Goodyera tesselata*, p. 102

## *Goodyera oblongifolia* Rafinesque

### giant rattlesnake orchis

forma *reticulata* (Boivin) P.M. Brown—
reticulated leaved form

*Canadian Field-Naturalist* 65: 20. 1951, as *Goodyera oblongifolia* var. *reticulata* B. Boivin, type: British Columbia

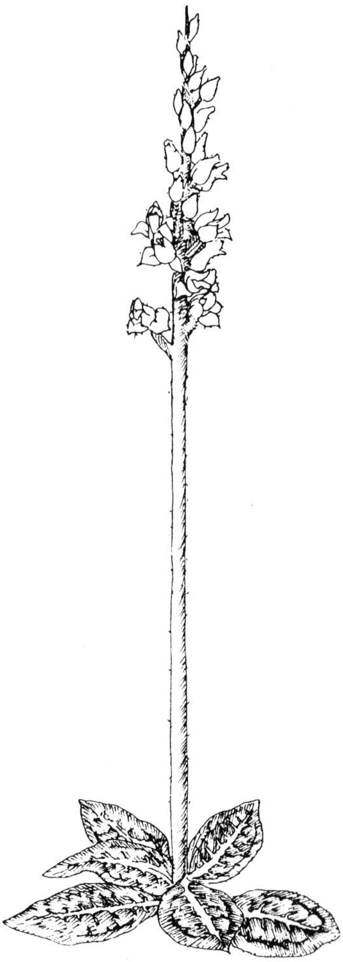

**Range:** southeastern Alaska east to Newfoundland, south to Maine, California, and New Mexico; Mexico

**In the Northeast: Maine, [Vermont]:** very rare and local

**Plant:** terrestrial, to 45 cm tall

**Leaves:** 3–7; in a basal rosette, dull bluish-green with a white central stripe or, in the forma *reticulata*, with handsome white reticulations; lanceolate, 2–4 cm wide × 5–11 cm long

**Flowers:** 10–30+; in a loosely flowered one-sided (secund) terminal spike; white with coppery-green overlays; dorsal sepal and petals forming a hood over the pointed lip, lateral sepals reflexed; individual flower size 4 × 5 mm

**Habitat:** dry mixed and deciduous woodlands

**Flowering period:** August

*Goodyera oblongifolia*, the **giant rattlesnake orchis,** is the largest of all the rattlesnake orchises in North America in both rosette size and height. Unfortunately it is also one of the less showy of the genus. The large, dull rosettes occasionally make colonies but more usually occur singly. The tall, few-flowered spike carries numerous off-white flowers in a loose, one-sided raceme.

In the forma *reticulata* the leaves take on a handsome appearance with beautiful, delicate reticulations. This variation occurs randomly throughout the range of the species, although it is more frequently encountered in western North America. *Goodyera oblongifolia* ranges eastward of the Great Lakes region in widely scattered, disjunct colonies and is confined in the Northeast to Aroostook County, Maine. Reports from other northeastern states usually prove to be hybrids between *G. pubescens* and *G. tesselata*.

typical leaf coloration

forma *reticulata*

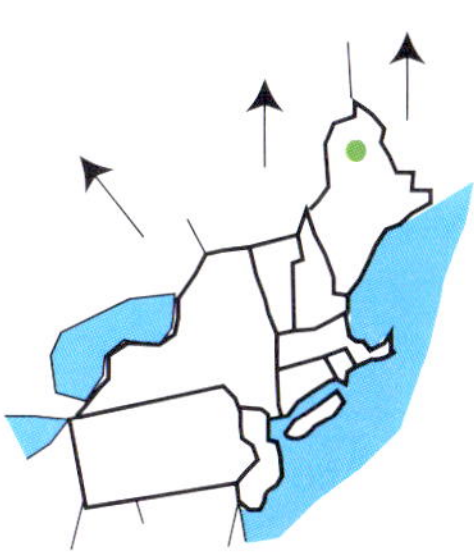

## *Goodyera pubescens* (Willdenow) R. Brown

### downy rattlesnake orchis

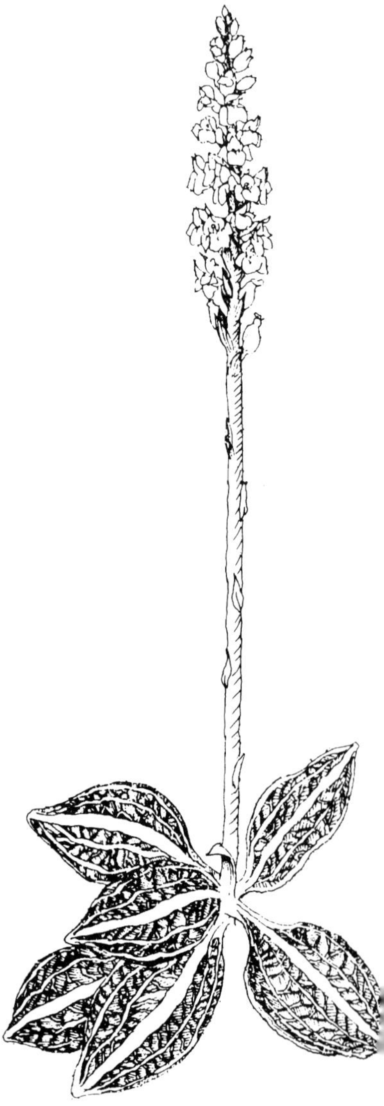

**Range:** Ontario east to Nova Scotia, south to Arkansas and Florida
**In the Northeast: Maine, New Hampshire, Vermont, Massachusetts, Connecticut, Rhode Island, New York, Pennsylvania, New Jersey:** widespread and often common in the southern portion of the range, becoming very rare northward
**Plant:** terrestrial, 20–50 cm tall
**Leaves:** 4–8; in a basal rosette, bluish-green with white reticulations on the veins, broadly lanceolate, 2–4 cm wide × 4–10 cm long; evergreen
**Flowers:** 20–50+; in a densely flowered terminal spike; white, copiously pubescent; petals and sepals ovate—somewhat similar and the upper ones forming a hood over the spreading sepals and saccate lip; individual flower size ca. 3 × 4 mm
**Habitat:** mixed and deciduous woodlands
**Flowering period:** August

*Goodyera pubescens*, the **downy rattlesnake orchis,** is a typically southern species reaching the northern limit of its range in the Northeast. It has the most handsomely marked foliage of any of our native orchids and also has the added feature of being evergreen. Large patches are often formed; when in flower the snow-white blooms atop the slender spikes make it the showiest of all the rattlesnake orchises in North America. The entire inflorescence is copiously pubescent and the neat little rounded buds form a fanciful appearance similar to that of the tail of a rattlesnake!

## *Goodyera repens* (Linnaeus) R. Brown

### lesser rattlesnake orchis

forma *ophioides* (Fernald) P.M. Brown—white-veined leaved form

*Rhodora* 1: 6. 1899, as *Goodyera repens* var. *ophioides* Fernald, type: northeastern United States and Canada

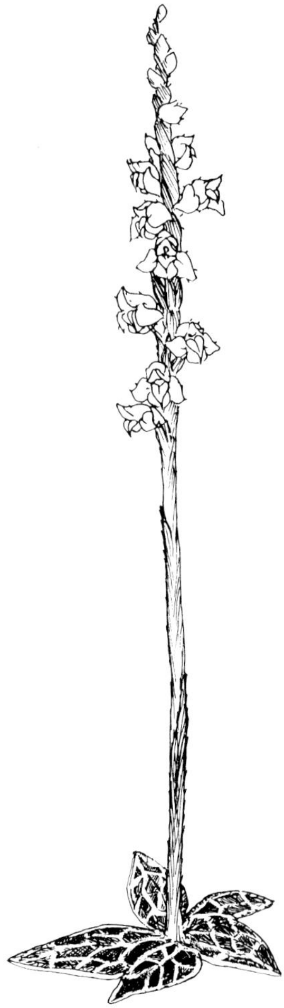

**Range:** Alaska east to Newfoundland, south to Wyoming, south in the Rocky and Appalachian Mountains; northern Eurasia

**In the Northeast: Maine, New Hampshire, Vermont, Massachusetts, Connecticut, New York:** rare and local but widespread in northern coniferous woodlands with few disjunct populations southward

**Plant:** terrestrial, 5–23 cm tall

**Leaves:** 3–6; in a basal rosette, dark green or, in the forma *ophioides*, marked with silver veining, ovate, 0.5–2.0 cm wide × 1.0–4.0 cm long

**Flowers:** 10–20; in a loosely flowered, single-ranked, terminal raceme; white, pubescent; dorsal sepal and petals forming a hood over the rounded lip, lateral sepals often reflexed; individual flower size 2 × 3(4) mm

**Habitat:** mixed and deciduous woodlands

**Flowering period:** July to August

*Goodyera repens*, the tiniest of the rattlesnake orchises, is the only North American species found in Eurasia as well. The small rosettes of the nominate variety are nearly plain with little or no contrasting veining. This is what is seen throughout most of the range in Europe and Asia and rarely seen in northernmost North America. The forma *ophioides*, with beautiful silver veining on the leaves, is the form most frequently seen through most of North America. Plants can be quite variable in the degree of veining. Fernald described this form as var. *ophioides* but as it passes into var. *repens* northward (especially in Canada) it is best treated as a form.

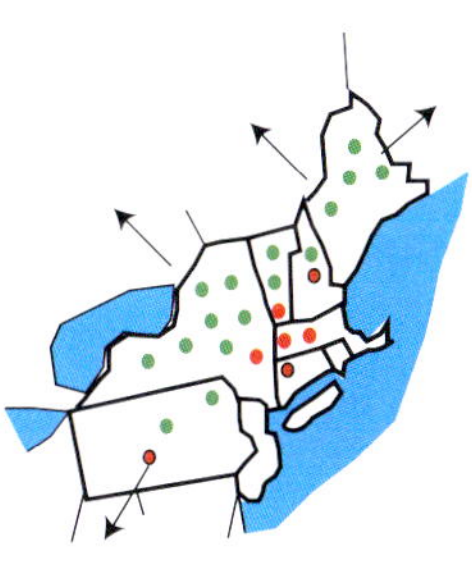

## *Goodyera tesselata* Loddiges

### checkered rattlesnake orchis

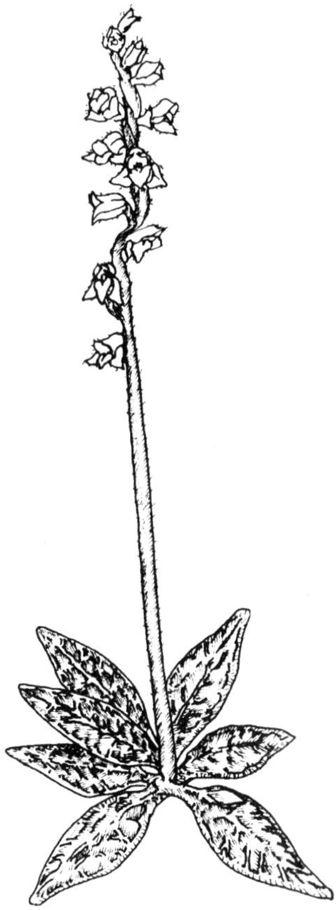

**Range:** Manitoba east to Newfoundland, south to Minnesota and Maryland
**In the Northeast: Maine, New Hampshire, Vermont, Massachusetts, Connecticut, Rhode Island, New York, Pennsylvania, New Jersey:** local to occasional throughout
**Plant:** terrestrial, 15–35 cm tall
**Leaves:** 4–8; in a basal rosette, dull bluish-green, finely reticulated with slender white markings, elliptic-lanceolate, 1.0–2.5 cm wide × 2.0–8.0 cm long
**Flowers:** 10–40; in a loosely flowered, usually one-sided terminal raceme; white, copiously pubescent; dorsal sepal and petals lanceolate and forming a hood over the short, rounded lip; individual flower size 3 × 4 mm
**Habitat:** mixed and deciduous woodlands
**Flowering period:** July to August

The **checkered rattlesnake orchis,** *Goodyera tesselata,* occupies an interesting position among the four species of *Goodyera* found in North America. For many years *G. tesselata* was assumed to be part of a hybrid swarm, although it does not range farther west than Manitoba and is really an eastern species. Research by Kalunki (1976) has hypothesized that the species originated as a hybrid between *G. repens* and *G. oblongifolia* and has subsequently established itself here in the East. Plants appearing to be hybrids between *G. tesselata* and *G. pubescens* have a striking resemblance to *G. oblongifolia* and are responsible for several erroneous eastern records of the latter species. *Goodyera tesselata* does appear to readily backcross with *G. repens,* resulting in plants that often challenge (and frustrate) the observer.

## *Gymnadeniopsis*

Formerly placed within the genera *Habenaria* and *Platanthera*, the three species that Rydberg used to comprise the genus *Gymnadeniopsis* have recently been revalidated (Brown, 2002). Stone (1910), in his exhaustive work on southern New Jersey, used the genus *Gymnadeniopsis* for these three species. Several differences are present that render them distinctive; tubers on the roots and small tubercles on the column are two major differences that separate them from the other genera.

### Key to the frog orchids, *Gymnadeniopsis*

1a flowers white; non-resupinate (lip uppermost) . . . . . **snowy orchis**, *Gymnadeniopsis nivea*, p. 112
1b flowers yellow or green to straw colored to nearly white; lip lowermost; spur swollen at the tip . . . 2

2a flowers bright yellow, lip erose at apex . . . . . **yellow fringeless orchis**, *Gymnadeniopsis integra*, p. 110
2b flowers straw yellow to greenish white . . . . 3

3a leaves multiple; inflorescence lax . . . . . **little club-spur orchis**, *Gymnadeniopsis clavellata* var. *clavellata*, p. 106
3b leaf solitary; inflorescence dense . . . . . **northern club-spur orchis**, *Gymnadeniopsis clavellata* var. *ophioglossoides*, p. 108

## *Gymnadeniopsis clavellata* (Michaux) Rydberg var. *clavellata*

### little club-spur orchis

forma *slaughteri* (P.M. Brown) P.M. Brown—white-flowered form

*North American Native Orchid Journal* 1(3): 200. 1995, as *Platanthera clavellata* var. *clavellata* forma *slaughteri* P.M. Brown, type: Arkansas

forma *wrightii* (Olive) P.M. Brown—spurless form

*Bulletin of the Torrey Botanical Club* 78(4): 289–291. 1951, as *Habenaria clavellata* var. *wrightii*, type: North Carolina

**Range:** Wisconsin east to Maine, south to Texas and Georgia
**In the Northeast: Maine, New Hampshire, Vermont, Massachusetts, Connecticut, Rhode Island, New York, Pennsylvania, New Jersey:** widespread and often frequent throughout
**Plant:** terrestrial, 15–35 cm tall
**Leaves:** 2; cauline, ovate-lanceolate, 1–2 cm wide × 5–15 cm long, passing upward into bracts
**Flowers:** 5–15; arranged in a loose terminal raceme, flowers usually twisted to one side; sepals ovate, petals linear, enclosed within the sepals and forming a hood; lip oblong, the apex obscurely three-lobed; perianth yellow-green or, in the forma *slaughteri*, white; individual flower size 0.5 cm, not including the 1 cm spur, the small tip swollen (clavate) or, in the forma *wrightii*, the spur absent
**Habitat:** damp woods, streamsides, open wet ditches
**Flowering period:** June to August

The small, pale greenish flowers of the **little club-spur orchis** are very different from any other orchid we have, and they also hold themselves at curious angles on the stem. The distinctive spur, with its swollen tip, is what gives this plant its common name. Plants of the nominate variety are found primarily in wooded swamps northward from Florida to the lower Great Lakes region and southern Maritimes, especially in southwestern Nova Scotia. *Gymnadeniopsis clavellata* var. *ophioglossoides* is found primarily in the northern and higher elevation areas of northeastern North America.

forma *wrightii*

forma *slaughteri*

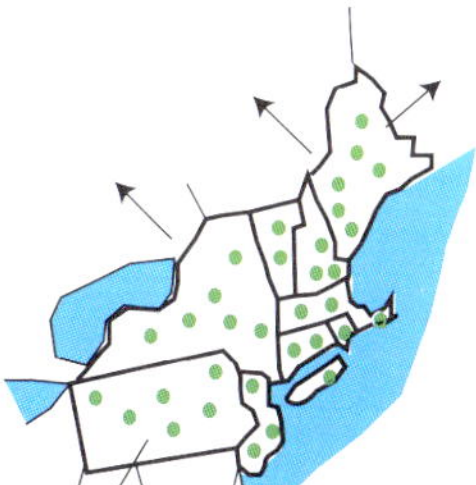

## *Gymnadeniopsis clavellata* (Michaux) Rydberg var. *ophioglossoides* (Fernald) W.J. Schrenk

**northern club-spur orchis**

**Range:** Ontario east to Newfoundland, south to northern New England
**In the Northeast: Maine, New Hampshire, Vermont, Massachusetts:** locally common in open, wet areas at northern and higher elevations
**Plant:** terrestrial, 5–15 cm tall
**Leaves:** 1; cauline, ovate, 1–2 cm wide × 3–5 cm long, an occasional slender bract also present on the stem.
**Flowers:** 3–10; arranged in a short, dense, crowded terminal raceme; flowers usually twisted to one side; sepals ovate, petals linear, enclosed within the sepals forming a hood; lip oblong, the apex obscurely three-lobed; perianth yellow-green to frosty-white; individual flower size 0.5 cm, not including the 0.5 cm spur, the small tip swollen (clavate)
**Habitat:** exposed areas at northern or higher elevations; gravelly barrens, tundra, streamsides, lakeshores
**Flowering period:** July to August

The **northern club-spur orchis**, *Gymnadeniopsis clavellata* var. *ophioglossoides*, a very distinctive variety of the more common club-spur orchis, is often found in very large colonies in wet gravels, roadside ditches, and mountain seeps throughout the northern portions and higher elevations of the Northeast. The little plants, especially when in bud, resemble the adder's-tongue fern, *Ophioglossum*, in both the single leaf and the short little crowded inflorescence. It is not unusual to find areas that are nearly paved with these little gems.

## *Gymnadeniopsis integra* (Nuttall) Rydberg

### yellow fringeless orchis

**Range:** southern New Jersey south to Florida and west to eastern Texas
**In the Northeast:** rare in southern New Jersey
**Plant:** terrestrial, to 60 cm tall
**Leaves:** 1–2, cauline, lanceolate 5–20 cm long × 1–3 cm wide
**Flowers:** 30–65; arranged in a densely flowered terminal raceme; sepals ovate, petals oblong-ovate, enclosed within the dorsal sepal forming a hood; lip ovate, the margin erose; perianth bright yellow-orange; individual flower size 5–6 mm, not including the 6 mm spur
**Habitat:** open wet meadows, savannas
**Flowering period:** late July to early September

Although the **yellow fringeless orchis,** *Gymnadeniopsis integra*, ranges from southern New Jersey to Texas, it is rapidly becoming one of the rarer orchids in North America. Habitat destruction, specifically the draining of wetlands for agriculture and business, is the primary cause of decline. There are still a few scattered sites in the heart of the Pinelands of southern New Jersey; here they are confined to the savannas that border the winding shallow rivers of these deep woodlands. The plants are very easy to distinguish from the similarly colored fringed orchises, *Platanthera cristata* and *P. ciliaris*, as they are considerably smaller and more slender, with a compact, conical raceme of flowers that lack the distinctive fringe on the lip of the *Platanthera* species.

## *Gymnadeniopsis nivea* (Nuttall) Rydberg

### snowy orchis

**Range:** southern New Jersey south to Florida and Texas
**In the Northeast**: confined to the southernmost tip of New Jersey, where it may be extirpated
**Plant:** terrestrial, to 60 cm tall
**Leaves:** 2–3, cauline, lanceolate 5–25 cm long × 1–3 cm wide
**Flowers:** 20–50; non-resupinate, arranged in a densely flowered terminal raceme; sepals and petals oblong-ovate; lip uppermost, linear-elliptic and bent backward midway; perianth stark, icy white; individual flower size 8–10 mm, not including the 1.5 cm spur
**Habitat:** open wet meadows, seeps
**Flowering period:** late August to early September

Similar in habit and habitat to the **yellow fringeless orchis**, *Gymnadeniopsis integra*, the **snowy orchis,** *G. nivea*, is at the northern limit of its range in southern New Jersey. Plants had been known for many years from the Bennett Bogs near Cape May, an orchid-rich area now owned by New Jersey Audubon Society. It is most unfortunate that the alteration of water levels and the invasion of several rampant graminoids over the years have all but eliminated the orchids of the open grasslands here. In 1984 a few plants were also found in a nearby gravel pit. In addition to the pristine beauty of the **snowy orchis**, it has the added feature of being deliciously fragrant. The uppermost lip is unique among our species of *Gymnadeniopsis* (and *Platanthera*).

## *Isotria*

The genus *Isotria* consists of only two species, both in the eastern United States and adjacent Canada. They are related to the genera *Pogonia* and, more distantly, *Triphora*; these were earlier placed in the genus *Pogonia*. We have both species in the Northeast.

### Key to the whorled pogonias, *Isotria*

1a sepals greenish-yellow; 1.5 times longer than the petals or shorter than the petals . . . . . **small whorled pogonia**, *Isotria medeoloides*, p. 116

1b sepals purple; 2 or more times longer than the petals . . . . . **large whorled pogonia**, *Isotria verticillata*, p. 118

## *Isotria medeoloides* (Pursh) Rafinesque

### small whorled pogonia

**Range:** Michigan east to Maine, south to Missouri and South Carolina
**In the Northeast: Maine, New Hampshire, Vermont, Massachusetts, Connecticut, Rhode Island, New York, Pennsylvania, New Jersey:** very rare in all states in which it occurs, often no more than a few plants
**FEDERALLY LISTED AS THREATENED**
**Plant:** terrestrial, mature plants up to 15 cm tall, shorter (8–12 cm) in flower
**Leaves:** 5 or 6; in a whorl at the top of the stem, up to 1 cm wide × 5 cm long
**Flowers:** 1 or 2; sepals and petals greenish-yellow, wide-spreading; lip white; individual flowers ca. 2–3 cm across
**Habitat:** various wooded habitats favoring beech, mixed pines, and hardwoods; often near seasonal runoffs
**Flowering period:** April to May, usually before the trees leaf out

This was one of the first orchids listed by the federal government under the Endangered Species Act. Although very rare, the **small whorled pogonia** is often known in most states from a single station, or even a single plant. In New Hampshire and western Maine, the small whorled pogonia can be locally abundant. Both states have sites in excess of several thousand plants. This is an excellent example of a species, long thought to be one of the very rarest in North America, turning up in new sites because more people, both professional and amateur, have been searching for it. Although historically widespread, the species is considered extirpated in New York and Vermont, where it has not been seen for nearly a century.

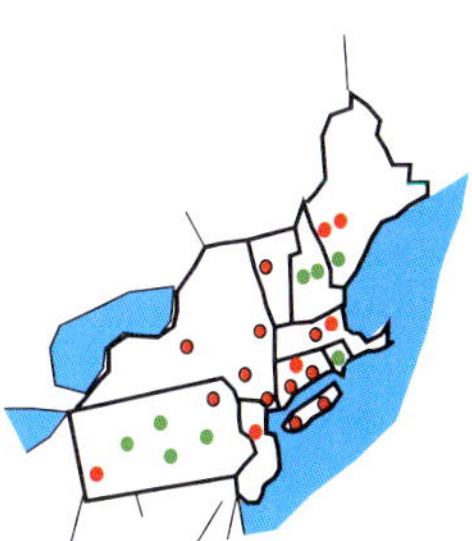

## *Isotria verticillata* (Mühlenberg *ex* Willdenow) Rafinesque

### large whorled pogonia

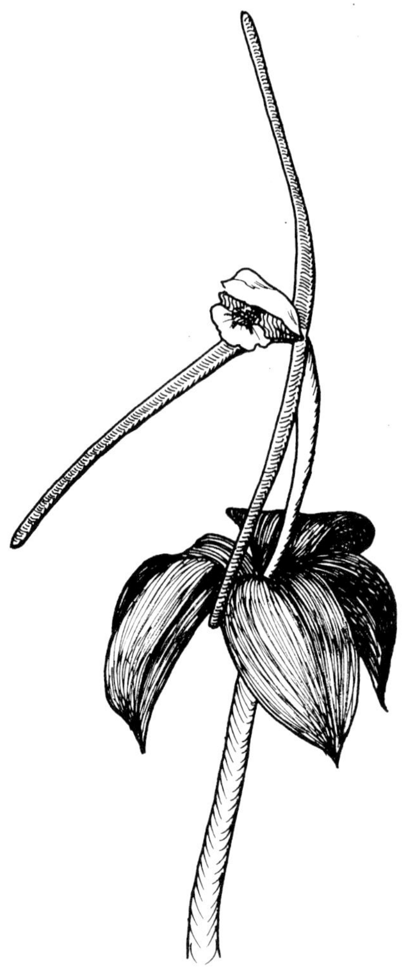

**Range:** Michigan east to Maine, south to Texas and Florida
**In the Northeast: Maine, New Hampshire, Massachusetts, Connecticut, Rhode Island, New York, Pennsylvania, New Jersey:** locally common in southern New England and southeastern New York southward
**Plant:** terrestrial, mature plants up to 40 cm tall, shorter (to 20 cm) in flower
**Leaves:** 5 or 6; in a whorl at the top of the stem, up to 3 cm wide × 9 cm long
**Flowers:** 1, rarely 2; sepals purplish, widespreading, slender and spidery; petals pale yellow, ovate, arched over the column; lip white, edged in purple, with a fleshy yellow central ridge; individual flowers ca. 10 cm across
**Habitat:** deciduous forests
**Flowering period:** late May through mid-June, usually before the trees fully expand their leaves

This is the third of the three species that are very common southward, but become increasingly rare at the northern limit of their range. *Isotria verticillata*, *Goodyera pubescens*, and *Gymnadeniopsis clavellata* form this trio, and all have a preference for southern affinity deciduous woodlands. Although not always sympatric, they often grow with the **pink lady's-slipper**, *Cypripedium acaule*. The fanciful flowers of *Isotria* are unmistakable and the plants have an unusual habit (as does the only other species in the genus, *I. medeoloides*) of nearly doubling in both leaf surface and height after flowering.

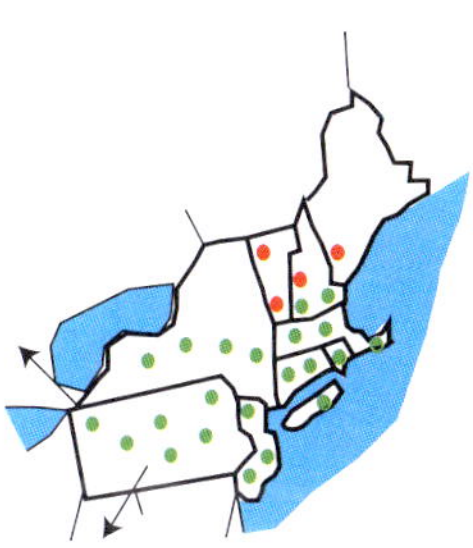

## *Liparis*

*Liparis* is a cosmopolitan genus of more than 200 species that occur in the widest variety of habitats throughout the world. All members of the genus are terrestrial or semi-epiphytic and have swollen leaf bases that form pseudobulb-like structures. These features are not unlike those of the genus *Malaxis*; they are more evident, and usually aboveground, in the subtropical and tropical species, whereas in the temperate and more northerly species the structure is belowground. Three species occur in the United States and Canada, but only two within the Northeast.

### Key to the greater twayblades, *Liparis*

1a flowers yellow-green; plants usually of moist areas, borrow pits, grassy fens, etc. . . . . . **Loesel's twayblade**, *Liparis loeselii*, p. 124

1b flowers chocolate-purple; plants of rich woodlands . . . . . **lily-leaved twayblade**, *Liparis liliifolia*, p. 122

## *Liparis liliifolia* (Linnaeus) Richard *ex* Lindley

### lily-leaved twayblade

forma *viridiflora* Wadmond—green-flowered form
*Rhodora* 34: 18. 1932, type: Wisconsin

**Range:** Minnesota and Ontario east to New Hampshire, south to Oklahoma and Georgia
**In the Northeast: New Hampshire, Vermont, Massachusetts, Connecticut, Rhode Island, New York, Pennsylvania, New Jersey:** scattered populations that can be locally abundant in rich woodlands
**Plant:** terrestrial, 9–30 cm tall
**Leaves:** 2; basal, green, strongly keeled, ovate 4 cm wide × 6–8 cm long
**Flowers:** 5–78; in a terminal raceme; sepals purple, ovate; petals and sepals green, slender and thread-like; lip chocolate-purple, broadly ovate or, in the forma *viridiflora*, flowers entirely green; individual flower size 1.2–2.4 cm
**Habitat:** rich, damp woodlands, mesic forest, shaded banks and roadsides; often occurring in calcareous soils
**Flowering period:** late spring; May to June

The **lily-leaved twayblade**, *Liparis liliifolia*, is a large, handsome orchid of rich mesic forests and streamsides. It is one of the prime components of the central and southern Appalachian woodlands. It is widespread in its distribution and often found growing with several other orchid species, including the **putty-root**, *Aplectrum hyemale*, and **showy orchis**, *Galearis spectabilis*.

forma *viridiflora*

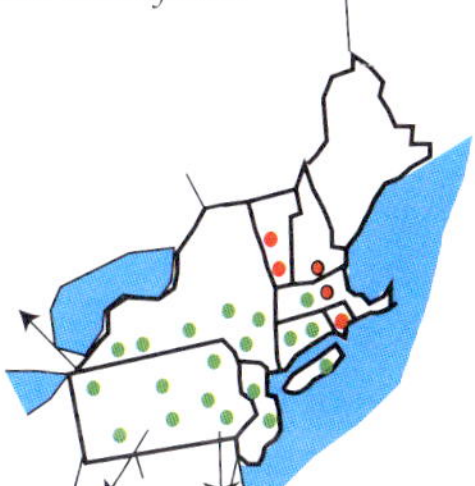

## *Liparis loeselii* (Linnaeus) Richard

### Loesel's twayblade, fen orchis

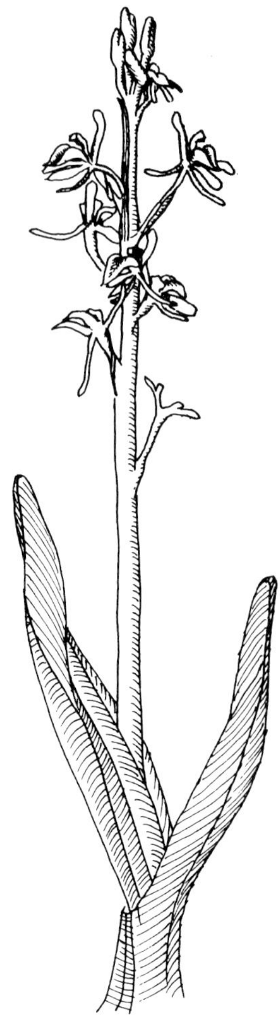

**Range:** British Columbia east to Nova Scotia and southwestern Newfoundland, south to Arkansas and Mississippi and in the southern Appalachian Mountains; Europe
**In the Northeast: Maine, New Hampshire, Vermont, Massachusetts, Connecticut, Rhode Island, New York, New Jersey:** local to occasional
**Plant:** terrestrial, 4–20 cm tall
**Leaves:** 2; basal, pale green, strongly keeled; oblanceolate, 2–3 cm wide × 4–6 cm long
**Flowers:** 5–15; in a terminal raceme; sepals and petals slender and thread-like; lip broadly ovate, watery-green; individual flower size 0.5–1.0 cm
**Habitat:** damp gravels, bogs, ditches, seepages, shaded banks, and roadsides; often in calcareous soils
**Flowering period:** late spring; May to June

The **fen orchis**, *Liparis loeselii,* is one of the few species that the eastern United States shares with northern Europe. And as rare as it is in Europe, it can be common in portions of our region. Because of its translucent coloring it is easily overlooked. Plants vary greatly in size and frequency. In a grassy sedge meadow larger individual plants may be seen but in the damp gravels of a borrow pit hundreds of tiny plants may cover the ground.

**Hybrid:**

*Liparis ×jonesii* S. Bentley

**Jones's hybrid twayblade**

(*L. liliifolia* × *L. loeselii*)

*Native Orchids of the Southern Appalachian Mountains* 1999: 138–39, type: North Carolina

This hybrid is very rare and although currently known only from the type locality along the Blue Ridge Parkway in southwestern North Carolina, both parents are often found growing nearby throughout much of the southern portion of the Northeast.

## *Listera*

The genus *Listera* comprises 25 species that occur in the cooler climes of both the Northern and Southern Hemispheres. Eight species in the genus grow in the United States and Canada; one, *L. ovata*, is a very common species in Europe that has become naturalized in southern Ontario. Five species are found in northeastern North America. Although plants of all species typically have two opposite leaves, many of these species also have variations with three or more leaves variously arranged. There is a current trend to place *Listera* in the genus *Neottia* (Szlachetko, 1995, Pridgeon et al., 2005).

### Key to the lesser twayblades, *Listera*

1a lip deeply cleft to more than half its length . . . 2
1b lip shallowly cleft to less than half its length . . . 3

2a lip about twice as long as petals . . . . . **heart-leaved twayblade**, *Listera cordata*, p. 134
2b lip about four times as long as petals . . . . . **southern twayblade**, *Listera australis*, p. 130

3a lip with parallel sides, auricled at base; lip entirely green with prominent auricles . . . . . **auricled twayblade**, *Listera auriculata*, p. 128
3b lip tapered from summit to base, not auricled at base . . . 4

4a leaves rounded, usually longer than the peduncle of the raceme; plants of northern, cool, mossy woods and streamsides . . . . . . **broad-lipped twayblade**, *Listera convallarioides*, p. 132
4b leaves kidney-shaped; plants of rhododendron thickets in northern New Jersey and mountains of Pennsylvania . . . . **Small's twayblade**, *Listera smallii*, p. 136

## *Listera auriculata* Wiegand

### auricled twayblade

forma *trifolia* (Lepage) Lepage—three-leaved form

*Naturaliste Canadien* 96: 770. 1969, as *Listera borealis* forma *trifolia* Lepage, type: Quebec

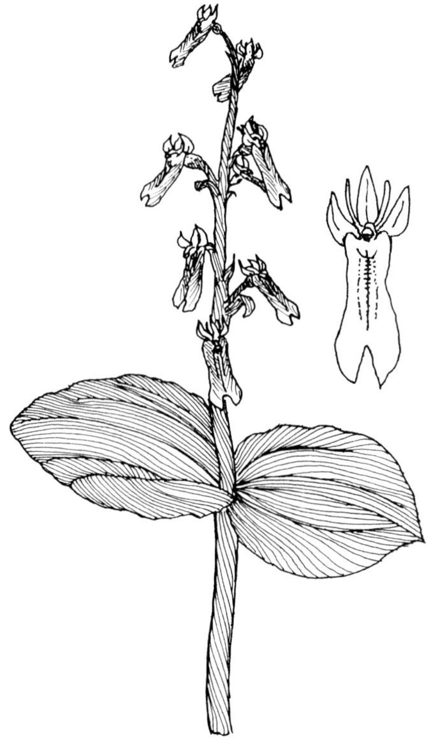

**Range:** Ontario east to Newfoundland, south to Michigan and Maine
**In the Northeast: Maine, New Hampshire, Vermont, New York:** rare and local, with several historical sites
**Plant:** terrestrial; 10–20 cm tall
**Leaves:** 2; opposite, midway on the stem or, in the forma *trifolia,* 3 in a whorl, green, ovate-oblong, 3.0 cm wide × 3.5 cm long
**Flowers:** 5–15; in a terminal raceme; sepals, petals watery-green, narrowly spatulate, reflexed; lip oblong with distinctive auricles clasping the ovary at the base and narrowly cleft at the apex, green; pedicles and ovary glabrous; individual flower size 0.6–1.0 cm
**Habitat:** gravel bars, alder thickets, and rocky river shores
**Flowering period:** late June through much of July

One of the rarest orchids in northeastern North America, the **auricled twayblade**'s distribution is limited to the northern Great Lakes region, Atlantic Canada, and northern New England. The diminutive plants prefer rocky gravels and riverbanks that are heavily scarred by winter ice. Because the plants of *Listera auriculata* are a consistent watery-green in color they are often overlooked, although they have much larger leaves and individual flowers than both *L. australis* and *L. cordata*. Hybrids with *L. convallarioides* are known as *L. ×veltmanii* and occur in several sympatric sites.

forma *trifolia*

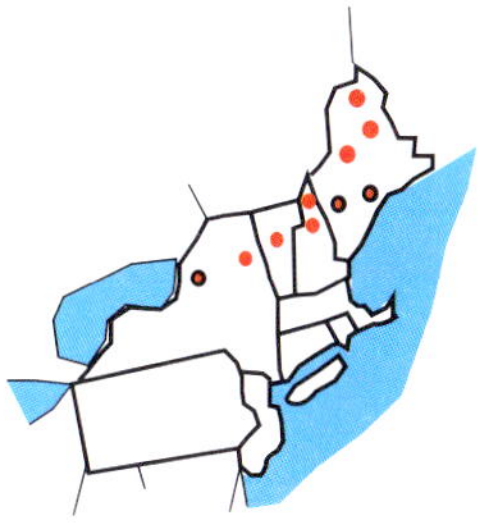

## *Listera australis* Lindley

### southern twayblade

forma *scottii* P.M. Brown—many-leaved form
*North American Native Orchid Journal* 6(1): 63–64. 2000, type: Florida

forma *trifolia* P.M. Brown—three-leaved form
*North American Native Orchid Journal* 1(1): 11. 1995, type: Vermont

forma *viridis* P.M. Brown—green-flowered form
*North American Native Orchid Journal* 6(1): 63–64. 2000, type: Florida

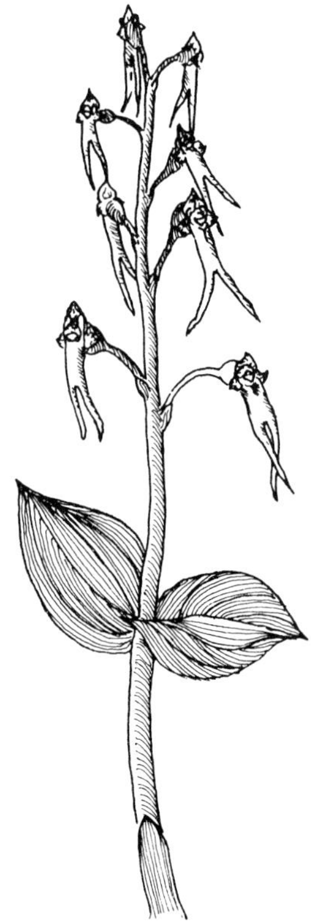

**Range:** Quebec to Nova Scotia, south to Florida and Texas
**In the Northeast: Vermont, New York, Pennsylvania, New Jersey:** rare and very local
**Plant:** terrestrial in damp soils, up to 35 cm tall
**Leaves:** 2; opposite, midway on the stem, green, usually flushed with red, ovate 2.0 cm wide × 3.5 cm long or, in the forma *scottii*, leaves several scattered along the stem or, in the forma *trifolia*, leaves 3 in a whorl
**Flowers:** 5–40; in a terminal raceme; sepals purple, ovate; petals purple, narrowly spatulate, recurved; lip purple, linear, split into 2 slender filaments or, in the forma *viridis*, flowers entirely green; individual flower size 6–10 mm
**Habitat:** open, damp woodlands and heaths, often in sphagnum moss
**Flowering period:** late May well into July northward

A spring ephemeral, the **southern twayblade** appears quickly in late spring or early summer. Most northeastern populations consist of less than a dozen plants and still contain an amazing degree of variation. Habitat is somewhat variable, with plants preferring seasonally wet woodlands in the southern portion of the range and open sphagnum bogs in the north. The species sets seed and senesces very quickly, so that a month after flowering there is usually no sign of the plants until next season.

forma *trifolia*

forma *scotti*

forma *viridens*

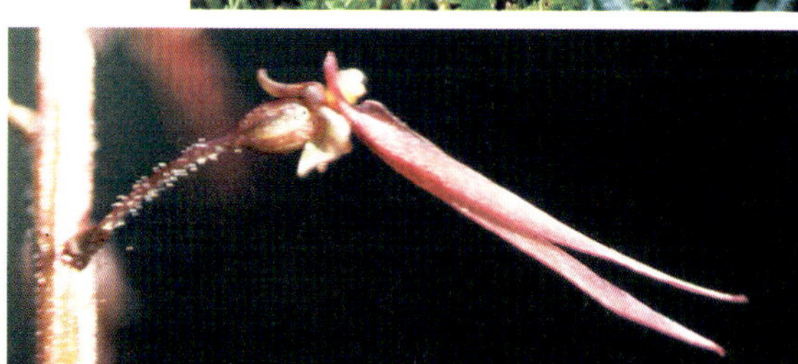

*Listera convallarioides*
(Swartz) Nuttall

**broad-lipped twayblade**

forma *trifolia* P.M. Brown—three-leaved form
*North American Native Orchid Journal,* 1(1): 11. 1995, type: Newfoundland

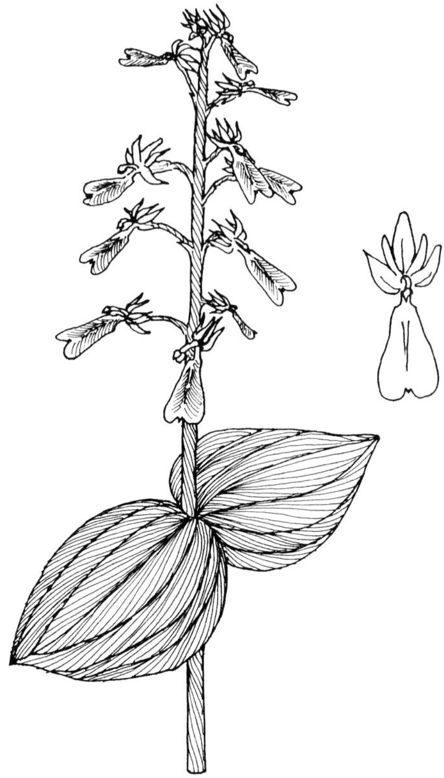

**Range:** southwestern Alaska; British Columbia east to Newfoundland, south to California and Wyoming, east to northern Michigan and Maine
**In the Northeast: Maine, New Hampshire, Vermont, New York:** local in northern New England and northeastern New York
**Plant:** terrestrial; 10–30 cm tall
**Leaves:** 2; opposite, midway on the stem or, in the forma *trifolia,* 3 in a whorl, green, ovate-oblong, 1–3 cm wide × 2–6 cm long
**Flowers:** 5–15; in a terminal raceme; sepals and petals watery-green, reflexed ; lip pale yellow-green, oblong, broadening to a deep cleft at the apex; pedicles and ovary pubescent; individual flower size 0.6–1.5 cm
**Habitat:** damp to wet, cold, mossy woodlands, thickets, and river shores
**Flowering period:** July

The **broad-lipped twayblade,** *Listera convallarioides***,** is the largest of the lesser twayblades (*Listera* spp.) that we have in northeastern North America. The plants are almost always colonial and may form large patches usually in open damp woods, in mossy glades, and on isolated little islets in flowing streams. When *Listera auriculata* is nearby the hybrid *Listera* ×*veltmanii* is almost always present. *Listera convallarioides* is often mistakenly called the broad-leaved twayblade when the correct common name is the **broad-lipped twayblade,** referring to the decidedly broadened apex of the lip that is unlike that of any other *Listera* in our region.

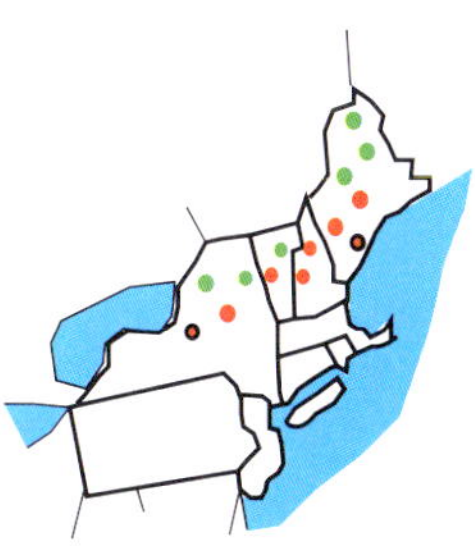

## *Listera cordata* (Linnaeus) R. Brown var. *cordata*

### heart-leaved twayblade

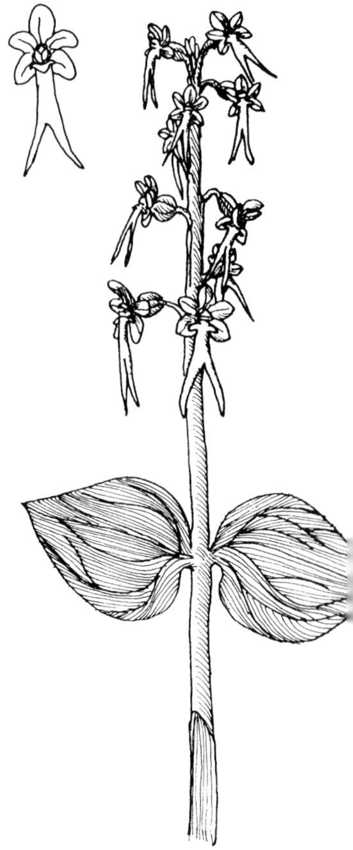

forma *disjuncta* Lepage—alternate-leaved form
*Naturaliste Canadien* 73: 16. 1946, type Quebec

forma *tetraphylla* Lavoie—four-leaved form
*Provancheria* 7: 92. 1984, type: Quebec

forma *trifolia* P.M. Brown—three-leaved form
*North American Native Orchid Journal* 1(1): 11. 1995, type: Newfoundland

forma *variegata* P.M. Brown—variegated-leaved form
*North American Native Orchid Journal* 1(1): 11. 1995, type: Vermont

forma *viridens* P.M. Brown—green-flowered form
*North American Native Orchid Journal* 1(4): 288. 1995, type: Vermont

**Range:** Alaska east to Newfoundland and Greenland, south to California, and the Rocky Mountains in New Mexico; south to North Carolina in the Appalachian Mountains; Eurasia

**In the Northeast: Maine, New Hampshire, Vermont, Massachusetts, Connecticut, New York, Pennsylvania:** local and scattered

**Plant:** terrestrial, 10–40 cm tall

**Leaves:** 2 or, in the forma *trifolia*, 3 in a whorl or, in the forma *tetraphylla*, 4 in a whorl; opposite, midway on the stem or, in the forma *disjuncta*, with an additional leaf above; green or, in forma *variegata*, with white variegations; ovate 2.0 cm wide × 3.5 cm long with a somewhat cordate base

**Flowers:** 5–40; in a terminal raceme; sepals purple, ovate, reflexed; petals purple, narrowly spatulate, strongly recurved; lip purple, linear, split beyond the middle into 2 slender filaments or, in the forma *viridens*, flowers entirely green; individual flower size 6–10 mm

**Habitat:** damp, often dark, coniferous woodlands, trailsides, heaths, and sphagnum bogs

**Flowering period:** June to August

The **heart-leaved twayblade** is the most frequently encountered twayblade throughout the northern portion of our region. It often grows in great numbers and the variability in both leaf placement and flower color is usually evident. Although individual plants may be easy to overlook, these large colonies, when struck by the sun, seem to dance on the woodland floor. The individual flowers, like all of those in the genus *Listera*, are all lip with the petals and sepals pulled back around the ovary, well out of the way.

Both typical red-flowered form and green-flowered forma *viridens*

forma *variegata*

forma *disjuncta*

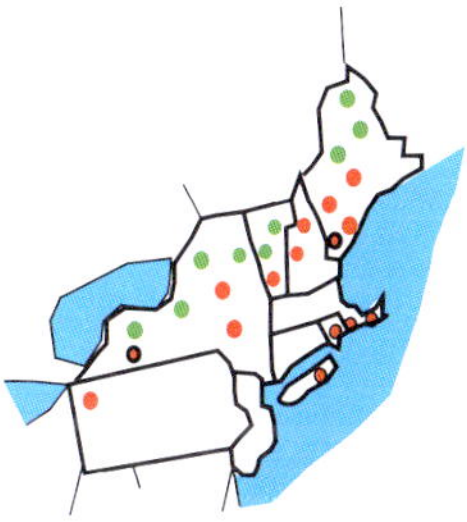

## *Listera smallii* Wiegand

### Small's twayblade

forma *variegata* P.M. Brown—variegated-leaved form
*North American Native Orchid Journal* 1(4): 289. 1995, type: West Virginia

**Range:** northern New Jersey; central Pennsylvania south to northern Georgia
**NATIONALLY SIGNIFICANT SPECIES**
**In the Northeast: Pennsylvania, New Jersey**: very rare in the northern and mountain counties
**Plant:** terrestrial in damp soils, up to 25 cm tall
**Leaves:** 2; opposite midway on the stem, reniform to ovate, 2.0 cm wide × 3.5 cm long, green or, in the forma *variegata*, with white markings
**Flowers:** 4–12; in a terminal raceme; greenish/yellow to beige; lip broadened at the summit and notched; individual flower size 6–12 mm
**Habitat:** rich, damp woodlands, and along stream runs, usually under *Rhododendron maximum*
**Flowering period:** late June well into July

This, the rarest twayblade in North America, is known from only deep within the Appalachian Mountains. The distribution of **Small's twayblade** is very specific from south central Pennsylvania near State College south to northeastern Georgia, with a disjunct site in the mountains of northern New Jersey.

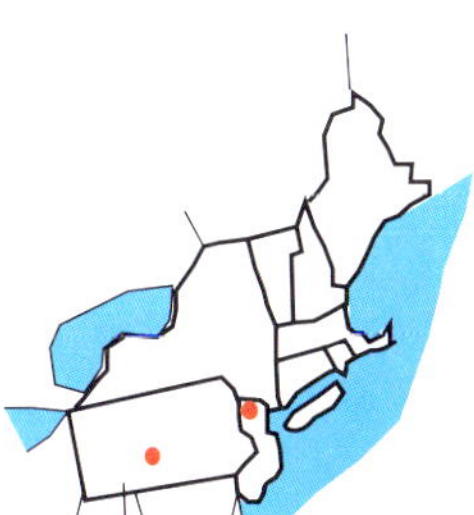

Hybrid:
*Listera ×veltmanii* Case
**Veltman's hybrid twayblade**
(*L. auriculata* × *L. convallarioides*)
*Michigan Botanist* 3: 67–70. 1964, type: Michigan

When infrequently encountered because of the rarity of *L. auriculata*, this hybrid is easily identified by the usually misshapen lip.

## *Malaxis*

The genus *Malaxis* is a cosmopolitan one of about 300 species. Eleven species are found in the United States and Canada, including three that occur in our region. All species have a pseudobulbous stem, which is more evident in the subtropical and tropical species. In the temperate species it appears more corm-like. The genus possesses some of the smallest flowers in the *Orchidaceae*, many not more than a few millimeters in any dimension.

### Key to the adder's-mouths, *Malaxis*

1a inflorescence a many-flowered slender spike . . . . . **white adder's-mouth**, *Malaxis brachypoda*, p. 142

1b inflorescence otherwise . . . 2

2a inflorescence an elongated cluster or raceme; lower flowers persisting after anthesis . . . . . **Bayard's adder's-mouth**, *Malaxis bayardii*, p. 140

2b inflorescence a flat-topped cluster; lower flowers withering after anthesis . . . . . **green adder's-mouth**, *Malaxis unifolia* p. 144

## *Malaxis bayardii* Fernald

### Bayard's adder's-mouth

forma *kelloggiae* P.M. Brown—albino form
*North American Native Orchid Journal* 11: 5. 2005, type: Massachusetts

**Range:** Nova Scotia; Massachusetts south to South Carolina, west to Ohio
**In the Northeast: Vermont, Massachusetts, Connecticut, Rhode Island, New York, Pennsylvania, New Jersey:** very rare with few extant sites
**Plant:** terrestrial in dry open ground; 4–18+ cm tall, stem swollen at the base into a (pseudo)bulb, green or, in the forma *kelloggiae*, white
**Leaves:** 1, ovate, keeled, to 6 cm wide × 9 cm long, midway on the stem, green or, in the forma *kelloggiae*, white
**Flowers:** 35–150; arranged in an elongated raceme; sepals oblanceolate, yellow-green or, in the forma *kelloggiae*, white; petals linear and positioned behind the flower; lip yellow-green, broadly ovate to cordate, with prominent auricles at the base and bidentate at the summit; individual flower size 2–4 mm, persisting after anthesis
**Habitat:** dry open woodlands, sandy roadsides, rocky barrens
**Flowering period:** July

**Bayard's adder's-mouth**, *Malaxis bayardii*, is perceived to be very rare, and perhaps is simply overlooked. Plants of **green adder's-mouth**, *M. unifolia*, found growing in atypical dry habitats should be carefully examined to see if they are *M. bayardii*, as the overall distribution is not well known. Recently revalidated as a species (Catling, 1991), this diminutive green orchid is currently known from only six extant sites in North America. Its discovery in Nova Scotia in 1994 and again in 1996 extends the range to Canada.

Historically *Malaxis bayardii* was vouchered from North Carolina, Virginia, New Jersey, Ohio, and extensively from Pennsylvania as well as New England and New York. Recent work (Brown, 2004) has located several herbarium specimens from South Carolina as well. The largest site, with about 400 individuals, occurs along an abandoned woodroad and adjacent field sides on Cape Cod, Massachusetts. Its similarity to *M. unifolia* makes for some problems in identification but Catling's article goes into great detail and supports all identification criteria. Unless more sites can be found this species is certainly one of the rarest orchids in North America.

forma *kellogiae*

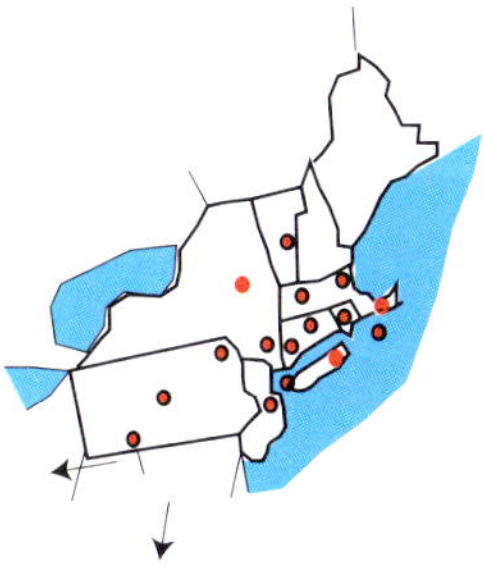

## *Malaxis brachypoda* (Gray) Fernald

**white adder's-mouth**

forma *bifolia* (Mousley) Fernald—two-leaved form
*Orchid Review* 35: 356. 1927, as *Malaxis monophyllos* forma *bifolia* Mousley, type: Quebec

**Range:** southern Alaska east to Newfoundland, south to California, Colorado, Indiana, Pennsylvania, and New England
**In the Northeast: Maine, New Hampshire, Vermont, Massachusetts, Connecticut, New York, Pennsylvania:** local to occasional but often overlooked
**Plant:** terrestrial; 8–25+ cm tall, stem swollen at the base into a (pseudo)bulb
**Leaves:** 1 or, in the forma *bifolia*, 2; ovate, keeled, to 6 cm wide × 9 cm long, midway on the stem; green
**Flowers:** 5–80+; arranged in a slender spike; sepals oblanceolate, yellow-green to whitish-green; petals linear and positioned behind the flower; lip white, broadly triangular; individual flower size ca. 1.5–3.0 mm
**Habitat:** moist open barrens, borrow pits, damp gravelly roadsides, fens, and sphagnum bogs
**Flowering period:** late June to August

Although the range of the **white adder's-mouth,** *Malaxis brachypoda*, in the Northeast overlaps that of the **green adder's mouth**, *M. unifolia*, it is a much rarer orchid. Most populations are small and usually amount to only a few dozen plants, if that. Several authors (Catling and Magrath, FNA 2002) consider *M. brachypoda* as a variety of the widespread *M. monophyllos*, a species found primarily in Eurasia. *Malaxis monophyllos* has the lip ovate, uppermost (non-resupinate), and the flowers yellowish-green in contrast to the whitish-green flowers of *M. brachypoda*.

forma *bifolia*

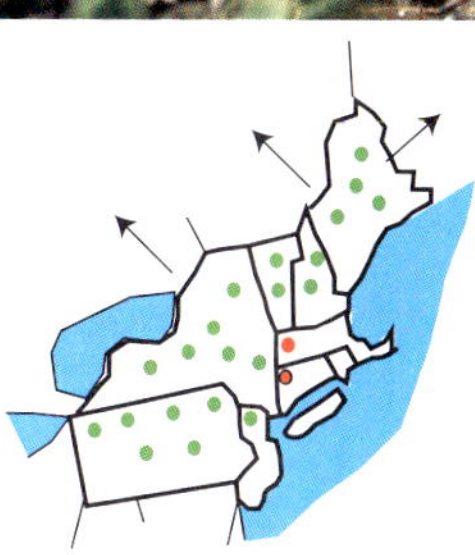

## *Malaxis unifolia* Michaux

### green adder's-mouth

forma *bifolia* Mousley—two-leaved form
*Orchid Review* 35: 163. 1927, type: Quebec
forma *variegata* Mousley—variegated-leaf form
*Orchid Review* 35: 164. 1927, type: Quebec

**Range:** Manitoba east to Newfoundland south to Texas and Florida; Mexico
**In the Northeast: Maine, New Hampshire, Vermont, Massachusetts, Connecticut, Rhode Island, New York, Pennsylvania, New Jersey:** local to occasional but often overlooked
**Plant:** terrestrial; 8–25+ cm tall, stem swollen at the base into a (pseudo)bulb
**Leaves:** 1 or, in the forma *bifolia*, 2; ovate, keeled, to 6 cm wide × 9 cm long, midway on the stem; green or, in the forma *variegata*, with white markings
**Flowers:** 5–80+; arranged in a compact raceme, elongating as flowering progresses; sepals oblanceolate, green; petals linear and positioned behind the flower; lip green, broadly ovate to cordate, with extended auricles at the base and bidentate at the summit; individual flower size 2–4 mm
**Habitat:** damp woodlands, moist open barrens, mossy glades, fens, and sphagnum bogs
**Flowering period:** late June to August

Often considered one of the most widespread and common orchids in eastern North America, *Malaxis unifolia* can be a real challenge to find. Plants vary greatly in size and their natural camouflage blends them in with much of the surrounding vegetation. Only when growing in open mossy barrens do they really stand out. Large plants are not uncommon and they, like most members of the genus, bear up to 100 flowers and present them over a long period of time—up to 2 months. Plants found in the eastern portion of the range growing in atypically dry habitats should be carefully compared for the possibility of *M. bayardii* (see pp. 000).

forma *variegata*

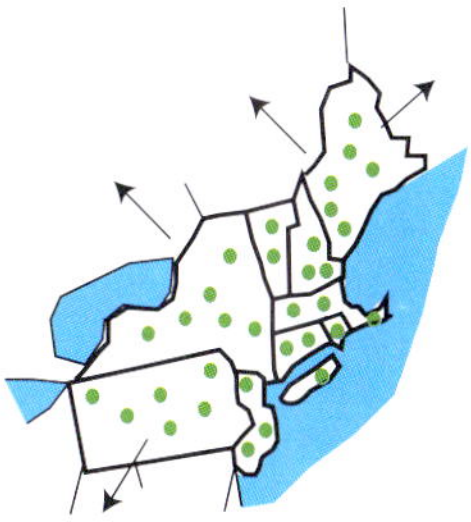

forma *bifolia*

## *Platanthera*

The genus *Platanthera* comprises about 40 North American and Eurasian species, primarily of temperate climes and is one of the major segregate genera traditionally placed by many botanists within *Habenaria*. It is the largest genus of orchids in the United States and Canada, with 13 species and varieties found within our range as well as several hybrids. It is also the largest genus in the region. Many of the species have large, colorful, showy flowers in tall spikes or racemes. There are several sections to the genus, but the showiest is the section Blephariglottis, the fringed orchises. There are two groups within this section: those species with an entire or unlobed lip and those with a three-parted lip. At various times in taxonomic history members of *Platanthera* have been included in *Habenaria* and *Piperia*.
Note: nearly all species of *Platanthera* can be found in both full sun and deeply shaded habitats. Plants in the sun tend to be shorter, with more densely flowered inflorescences and leaves more upright, whereas those growing in shaded areas tend to be taller and have elongated, loosely flowered inflorescences with spreading leaves. The individual flower size remains the same, but the overall appearance of the plants can be markedly different, to the point that some observers initially think they have two different species!

### Key to the fringed, bog, and rein orchises, *Platanthera*

1a margins of lips entire . . . 2
1b margins of lips fringed, lacerated, or erose . . . 10

2a lip with a prominent tubercle . . . 3
2b lip lacking a prominent tubercle . . . 4

3a lip ovate; bracts generally equal to or shorter than the flowers . . . . . **southern tubercled orchis,** *Platanthera flava* var. *flava*, p. 162
3b lip oblong; bracts generally longer than the flowers . . . . . **northern tubercled orchis,** *Platanthera flava* var. *herbiola*, p. 164

4a leaves cauline (along the stem) . . . 5
4b leaves basal (at or close to the ground) . . . 7

5a flowers white . . . . . **white bog orchis; bog candles**, *Platanthera dilatata*, p. 160
5b flowers green . . . 6

6a lip yellowish to yellowish-green, rhombic-lanceolate . . . . . **northern green bog orchis,** *Platanthera aquilonis*, p. 150

6b lip whitish-green, lanceolate, usually obscurely rounded or slightly dilated at base . . . . . **green bog orchis,** *Platanthera huronensis*, p. 171

Note: *P. aquilonis* and *P. huronensis* are an endless source of confusion for many orchid enthusiasts. Until both are clearly seen in the field it can be difficult. Carefully examine each potential plant, meticulously comparing the criteria. Additional information is found in FNA volume 26.

7a leaf 1; at base of stem . . . . . **blunt-leafed rein orchis**, *Platanthera obtusata*, p. 178

7b leaves 2; ovate and pad-like lying close to the ground . . . 8

8a dorsal sepal and lip arching forward, appearing like ice tongs . . . . . **Hooker's orchis**, *Platanthera hookeri* p. 168

8b lips descending . . . 9

9a spur less than 28 mm long . . . . . **pad-leaved orchis**, *Platanthera orbiculata* p. 180

9b spur greater than 28 mm long . . . . . **Goldie's pad-leaved orchis,** *Platanthera macrophylla* p. 176

Note: see drawings at species account for shape and position of petals

10a lip entire, not divided into segments . . . 11

10b lip tripartite, divided into 3 segments . . . 14

11a flowers white . . . . . **northern white fringed orchis**, *Platanthera blephariglottis* p. 154

11b flowers yellow, orange, or cream . . . 12

12a spur exceeding the lip in length . . . . . **orange fringed orchis**, *Platanthera ciliaris* p. 156

12b spur equal to or less than the lip in length . . . 13

13a lip thrust forward, flowers bright orange to lemon-yellow in color . . . . . **orange crested orchis**, *Platanthera cristata* p. 158

13b lip descending and recurved at tip; flowers ivory-cream in color . . . . . **pale fringed orchis**, *Platanthera pallida* p. 182

14a flowers green or white . . . 15

14b flowers purple . . . 16

15a petals entire, lip deeply lacerate; flowers greenish-white to creamy green ..... **green fringed orchis; ragged orchis**, *Platanthera lacera* p. 172

15b petals shallowly fringed at the apex, ovate; sepals green to whitish-green; very rare ..... **eastern prairie fringed orchis**, *Platanthera leucophaea* p. 174

Note: beware of white-flowered forms of *P. grandiflora* and the hybrid *P.* ×*andrewsii*!

16a lip margin fringed to more than 1/3 the length; spur orifice circular ..... **large purple fringed orchis**, *Platanthera grandiflora* p. 166

16b lip margin fringed to less than 1/3 the length **OR** merely erose . . . 17

17a lip margin merely erose, spur orifice rounded ..... **purple fringeless orchis**, *Platanthera peramoena* p. 184

Note: beware of fringeless forms of both *P. grandiflora* and *P. psycodes*

17b lip margin distinctly fringed but to less than 1/3 the length, spur orifice a transverse dumbbell ..... **small purple fringed orchis**, *Platanthera psycodes* p. 186

## *Platanthera aquilonis* Sheviak

### northern green bog orchis

forma *alba* (Light) P.M. Brown—albino form
*Lindleyana* 4: 158–160; figs. 1–3. 1989, as *Platanthera hyperborea* forma *alba* M.H.S. Light, type: Quebec

**Range:** Alaska east to Newfoundland, south to California, New Mexico, and Iowa, east to Massachusetts
**In the Northeast: Maine, New Hampshire, Vermont, Massachusetts, Connecticut, Rhode Island, New York, Pennsylvania, New Jersey:** rare to local; more frequent northward
**Plant:** terrestrial, 5–60 cm tall
**Leaves:** 2–4; cauline, linear-lanceolate, gradually reduced to bracts; 1–4 cm wide × 3–20 cm long
**Flowers:** 20–45; arranged in a loose to dense terminal spike; dorsal sepal obovate, arching; lateral sepals linear-oblong, spreading to recurved, petals rhombic-linear, somewhat enclosed within the dorsal sepal forming a hood; lip rhombic-lanceolate to lanceolate, descending, projecting or the apex caught within the tip of the dorsal sepal and petals; flowers yellow-green to whitish-green in cooler climes; lip usually a dull yellow-green; individual flower size 0.8 × 1.3 cm, not including the 0.2–0.5 cm clavate to somewhat cylindric spur; flowers autogamous, with the pollinia rotating forward and falling out of the anther sacs, spilling onto the stigma of the column.
**Habitat:** open wet meadows, roadside ditches and seeps, fens, bogs, and river gravels
**Flowering period:** late June to August

Plants formerly identified as *Platanthera hyperborea* in much of North America were described as a new species, *P. aquilonis* Sheviak in 1999. True *P. hyperborea* is known in North America only from Greenland, and all plants previously correctly assigned to that species are *P. aquilonis*. In eastern North America the problem of the basic green *Platanthera* is not nearly as compounded as in western North America. Here we only have two green species, *P. aquilonis* and *P. huronensis*, as well as the closely related white-flowered *P. dilatata*. In western North America several other species occur as well. For many years both green-flowered species were simply referred to as *P. hyperborea* and usually in two varieties—var. *hyperborea* and var. *huronensis*. Unfortunately too many people, and authors alike, placed the smaller, more slender, "poorly flowered" plants into *P. hyperborea* and the robust, lush-flowered plants into *P. huronensis*. That this was incorrect only compounded the problem. Sheviak's description of *P. aquilonis* greatly helped in solving this problem, and recent work by Wallace (2002, 2003, 2004) validates both the origins and the identifications of the three species. In a more simplistic form *P. aquilonis* may be differentiated from *P. huronensis* by the color and shape of the lip, position of the pollinia, and overall aspect of the plant. Range and habitat are also helpful but should not be relied upon too heavily.

The chart on page 152, prepared by Lorne Heshka of Winnipeg, Manitoba, will help in comparing characteristics of the two species. This excellent chart was previously published as part of a longer article in *Native Orchid News*, volume 5, issue 4, 2003, and reprinted here by permission.

forma *alba*

| | *Platanthera aquilonis* | *Platanthera huronensis* |
|---|---|---|
| **Lip/flower colour** | Green flower with yellow lip | Whitish-green flower, lip not yellow |
| **Lip shape** | Sides nearly straight, angles rounded but not dilated | Lance shaped, base moderately to roundly dilated |
| **Spur** | Club shaped, approximately 3/4 length of lip, strongly forward curved | Slender to thickened cylindrical shape, equal in length to the lip, pendant to slightly forward curved |
| **Scent** | Absent | Fragrant |
| **Pollination** | Autogamous - pollinia rotate forward out of anther sacs, pollinia may break apart spilling the pollen | Autogamous - pollinia rotate forward out of anther sacs, pollinia may fragment spilling the pollen; *or may be* Allogamous - pollinia remain in the anther sacs until removed by a pollinator |
| **Anther sac position** | Anther sacs low, widely diverging at the base and in close proximity at the apex | Anther sacs elevated, almost parallel, slightly diverging at the base and separated at the apex |

*P. aquilonis*

*P. huronensis*

## *Platanthera blephariglottis* (Willdenow) Lindley

### northern white fringed orchis

forma *holopetala* (Lindley) P.M. Brown—entire-lip form
*Genera and Species of Orchidaceous Plants* 291. 1835, as *Platanthera holopetala*, type: Canada.

**Range:** Michigan east to Newfoundland, south to Georgia
**In the Northeast: Maine, New Hampshire, Vermont, Massachusetts, Connecticut, Rhode Island, New York, Pennsylvania, New Jersey:** widespread and local
**Plant:** terrestrial, 25–60 cm tall; plants much shorter in northern, exposed situations
**Leaves:** 2–4; cauline, lanceolate 2–4 cm wide × 8–20 cm long
**Flowers:** 20–45; arranged in a dense terminal raceme; sepals ovate, petals linear, enclosed within the sepals forming a hood; lip spatulate with a coarse, fringed margin or, in the forma *holopetala*, the margin slightly if all at fringed; lip narrowed to an obscure isthmus at the base; perianth pure white; individual flower size 1.75–2.0 cm, not including the 1.5–2.0 cm spur
**Habitat:** open wet meadows, roadside ditches and seeps, fens, and bogs
**Flowering period**: late July to August

This large, showy member of the fringed-lipped section Blephlariglottis is widespread throughout eastern North America. It, like several other *Platanthera*, is affected by successional habitats and often flowers best a few years after the disturbance of adjacent woody plant material by burning, mowing, or the like. Large masses of the **northern white fringed orchis** may be seen in the open northern bogs and heaths of the northern counties and often under power lines in swales. It is a major attraction of the summer-flowering orchids. Plants vary greatly from those that are short and few-flowered in the northern bogs and muskegs to large thrifty specimens from the southern coastal plain. It was these larger plants that were mistaken for the variety *conspicua* in previous publications. The potential for the very rare cross-generic hybrid, X*Platanthopsis vossii*, described from Michigan, is nearly everywhere within our range because the other parent, *Gymnadeniopsis clavellata*, readily occurs here. Despite many searches, the hybrid remains rare and elusive.

Large coastal form

northern wetland form

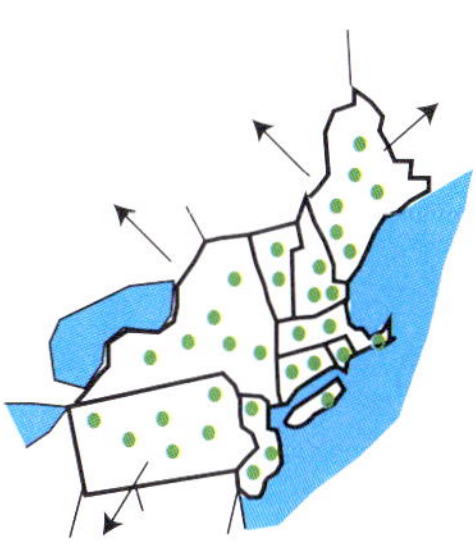

## *Platanthera ciliaris* (Linnaeus) Lindley

### orange fringed orchis

**Range:** southern Michigan east to Massachusetts, south to Florida and Texas

**In the Northeast: [New Hampshire], [Vermont], Massachusetts, Connecticut, Rhode Island, New York, Pennsylvania, New Jersey:** rare and local, although some populations are very large

**Plant**: terrestrial, 25–100+ cm tall

**Leaves**: 2–5; cauline, lanceolate, 1–5 cm wide × 5–30 cm long, gradually reduced to bracts within the inflorescence

**Flowers**: 30–75; arranged in a dense terminal raceme; sepals ovate, petals linear, fringed at the tip, enclosed within the sepals forming a hood; lip ovate with a delicately fringed, filiform margin; perianth deep yellow to orange; individual flower size 4 cm, not including the 2.5–3.5 cm spur, which typically is loosely descending; the column tapering to a point

**Habitat**: open wet meadows, roadside ditches, and seeps

**Flowering period**: late July to late August

A near mirror-image of the **northern white fringed orchis**, *Platanthera blephariglottis*, the brilliant, deep yellow to orange plumes of the **orange fringed orchis** can be a meter in height. Scattered populations are well known from southern New England and Long Island. With a preference for areas that stay wet to damp in the hot, dry days of summer, populations vary from year to year in how thrifty they are. This species often grows with its white cousin and the hybrid, *P.* ×*bicolor*, may frequently be found as well. Rare hybrids with *P. cristata* are known as *P.* ×*channellii*. See page 189 for additional information.

The New Hampshire specimen from an area known as the Bottomless Pit near Hanover has been discounted as an error in labeling and the report by Niles from southern Vermont has never been substantiated.

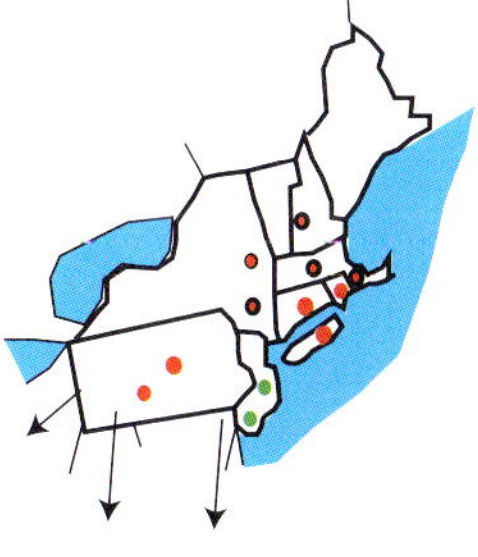

## *Platanthera cristata* (Michaux) Lindley

### orange crested orchis

forma *straminea* P.M. Brown—pale yellow-flowered form
*North American Native Orchid Journal* 1(1): 12. 1995, type: New Jersey

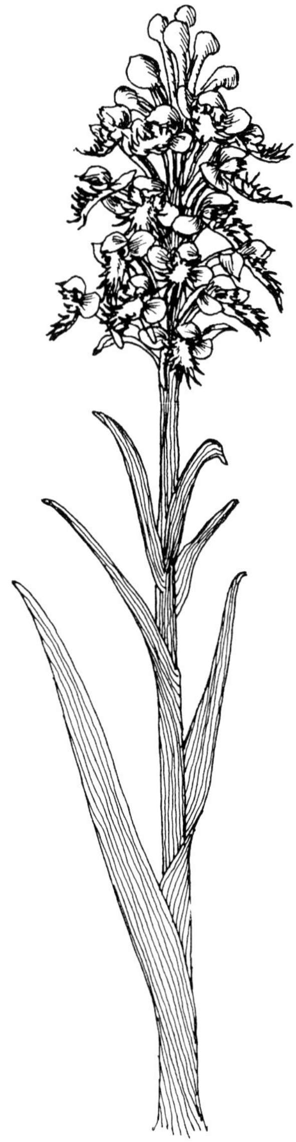

**Range:** southeastern Massachusetts south to Florida and west to eastern Texas, primarily on the Coastal Plain
**In the Northeast: Massachusetts, Rhode Island, New York, Pennsylvania, New Jersey:** rare and scattered throughout our area, primarily in the Coastal Plain region
**Plant**: terrestrial, to 80 cm tall
**Leaves**: 2–4; cauline, lanceolate, 1–3 cm wide × 5–20 cm long, rapidly reduced to bracts within the inflorescence
**Flowers**: 30–80; arranged in a loose to dense terminal raceme; sepals ovate, petals spatulate with margin of the apex crested, enclosed within the sepals forming a hood; lip long, triangular-ovate with a coarsely lacerate margin; perianth deep yellow to orange or, in the forma *straminea*, pale yellow; individual flower size 5–7 mm, not including the 7 mm spur which is typically curved; the column is very short and the face flattened
**Habitat**: open wet meadows, roadside ditches, Atlantic white cedar woodlands
**Flowering period**: late June to late September

A smaller, and perhaps more refined version of the **orange fringed orchis**, *Platanthera ciliaris*, the **orange crested orchis** is very rare and widespread throughout the Coastal Plain and often occurs without other related species nearby. Only in the Pinelands of New Jersey are plants seen with any regularity. The raceme is usually about 2.5 cm in diameter and the spur is always shorter than the lip and typically curved forward, whereas *P. ciliaris* always has the loosely descending spur much longer than the lip, and the raceme is 4.5+ cm in diameter.

forma *straminea*

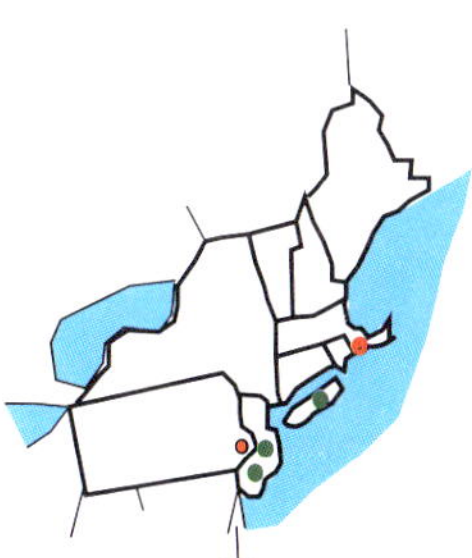

## *Platanthera dilatata* (Pursh) Lindley var. *dilatata*

### white bog orchis; bog candles

**Range:** Alaska east to Newfoundland, south to California and New Mexico; Minnesota south to Indiana, Pennsylvania, and New England
**In the Northeast: Maine, New Hampshire, Vermont, Massachusetts, Connecticut, Rhode Island, New York, Pennsylvania, New Jersey:** widespread and relatively common in the north to very rare in the southern counties
**Plant**: terrestrial, 25–100+ cm tall
**Leaves**: 4–12; cauline, passing into bracts on the stem, lanceolate, 4–7 cm wide × 15–30 cm long
**Flowers**: 20–100+; arranged in a dense terminal spike; dorsal sepal ovate, lateral sepals linear; petals linear-falcate, enclosed within the sepals forming a hood; lip linear-lanceolate, dilated at the base; perianth pure white; individual flower size 1.75–2.0 cm, not including the cylindric spur which is about equal to the length of the lip
**Habitat**: open wet meadows, roadside ditches and seeps, fens, and bogs
**Flowering period**: late June to August

*Platanthera dilatata* is the showiest of the slender bog or rein orchids. Its tall, white, fragrant spikes may occur in great numbers throughout the range of the species. Size is variable and smaller plants often have only a few flowers. Mixed colonies of *P. dilatata*, *P. huronensis*, and/or *P. aquilonis* are not uncommon. *Platanthera dilatata* is by far the most frequently seen of the three. Hybridization among these species is minimal today because of the evolution of self-pollinating breeding systems in the green-flowered species. Plants known as *P.* ×*media* were once thought to represent frequent hybrids between *P. dilatata* and *P. hyperborea*, and although that is technically correct, they actually represent plants of *P. huronensis* (Sheviak, 1999; Wallace, 2004). *Platanthera dilatata* var. *albiflora* and var. *leucostachys* both occur in western North America. A primary difference from the nominate variety is in the length of the spur.

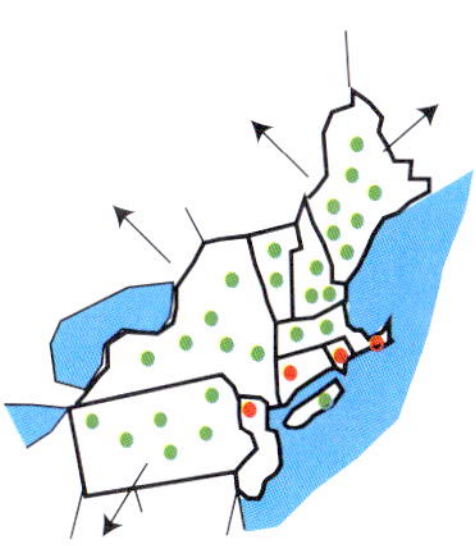

## *Platanthera flava* (Linnaeus) Lindley var. *flava*

### southern tubercled orchis

**Range:** Ontario, Nova Scotia; Missouri east to Maryland, south to Florida and Texas
**In the Northeast: New Jersey:** local in the southern counties
**Plant**: terrestrial, 10–60 cm tall
**Leaves**: 2–4; cauline, lanceolate, 1–4 cm wide × 5–20 cm long
**Flowers**: 10–40; arranged in a loose to dense terminal raceme and subtended by bracts rarely exceeding the combined length of the ovary and flower; sepals and petals ovate, enclosed within the dorsal sepal forming a hood; lip ovate with a prominent tubercle in the center; perianth yellow-green; individual flower size 6–7 mm, not including the 8 mm spur
**Habitat**: open wet meadows and lakeshores
**Flowering period**: late June to July

Reaching the northern limit of its contiguous range in southern New Jersey, *Platanthera flava* var. *flava*, the **southern tubercled orchis**, extends it range in disjunct colonies in southwestern Nova Scotia and southwestern Ontario. The two varieties are easily distinguished primarily by the shape of the lip and, more noticeably, by the length of the subtending floral bracts. In the variety *flava* the bracts rarely exceed the length of the flower. The lip in variety *flava* is square to broadly ovate rather than distinctly oblong as in the variety *herbiola*.

## *Platanthera flava* (Linnaeus) Lindley var. *herbiola* (R. Brown) Luer

### northern tubercled orchis

forma *lutea* (Boivin) Whiting & Catling—yellow-flowered form
*Naturaliste Canadien* 109(2): 278. 1982, type: Ontario

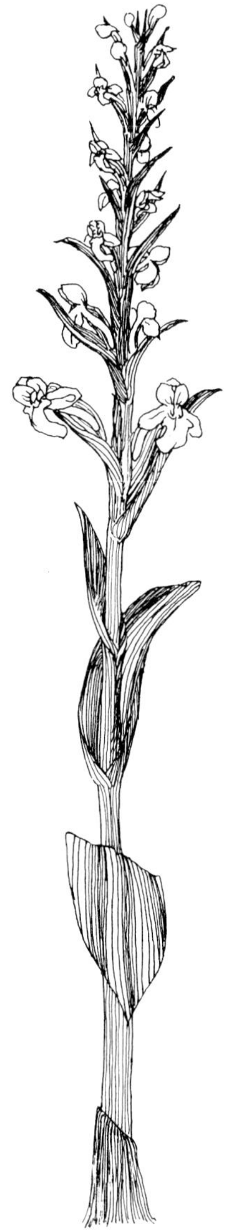

**Range:** Minnesota east to Nova Scotia, south to Missouri and Georgia; south in the Appalachian Mountains
**In the Northeast: Maine, New Hampshire, Vermont, Massachusetts, Connecticut, New York, Pennsylvania, New Jersey:** local to occasional throughout
**Plant**: terrestrial, 10–50 cm tall
**Leaves**: 3–5; cauline, lanceolate 2–5 cm wide × 8–20 cm long
**Flowers**: 15–45; arranged in a loose to dense terminal raceme and subtended by bracts usually exceeding the combined length of the ovary and flower; sepals and petals ovate, enclosed within the dorsal sepal forming a hood; lip oblong with a prominent tubercle near the base and triangular lobes on either side; perianth grassy-green or, in the forma *lutea*, distinctly yellow; individual flower size 6–7 mm, not including the 5–7 mm spur
**Habitat**: open wet meadows, roadside ditches and seeps, swamps, and shaded floodplains
**Flowering period**: late July

*Platanthera flava* var. *herbiola,* the **northern tubercled orchis,** is an obscure, grass-green, fragrant species once considered one of the rarer orchids in eastern North America. As the result of intensive field searches by many individuals we now know of some large, stable populations in several states.

forma *lutea*

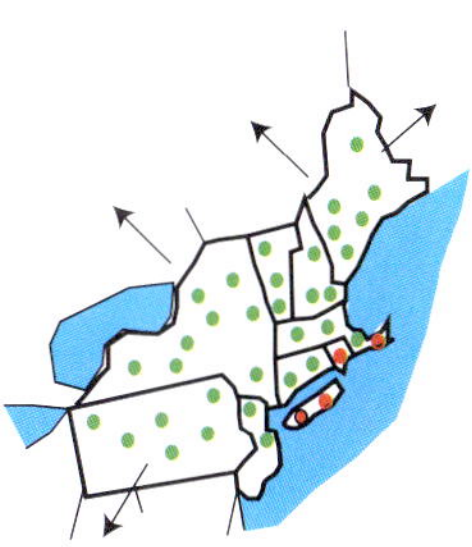

## *Platanthera grandiflora* (Bigelow) Lindley

### large purple fringed orchis

forma *albiflora* (Rand & Redfield) Catling—white-flowered form
*Flora of Mt. Desert Island* 152. 1894, type: Maine

forma *bicolor* P.M. Brown—bicolor-flowered form
*North American Native Orchid Journal* 1(4): 289. 1995, type: Newfoundland

forma *carnea* P.M. Brown—pink-flowered form
*North American Native Orchid Journal* 1(4): 289. 1995, type: Newfoundland

forma *mentotonsa* (Fernald) P.M. Brown—entire-lip form
*Rhodora* 48: 184. 1946, as *Habenaria fimbriata* (Aiton) R. Brown forma *mentotonsa* Fernald, type: Nova Scotia

**Range:** Ontario east to Newfoundland, south to West Virginia and New Jersey; south in the Appalachian Mountains to Georgia
**In the Northeast: Maine, New Hampshire, Vermont, Massachusetts, Connecticut, New York, Pennsylvania, New Jersey:** more frequent northward becoming very rare to the south
**Plant**: terrestrial, 25–100+ cm tall
**Leaves**: 2–6; cauline, lanceolate, keeled, 1.5–7.0 cm wide × 8.0–24.0 cm long
**Flowers**: 30–65; arranged in a loose to dense terminal raceme usually 3–5 cm in diameter with all flowers open simultaneously; sepals ovate, petals spatulate with dentate margins; lip three-parted with a coarsely fringed margin usually to more than 1/3 the depth of the lip or, in the forma *mentotonsa*, the margin essentially entire; perianth various shades of purple from pale lavender to deep, rich magenta or, in the forma *albiflora*, white or, in the forma *bicolor*, purple and white or, in the forma *carnea*, a delicate fresh pink; individual flower size 3 cm, not including the 2.5 cm spur; spur orifice rounded
**Habitat**: open wet meadows, roadside ditches and seeps, mountain meadows
**Flowering period**: late June to early July

The **large purple fringed orchis** is widespread throughout much of central and northeastern North America. This tall (to 1 meter), stately species is often a feature of the summer open woodlands and, northward, damp meadows and roadsides. It usually occurs in small numbers, often only a single plant, but every once in a while large stands of more than 100 plants can be found. Although these are similar in overall appearance to the small purple fringed orchis *P. psycodes*, several points will aid in identification. Be sure to carefully note the shape of the orifice, depth of the fringing, and overall shape of the inflorescence. Hybrids with *P. lacera* are known as *P.* ×*keenanii*.

forma *bicolor*

forma *albiflora*

forma *carnea*

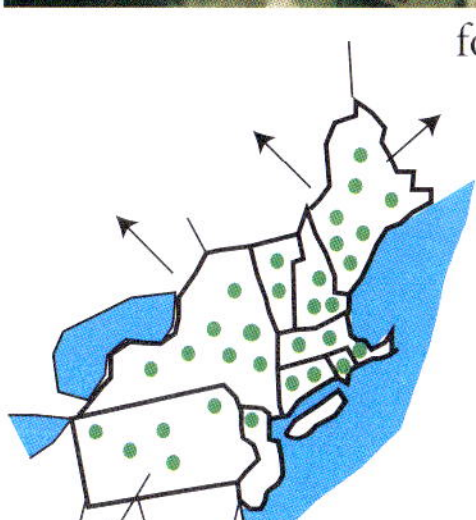

## *Platanthera hookeri* (Torrey) Lindley

### Hooker's orchis

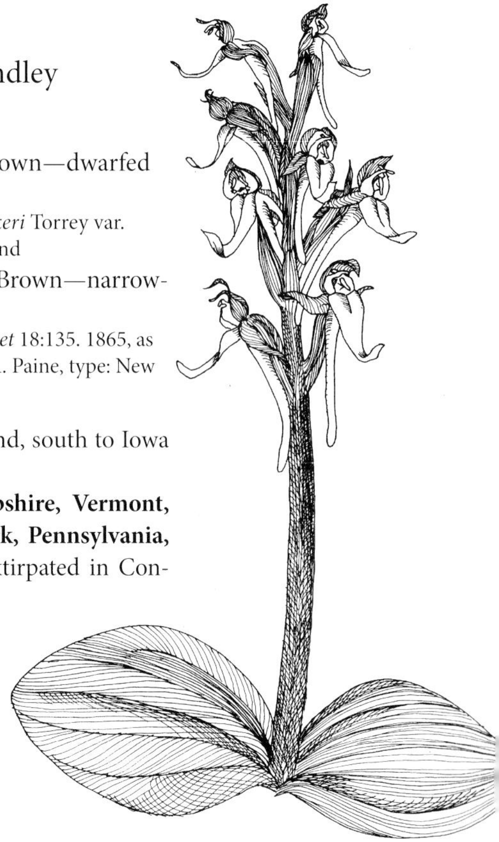

forma *abbreviata* (Fernald) P.M. Brown—dwarfed form

*Rhodora* 35: 239. 1933, as *Habenaria hookeri* Torrey var. *abbreviata* Fernald, type: Newfoundland

forma *oblongifolia* (J.A. Paine) P.M. Brown—narrow-leaved form

*Annual Report of the New York State Cabinet* 18:135. 1865, as *Platanthera hookeri* var. *oblongifolia* J.A. Paine, type: New York

**Range:** Minnesota east to Newfoundland, south to Iowa and New Jersey

**In the Northeast: Maine, New Hampshire, Vermont, Massachusetts, Connecticut, New York, Pennsylvania, New Jersey**: rare and local; possibly extirpated in Connecticut, Rhode Island, and New Jersey

**Plant**: terrestrial, 10–50 cm tall or, in the forma *abbreviata*, to 18 cm tall, the inflorescence occupying nearly half the height; bracts absent from stem

**Leaves**: 2; basal, oblong-ovate up to 12 cm wide × 15 cm long or, in the forma *oblongifolia*, 5 cm wide x 12 cm long; light green above and pale beneath

**Flowers**: 5–25; arranged in a loose terminal raceme; dorsal sepal concave, ovate, and tapering to a point; lateral sepals lanceolate and strongly reflexed; petals linear-lanceolate, tapering, falcate, projecting forward; lip long-triangular curving upward at the tip; the overall appearance that of ice tongs; perianth lime-green; flower size ca. 2 × 3 cm not including the slender 1.5–2.5 cm spur; plants of the forma *abbreviata* smaller and more crowded in all aspects with the color nearly yellow-bronze

**Habitat**: rich deciduous and mixed woodlands; forma *abbreviata* from western Newfoundland is found on limestone barrens growing among the various heaths and dwarf shrubs

**Flowering period**: July

No native orchid flowers are so curious in their appearance as those of **Hooker's orchis**, *Platanthera hookeri*. Striking some as looking like gargoyles or ice tongs, the flowers have lower lip curling upward and dorsal sepal projecting forward while the petals spread wing-like to give this appearance. Plants found in woodlands often occur in colonies and although the plants are monochromatic—a decided shade of chartreuse—they usually grow where there is little competing ground cover. **Hooker's orchis** is one of three species of *Platanthera* that produce oval to round basal leaves. The other two, *P. orbiculata* and *P. macrophylla*, are both larger in overall dimensions, have much rounder leaves, and flower later than *P. hookeri*.

forma *oblongifolia*

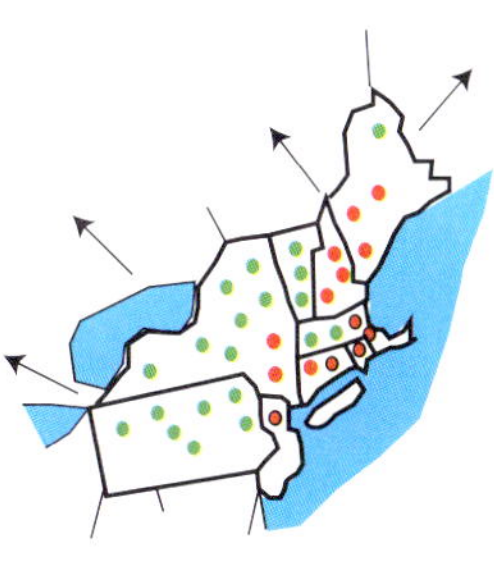

## *Platanthera huronensis* (Nuttall) Lindley

### green bog orchis

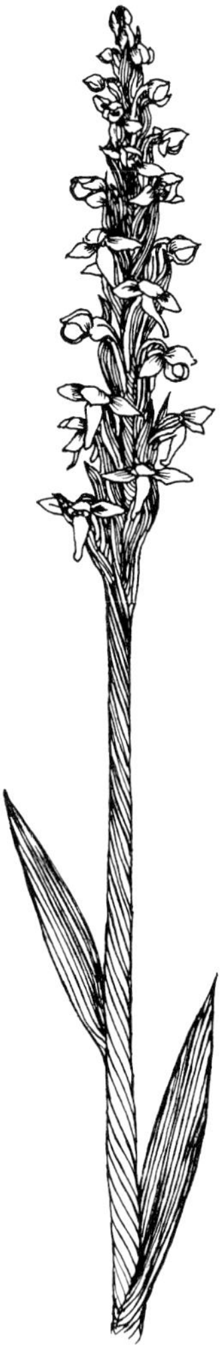

**Range:** Alaska east to Newfoundland, south to California and Pennsylvania
**In the Northeast: Maine, New Hampshire, Vermont, Massachusetts, Connecticut, Rhode Island, New York, Pennsylvania, New Jersey:** scattered to occasional throughout; more frequent northward
**Plant**: terrestrial, 10–100+ cm tall
**Leaves**: 2–4; cauline, linear-lanceolate, gradually reduced to bracts; 1–6 cm wide × 5–30 cm long
**Flowers**: (8)20–75+; arranged in a loose to dense terminal spike; dorsal sepal obovate, arching; lateral sepals linear-oblong, spreading to recurved, petals ovate to lance-falcate, somewhat enclosed within the dorsal sepal forming a hood; lip lanceolate, descending, or the apex caught within the tip of the dorsal sepal and petals; sepals whitish-green, petals and lip pale greenish-white but markedly whiter than the sepals; individual flower size 0.8 × 1.3 cm, not including the 0.4–1.2 cm somewhat cylindric spur; flowers are autogamous, with the downward-pointing pollinia remaining in the anther sacs.
**Habitat**: open wet meadows, roadside ditches and seeps, fens, bogs, and river gravels
**Flowering period**: late June to August

*Platanthera huronensis*, the **green bog orchis**, is the most widespread and frequently encountered of all of the green-flowered rein orchises in northeastern North America. The tall spikes are frequently found in a wide variety of habitats and, like many species of *Platanthera*, their habit varies with the habitat. Plants of open wet areas have densely flowered tall spikes with many flowers whereas those of woodlands often have few-flowered, slender spikes. The flowers are usually intensely fragrant. Sheviak (2002) states that although hybrids with *P. dilatata* may occur the name traditionally used for them, *P. ×media*, is actually a synonym for *P. huronensis*. See the chart on page 000 for a comparison with *P. aquilonis*.

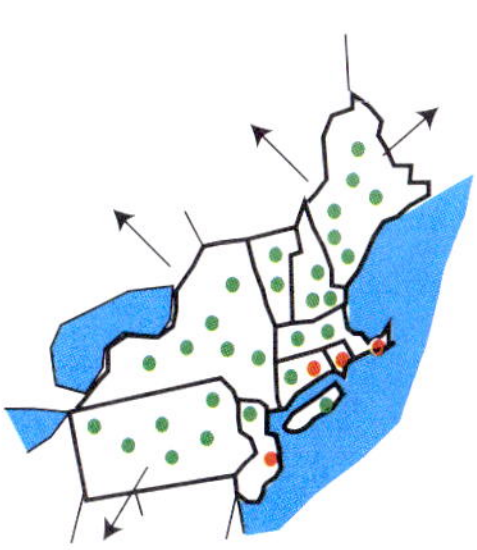

## *Platanthera lacera* (Michaux) G. Don

### green fringed orchis; ragged orchis

**Range:** Manitoba east to Newfoundland, south to Texas and Georgia
**In the Northeast: Maine, New Hampshire, Vermont, Massachusetts, Connecticut, Rhode Island, New York, Pennsylvania, New Jersey:** scattered to occasional throughout; more frequent northward
**Plant**: terrestrial, 20–80 cm tall
**Leaves**: 3–6; cauline, lanceolate, keeled, 2.5–5.0 cm wide × 8–24 cm long, passing into bracts
**Flowers**: 12–40+, highly variable; arranged in a loose to dense terminal raceme; sepals obovate, the petals oblong, upright, usually with entire margins; lip three-parted and deeply lacerate; perianth various, green to nearly yellow or white; individual flower size ca. 1.5–3.0 cm, not including the 1.6–2.3 cm spur, the orifice nearly square
**Habitat**: open wet meadows, roadside ditches and seeps, mountain meadows
**Flowering period**: late June to early August

The least conspicuous of the fringed orchises, *Platanthera lacera* is scattered throughout the region. It can be found throughout the summer in damp meadows, open wet woods, and roadside ditches. Flower color is highly variable in many shades of green and some plants are nearly white. In many places in the northern portion of the Northeast *P. lacera* is found growing with either or both *P. grandiflora* and *P. psycodes*. Those plants whose flowers show a wash of lavender may represent hybrids with either *P. psycodes* (*P. ×andrewsii*) or *P. grandiflora* (*P. ×keenanii*). *Platanthera ×hollandii*, which was described from north of the range of this field guide, is the hybrid with *P. leucophaea* and, at least in theory, could be found in the only extant site for *P. leucophaea* within the field guide range. See page 174 for more details.

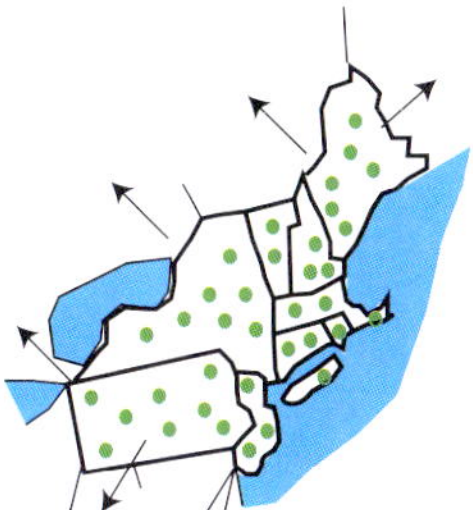

## *Platanthera leucophaea* (Nuttall) Lindley

### eastern prairie fringed orchis

**Range:** Nebraska east to Ontario and Maine, south to Oklahoma, Louisiana, and Virginia
**In the Northeast: Maine, New York, Pennsylvania**
**Plant**: terrestrial, 50–120 cm tall
**Leaves**: 2–5; cauline, lanceolate, keeled, 2.5–5.0 cm wide × 8–20 cm long, passing into bracts
**Flowers**: 12–27; arranged in a loose to dense terminal raceme; sepals ovate, the petals spatulate and broadly rounded, the margin finely serrate, partially enclosed within the sepals to form a cup-shaped hood; lip three-parted and deeply fringed; perianth cream shaded to whitish-green; individual flower size ca. 2–3 cm, not including the 3–5 cm spur, the orifice broadly crescent-shaped
**Habitat**: wet prairies, fens
**Flowering period**: July

Long considered one of the rarest and most vulnerable species of orchid in North America, the **eastern prairie fringed orchis**, *Platanthera leucophaea*, has few extant sites in the eastern United States. Crystal Bog, in Aroostook County, Maine, is the last remaining extant site in the Northeast, although numerous records exist from western New York and Pennsylvania. The tall, fragrant flowers of the **eastern prairie fringed orchis** wave gently in the breeze in the fen. Globally, *Platanthera leucophaea* occupies two somewhat different ecological niches. It is found primarily in the prairies in the Midwest and less frequently in fens and along lakeshores near Lake Huron. Reports of this species from additional sites in eastern Canada and the northeastern United States have always proven to be white-flowered forms (forma *albiflora*) of *Platanthera grandiflora*. Two interesting hybrids with *P. leucophaea* have recently been described from southwestern Ontario, *Platanthera* ×*hollandii*, with *P. lacera* (Catling, 2001), and *P.* ×*reznicekii*, with *P. psycodes* (Catling 2002). These sites are the only documented instances of the two hybrid combinations having been found. Both of the other parents are found flowering near Crystal Bog at the time that *P. leucophaea* is in flower. The best field marks would be an overlay of pink or pink tinges in the lip or a *P. leucophaea* with deeply cut or lacerate segments. The petals and sepals are also intermediate with the respective parents. Remember, though, that hybrids usually favor one parent or the other, so differences may be slight.

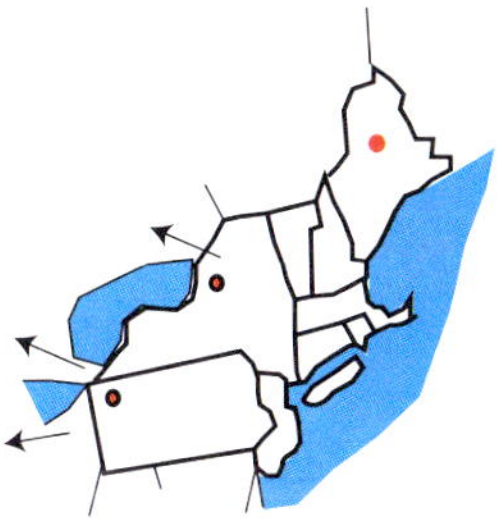

## *Platanthera macrophylla* (Goldie) P.M. Brown

### Goldie's pad-leaved orchis

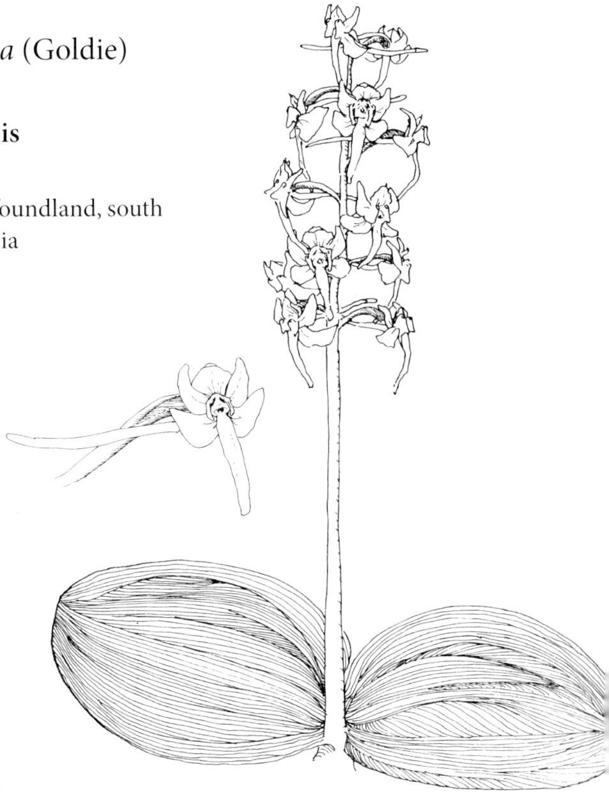

**Range:** Ontario east to Newfoundland, south to Michigan and Pennsylvania
**In the Northeast: Maine, New Hampshire, Vermont, Massachusetts, Connecticut, Rhode Island, New York, Pennsylvania, New Jersey**
**Plant**: terrestrial, 25–85 cm tall, the inflorescence occupying the upper third of the height; slender bracts present on the stem
**Leaves**: 2; basal, lying on the ground, ovate, up to 7–18 cm wide × 8–24 cm long; dark green above and pale beneath
**Flowers**: 9–23; arranged in a loose terminal raceme; dorsal sepal broadly ovate tapering to a point and concave; lateral sepals ovate-falcate and strongly reflexed; petals linear-lanceolate, tapering, falcate, erect and arching outward; lip linear-oblong, 1.0–2.3 cm long, descending or rarely recurved; sepals greenish-white; petals and lip whiter; flower size ca. 3 x 5 cm not including the slenderly clavate 2.8–4.6 cm spur
**Habitat**: rich deciduous and mixed woodlands
**Flowering period**: July to mid-August

For many years *Platanthera macrophylla* was considered a variety of *P. orbiculata*, although it was originally described as a full species. This giant of the northeastern woodlands is one of the most spectacular of all our native orchids. From leaves nearly the size of dinner plates to elephantine flowers it cannot help but take one's breath away. Populations can vary from single individuals to several hundred plants. In several other species of *Platanthera* where common names often include the adjectives large, small, big, etc., the overall size of the plant is *not* what matters. In this case, although plants of *P. macrophylla* are *usually* larger than those of *P. orbiculata*, it is the length of the spur that is the critical measurement. Also the position and shape of the petals is diagnostic. In one of the very best papers written on species pairs, Reddoch and Reddoch (1993) clearly explain the differences and similarities.

With flash

With flash

with natural light

## *Platanthera obtusata* (Banks *ex* Pursh) Lindley subsp. *obtusata*

### blunt-leafed rein orchis

forma *collectanea* (Fernald) P.M. Brown—dwarfed form

*Rhodora* 28: 175. 1926, as *Habenaria obtusata* var. *collectanea* Fernald, type: northern North America

forma *foliosa* P.M. Brown—multiple-leaved form

*North American Native Orchid Journal* 1(1): 13. 1995, type: Maine

**Range:** Alaska east to Newfoundland, south to Colorado and the upper Great Lakes region, east to western Massachusetts
**In the Northeast: Maine, New Hampshire, Vermont, Massachusetts, New York:** scattered populations particularly in the northernmost counties; historical in Massachusetts
**Plant**: terrestrial, 15–37 cm tall; in the forma *collectanea* 5–12 cm tall
**Leaves**: 1; basal or, in the forma *foliosa*, multiple, decreasing in size upward; linear oblanceolate and up to 0.9–5.5 cm wide × 4.0–15.0 cm long, blunt at the apex and tapering to the base or, in the forma *collectanea*, the single leaf usually oval-ovate and nearly equaling the scape in height; green
**Flowers**: 9–15; arranged in a loose terminal raceme or, in the forma *collectanea*, fewer flowers in a short, dense raceme; dorsal sepal broadly ovate tapering to a blunt apex; lateral sepals ovate-falcate and strongly reflexed; petals linear-lanceolate, with a dilated base, erect and arching outward in a horn-like manner; lip linear, broadened at the base, 3–6 mm long, descending; perianth green to greenish-white or, in the forma *collectanea*, yellowish-green; flower size to ca. 1 x 1 cm not including the 0.3–1.0 cm long acuminate spur
**Habitat**: mixed woodlands, usually in conifers, or, in the forma *collectanea*, open headlands, river gravels, tundra, and heaths
**Flowering period**: July to August

This highly variable circumpolar species is rare in the southern limit of its range but becomes one of the most common orchids in the far north. There it is not unusual to find plants of the forma *collectanea* in the open, exposed barrens. Within the woodlands the plants are much larger and more typical of the species. The moss- and lichen-covered coniferous woodlands that also support **heart-leaved twayblade**, *Listera cordata*, **lesser rattlesnake orchis**, *Goodyera repens*, and a variety of other orchids usually are home to the **blunt-leafed rein orchis**.

forma *collectanea*

forma *foliosa*

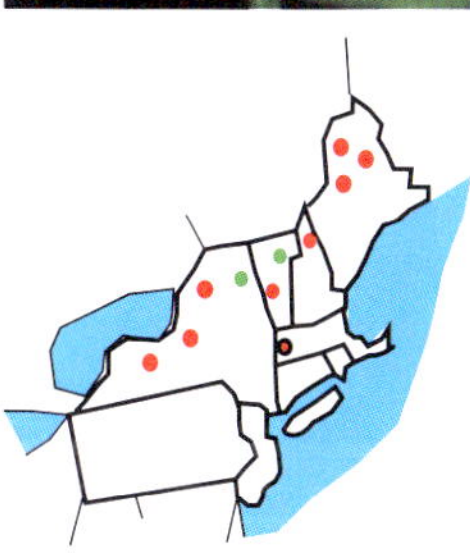

## *Platanthera orbiculata* (Pursh) Lindley

### pad-leaved orchis

forma *lehorsii* (Fernald) P.M. Brown—dwarfed form
*Rhodora* 52: 61. 1950, as *Habenaria orbiculata* var. *lehorsii* Fernald, type: St. Pierre et Miquelon

forma *longifolia* (Clute) P.M. Brown—narrow-leaved form
*American Botanist* (Binghampton) 7: 56. 1904, as *Habenaria orbiculata* var. *longifolia* Clute, type: Vermont

forma *pauciflora* (Jennings) P.M. Brown—few-flowered form
*Journal of the Washington Academy of Science* 10: 453. 1920, as *Lysias orbiculata* Rydberg var. *pauciflora* Jennings, type: Ontario

forma *trifolia* (Mousley) P.M. Brown—three-leaved form
*Orchid Review* 42: 112. 1934, as *Habenaria orbiculata* var. *trifolia* Mousley, type: Quebec

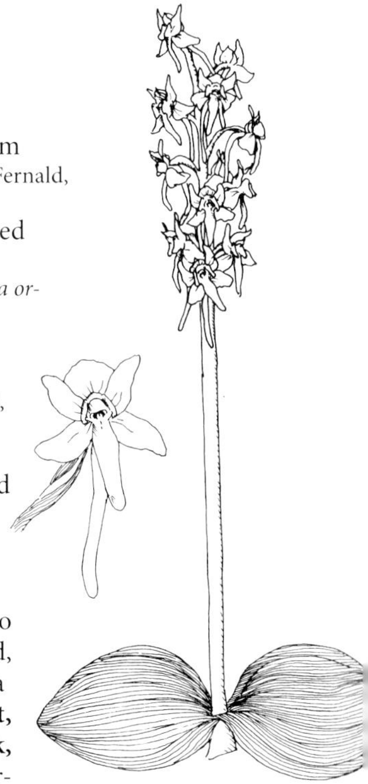

**Range:** southeastern Alaska, British Columbia east to Newfoundland, south to Washington and Maryland, south in the Appalachian Mountains to North Carolina
**In the Northeast: Maine, New Hampshire, Vermont, Massachusetts, Connecticut, Rhode Island, New York, Pennsylvania, New Jersey:** rare to local, but often occurring in large colonies
**Plants**: 12–75 cm tall; stem bracts present
**Leaves**: 2, basal, lying on the ground, or, in the forma *trifolia*, 3, the third leaf on the stem; ovate up to (4)10–20 cm wide × (5)12–22 cm long or, in the forma *longifolia*, oblong to nearly linear; dark green above and pale beneath
**Flowers**: 8–14, or in the forma *pauciflora*, 3–5 on shorter plants; arranged in a loose terminal raceme; dorsal sepal broadly ovate tapering to a point and concave; lateral sepals ovate-falcate and strongly reflexed; petals linear-lanceolate, tapering, falcate, erect; lip linear-oblong, descending or rarely recurved; sepals greenish-white; petals and lip whiter; flower size ca. 3 x 5 cm not including the slender 1.4–1.7 cm spur
**Habitat**: mixed woodlands; forma *lehorsii* in exposed sites on headlands
**Flowering period**: July to early August

*Platanthera orbiculata* and *P. macrophylla* presented, until recently, one of the most misunderstood species pairs in North American orchids. The work of Allan and Joyce Reddoch (1993) clearly revalidated *P. macrophylla* as a full species and helped to delineate the bounds of *P. orbiculata*. As mentioned here in the account for *P. macrophylla*, size does not matter as a distinguishing character of orchids except in the length of the spur. Spurs of *P. orbiculata* are 1.4–2.7 cm long, the lesser measurement found usually in plants of forma *lehorsii* and forma *pauciflora*. Mixed colonies of the two species are not uncommon in the eastern portion of the range, but as one progresses westward *P. macrophylla* becomes less common and pure stands of *P. orbiculata* are the norm. The large round leaves are always distinctive, but in areas where the two species overlap, identification of plants without flowers (or, in some situations, with withered flowers and fruit) cannot be certain.

With flash

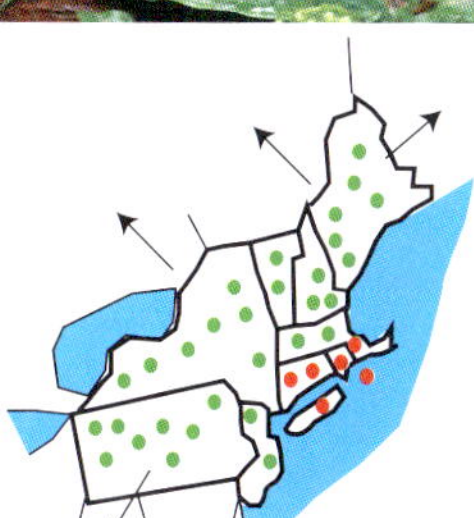

## *Platanthera pallida* P.M. Brown

### pale fringed orchis

**Range:** eastern Long Island, New York
**In the Northeast: New York:** local in interdunal hollows near Montauk, Long Island
**Plant**: terrestrial, to 80 cm tall
**Leaves**: 2–4; cauline, conduplicate, lanceolate, 1–3 cm wide × 5–20 cm long, rapidly reduced to bracts within the inflorescence
**Flowers**: 30–80; arranged in a loose to dense terminal raceme; sepals ovate, petals spatulate with margin of the apex crested, enclosed within the sepals forming a hood; lip 3–5 mm long, ovate-oblong, distinctively descending and recurved and with a finely lacerate margin; perianth pale ivory-yellow; individual flower size 5–7 mm, not including the 3 mm spur, which is typically curved
**Habitat:** near-xeric, interdunal hollows under pitch pines
**Flowering period**: late July into August

Known only from two sizable colonies near the eastern tip of Long island, the **pale fringed orchis**, *Platanthera pallida,* is a distinctive and showy component of the orchid flora of Long Island. Although superficially resembling the **orange crested orchis**, *P. cristata*, and considered a cline of *P. cristata* by Sheviak (FNA, 2002), the **pale fringed orchis** found on Long Island differs in several critical aspects. The flowers, apart from their creamy-ivory coloration, have descending, recurved lips and very short spurs. Plants of *P. cristata* forma *straminea*, with similar coloration, do not exhibit either of these characteristics. The pale green, conduplicate leaves of *P. pallida*, in contrast to the rich green, broad leaves of *P. cristata*, may represent an adaptation to the drier habitat of *P. pallida*. *Platanthera cristata* has not been found in or near the populations of *P. pallida* and inversely *P. pallida* has not been found elsewhere within or near populations of *P. cristata*. See Brown (1992) for more details.

## *Platanthera peramoena* (A. Gray) A. Gray

### purple fringeless orchis

forma *doddsiae* P.M. Brown—white-flowered form

*North American Native Orchid Journal* 8: 30–31. 2002, type: Missouri

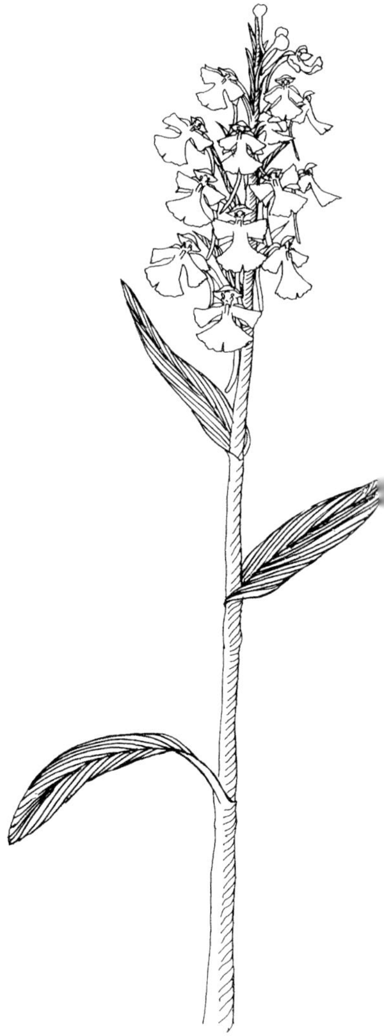

**Range:** Missouri east to New Jersey, south to Mississippi and Georgia

**In the Northeast: Pennsylvania, New Jersey:** very rare and extirpated from many previous locations

**Plant**: terrestrial, 75–105 cm tall

**Leaves**: 2–5; cauline, elliptic-lanceolate, keeled, 2.5–5.0 cm wide × 8–14 cm long, gradually reduced to bracts within the inflorescence

**Flowers**: 27–50+; arranged in a dense terminal raceme; sepals elliptic, reflexed; petals spatulate and rounded, the margin finely serrate, partially enclosed with the dorsal sepal to form a hood; lip three-parted, apically notched and faintly erose; perianth a brilliant rosy-purple or, in the forma *doddsiae*, pure white; individual flower size ca. 2–3 cm, not including the 2.5–3.0 cm spur, the orifice rounded

**Habitat**: damp meadows, low wet woods, streamsides

**Flowering period**: midsummer; late June to early August

One of the tallest and most striking of the tripartite-lipped fringed orchis group, *Platanthera peramoena*, the **purple fringeless orchis**, is a characteristic species of the east central United States. Not necessarily common anywhere, it can be locally abundant. Here in the Northeast it barely reaches into our area in southern Pennsylvania and scattered sites in New Jersey. Encountering these plants in flower is a real delight and, despite careful searching, the white-flowered form has been reported only once, and then from Missouri. Not easy to overlook, it should be carefully sought elsewhere. Reports of *P. peramoena* form New York and elsewhere have proven to be the fringeless forma of *P. grandiflora* (forma *mentotonsa*).

forma *doddsiae*

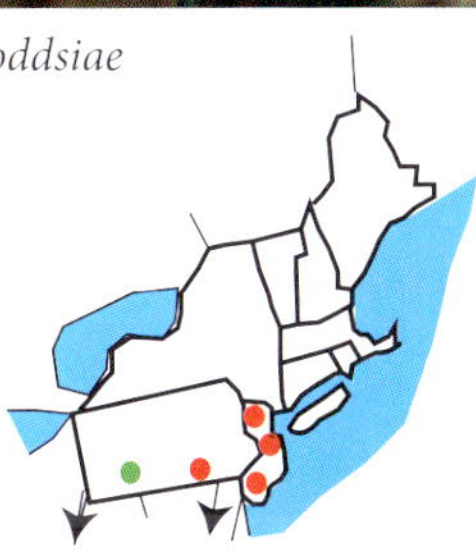

## *Platanthera psycodes* (Linnaeus) Lindley

### small purple fringed orchis

forma *albiflora* (R. Hoffman) Whiting & Catling—white-flowered form
*Proceedings of the Boston Society of Natural History* 36: 248. 1922, as *Habenaria psycodes* forma *albiflora*, type: Massachusetts

forma *ecalcarata* (Bryan) P.M. Brown—spurless form
*Annals of the Missouri Botanical Garden* 4: 38. 1917, as *Habenaria psycodes* var. *ecalcarata*, type: Michigan

forma *fernaldii* (Rousseau & Rouleau) P.M. Brown—dwarf form
*Bulletin du Jardin Botanique de l'État* 27: 370. 1957, as *Habenaria psycodes* var. *fernaldii* Rousseau & Rouleau, type Quebec

forma *rosea* P.M. Brown—pink-flowered form
*North American Native Orchid Journal* 1(4): 289. 1995, type: Vermont

forma *varians* (Bryan) P.M. Brown—entire-lip form
*Annals of the Missouri Botanical Garden* 4: 37. 1917, as *Habenaria psycodes* var. *varians*, type: Michigan

**Range:** Ontario east to Newfoundland, south to West Virginia and New Jersey; south in the Appalachian Mountains to Georgia
**In the Northeast: Maine, New Hampshire, Vermont, Massachusetts, Connecticut, Rhode Island, New York, Pennsylvania, New Jersey:** locally common
**Plant**: terrestrial, to 90 cm tall or, in the forma *fernaldii*, to only 25 cm
**Leaves**: 2–6; cauline, lanceolate, keeled 1.5–7.0 cm wide × 8–24 cm long
**Flowers**: 30–125; arranged in a loose to dense terminal raceme usually 2.5–3.0 cm in diameter with flowers open successively, i.e., the lower ones usually withering before the upper ones have opened, giving the inflorescence a conical appearance or, in the forma *fernaldii*, the raceme more compact and few-flowered; sepals elliptic, petals obovate with finely dentate margins; lip three-parted with a margin usually finely fringed to less than a third of the depth of the lip, or in the forma *varians* the margin essentially entire; perianth various shades of purple from pale lavender to deep, rich rosy-magenta; or, in the forma *albiflora*, white; or, in the forma *rosea*, a pale pink; individual flower size 0.5–1.5 cm, not including the 1.2–1.8 cm spur, or in the forma *ecalcarata*, the spur lacking; spur orifice likened to a transverse dumbbell in all forms
**Habitat**: open wet meadows, roadside ditches and seeps, mountain meadows or, in the forma *fernaldii*, river gravels
**Flowering period**: late June to August

The common names **large** and **small purple fringed orchis** are very misleading as the **small purple fringed orchis,** *Platanthera psycodes*, can often be "larger" than the **large purple fringed orchis**, *P. grandiflora*. It is usually both taller and more floriferous than *P. grandiflora*, although the individual flowers are smaller. The **small purple fringed orchis** is also widespread throughout much of central and northeastern North America. This often-tall, slender species is at home in open meadows as well as along wooded streamsides. It frequently occurs in small numbers, but is rarely found as a single plant. For comparisons to the **large purple fringed orchis**, *P. grandiflora*, see details at that entry on page 166. Hybrids with *P. lacera* are known as *P.* ×*andrewsii*.

forma *albiflora*

forma *varians*

Hybrids:

*Platanthera* ×*andrewsii* (Niles) Luer

**Andrews' hybrid fringed orchis**

(*P. lacera* × *P. psycodes*)

*Bog-trotting for Orchids*. 258. 1904, as *Habenaria* ×*andrewsii*, type: Vermont

Not at all uncommon throughout most of the range of the two parents. Plants formerly identified as *Platanthera lacera* var. *terra-novae* Fernald have proven to be *P.* ×*andrewsii*.

*Platanthera* ×*bicolor* (Rafinesque) Luer

**bicolor hybrid fringed orchis**

(*P. blephariglottis* × *P. ciliaris*)

*Flora Telleuriana*. 2: 39. 1839, as *Blephariglottis bicolor*, type: New Jersey

Plants usually have lemon, pale tan, or bicolored flowers and retain the overall dimensions of the parents.

*Platanthera* ×*canbyi* (Ames) Luer

**Canby's hybrid fringed orchis**

(*P. blephariglottis* × *P. cristata*)

*Rhodora* 10: 70. 1908, as *Habenaria canbyi*, type: Delaware

Plants vary in color from nearly white to pale yellow to light orange. The spur is usually about as long as the lip.

*Platanthera* ×*channellii* Folsom
**Channell's hybrid fringed orchis**
(*P. ciliaris* × *P. cristata*)
*Orquidea* (Mex.) 9(2): 344. 1984, type: Alabama

This hybrid and the southern species *Platanthera chapmanii* can be difficult to tell apart. Within the southeastern portion of the range of this book only true *P.* ×*channellii* would be a possibility.

*Platanthera* ×*keenanii* P.M. Brown
**Keenan's hybrid fringed orchis**
(*P. grandiflora* × *P. lacera*)
*A Field and Study Guide to the Orchids of New England and New York*, p. 189. 1994, type: Maine

Uncommon throughout the northeastern states and usually occurring as individuals in mixed populations of both parents.

X*Platanthopsis vossii* (Case) P.M Brown
**Voss' hybrid rein orchis**
(*Gymnadeniopsis clavellata* × *Platanthera blephariglottis*)
*Michigan Botanist*. 22: 141–144. 1983, as *Platanthera* ×*vossii*, type: Michigan.

see page 154 for a full account of this rare intergeneric hybrid

## *Pogonia*

This is a small genus of only three species, and is found in both Asia and North America. Formerly the genus included those species, among others, that are now treated in *Triphora*, *Isotria*, and *Cleistes*, although some current authors are again including *Isotria* and *Cleistes*. We have only one species in the United States and Canada, *Pogonia ophioglossoides*, which has one of the broadest ranges throughout all of eastern North America. Although variable in color, form, and size, the unmistakable flower form with the large spatulate lip makes them easy to identify, even from a distance. **Rose pogonias** are often seen in the company of **grass-pinks**, *Calopogon*, and several of the carnivores such as pitcher-plants and sundews.

## *Pogonia ophioglossoides* (Linnaeus) Ker-Gawler

### rose pogonia; snakemouth orchid

forma *albiflora* Rand & Redfield—white-flowered form

*Flora of Mount Desert Island* 152. 1894, type: Maine

forma *brachypogon* (Fernald) P.M. Brown—short-bearded form

*Rhodora* 23: 245. 1922, as *Pogonia ophioglossoides* (Linnaeus) Ker-Gawler var. *brachypogon* Fernald, type: Nova Scotia

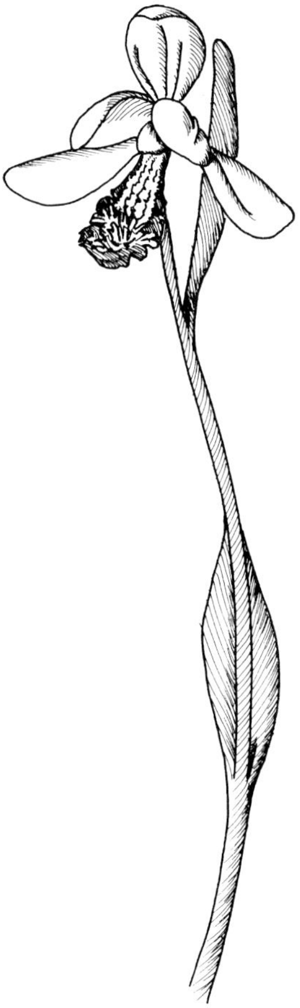

**Range:** Manitoba east to Newfoundland, south to Texas and Florida

**In the Northeast: Maine, New Hampshire, Vermont, Massachusetts, Connecticut, Rhode Island, New York, Pennsylvania, New Jersey:** locally common

**Plant**: terrestrial, 8–35 cm tall

**Leaves**: 1, rarely 2; cauline, ovate, placed midway on the stem, 2 cm wide × 6–10 cm long

**Flowers**: 1–3 (4) terminal; subtended by a foliaceous bract; sepals and petals similar, lanceolate to obovate; the sepals wide-spreading; lip spatulate with a deeply fringed margin and bright yellow beard or, in the forma brachypogon the beard reduced to a few knobs, to 2 cm; perianth from light to dark, rosy-pink or lavender or, in the forma *albiflora*, pure white; individual flower size ca. 4 cm

**Habitat**: moist meadows, open bogs and heaths, roadside ditches, and sphagnous seeps

**Flowering period**: late June to early August

From Newfoundland to Florida and westward to the Mississippi Valley, this little jewel adorns open bogs and meadows, roadside ditches, borrow pits, and sphagnous seeps. Color and form vary greatly from colony to colony. It is not unusual to find plants with the petals and sepals very narrow and, within the same colony, individuals with the sepals and petals broad and rounded. Plants with coloring from pale lilac to intense magenta occasionally have white-flowered, forma *albiflora*, plants growing among them. Although most plants have solitary flowers, it can be interesting, especially in a large population, to search for those with multiple flowers. Stems with two flowers are not that unusual and upon rare occasion a three-flowered stem will be seen. Only once has the author seen a stem with four flowers!

forma *albiflora*

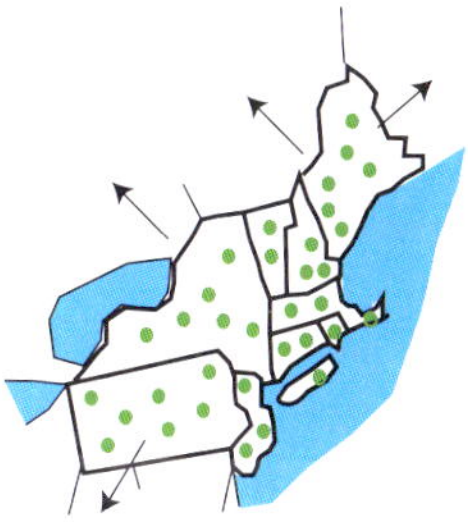

forma *brachypogon*

## *Spiranthes*

*Spiranthes* is a cosmopolitan genus of about 50 species. Treated in the strictest sense it is one of the most easily recognized genera, but includes some of the more difficult plants to identify to species. The relatively slender, often twisted stems and spikes of small white or creamy-yellow (or pink in *S. sinensis*) flowers are universally recognizable. In the United States and Canada we have 24 species, including 14 found in our area.

Note: *Spiranthes cernua* is a compilospecies with gene flow from several other species, depending on the plants' geographic location. Occasionally these plants prove problematic to key out. Plants of *S. cernua* from coastal New Jersey strongly resemble *S. odorata* and those of southern and western Pennsylvania in open prairie-like habits may resemble *S. magnicamporum*.

### Key to the ladies'-tresses, *Spiranthes*

1a plants summer flowering . . . 2
1b plants autumn flowering . . . 8

2a plants of wet habitats . . . 3
2b plants of dry habitats; flowers white or with green throats . . . 5

3a plants with broad shining leaves; plants of calcareous meadows and river banks; flowers with a brilliant yellow lip/throat . . . . . **shining ladies'-tresses**, *Spiranthes lucida*, p. 206
3b plants of swamps, meadows, and wet ditches; leaves slender and grass-like . . . 4

4a sepals divergent, plants of southern New Jersey . . . . . **lace-lipped ladies'-tresses**, *Spiranthes laciniata*, p. 204
4b sepals appressed, the flower tubular; green veining on the lip . . . . . **giant ladies'-tresses**, *Spiranthes praecox*, p. 231

5a flowers pure white, leaves absent at flowering time . . . . . **little ladies'-tresses**, *Spiranthes tuberosa*, p. 216
5b flowers with green throats or lip cream-colored . . . 6

6a leaves (slender and grass-like) present at flowering time . . . . . **grass-leaved ladies'-tresses**, *Spiranthes vernalis*, p. 218
6b leaves ovate; basal or absent at flowering time . . . 7

7a leaves present at flowering time; inflorescence loosely arranged; flowers spaced out; northerly in distribution . . . . . **northern slender ladies'-tresses**, *Spiranthes lacera* var. *lacera*, p. 200
7b leaves absent at flowering time; flowers tightly arranged; southerly in distribution . . . . . **southern slender ladies'-tresses**, *Spiranthes lacera* var. *gracilis*, p. 202

8a flowers small, 5 mm or less in length . . . 9
8b flowers large, 5 mm or more in length . . . 10

9a plants of open shales and grasslands; flowers, ca. 5 mm long, usually arranged in a single rank . . . . . **Case's ladies'-tresses**, *Spiranthes casei*, p. 196
9b plants of shaded woodlands and disturbed areas; flowers lacking a rostellum . . . . . **northern oval ladies'-tresses**, *Spiranthes ovalis* var. *erostellata*, p. 212

10a lip constricted in the middle, panduriform . . . . . **hooded ladies'-tresses**, *Spiranthes romanzoffiana*, p. 214
10b lip not constricted in the middle . . . 11

11a entire flower white and/or cream . . . 12
11b flowers with green or yellow on the lip . . . 13

12a lateral sepals and petals appressed . . . . . **nodding ladies'-tresses**, *Spiranthes cernua*, p. 198
12b lateral sepals and petals approximate or divergent; lower surface of lip butterscotch-colored . . . . . **yellow ladies'-tresses**, *Spiranthes ochroleuca*, p. 210

13a lateral sepals arched and incurved; plants of dry, calcareous prairie-like areas (historical in southern Pennsylvania). . . . . **Great Plains ladies'-tresses**, *Spiranthes magnicamporum*, p. 208
13b lateral sepals projecting forward; plants of coastal wetlands (possibly in coastal New Jersey) . . . . . **fragrant ladies'-tresses**, *Spiranthes odorata*, p. 231

## *Spiranthes casei* Catling & Cruise var. *casei*

### Case's ladies'-tresses

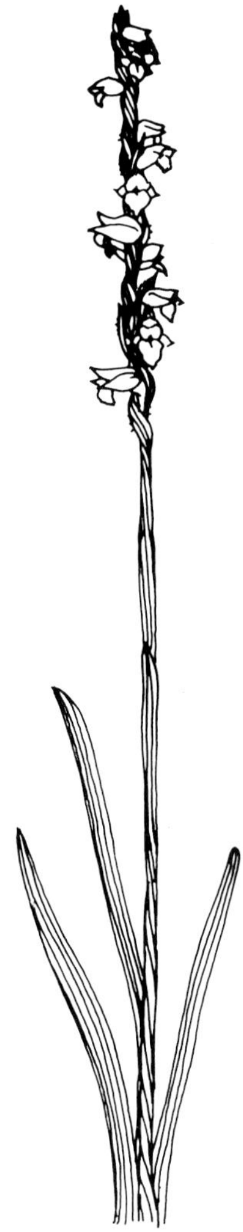

**Range:** Ontario east to Nova Scotia, south to Wisconsin, northern Pennsylvania, and western Maine
**In the Northeast: Maine, New Hampshire, Vermont, New York, Pennsylvania:** rare and local
**Plants**: terrestrial, 8–50 cm tall, sparsely pubescent
**Leaves**: 3–5; appearing basal or on the lower portion of the stem; linear-oblanceolate, up to 2 cm wide × 20 cm long; ascending to spreading; leaves present at anthesis
**Flowers**: 10–50; in a spike, loosely spiraled with 5 or more flowers per cycle, nodding from the base of the perianth; floral bracts green; sepals lanceolate; lateral sepals slightly spreading; petals ovate to oblanceolate; perianth ivory or greenish-white; lip oblong, 5.0–7.5 mm, the central portion often a deeper creamy yellow, with thin, fringed margins, the apex truncate; overall flower size 6–9 mm long
**Habitat**: dry open sites usually on the Canadian Shield in shaley soils, road scrapes, or thin-soil grasslands
**Flowering period**: late August to September

Although plants had been known for many years, it was only in 1974 that they were described as a species. Formerly these plants were often known as the "northern [*Spiranthes*] *vernalis*," a species that grows considerably farther to the south. For a short time plants of *S. casei* were also known as *S. intermedia*, again a completely different plant that is actually a hybrid between *S. vernalis* and *S. lacera* var. *gracilis* and does not range northward. With the publication by Catling and Cruise in 1974, the mystery of the so-called northern *vernalis* was solved and the species was named in honor of Fred Case, orchidist and botanist from Michigan and author of *Orchids of the Western Great Lakes Region*. Plants of *S. casei*, like most other species of *Spiranthes*, vary greatly in size, vigor, and number of flowers. The small, nodding, partially open flowers in a single rank make them reasonably easy to spot and if growing among other species of *Spiranthes* they are very distinctive. The only possible confusion would be with *S.* ×*borealis*, the hybrid between *S. casei* and *S. ochroleuca*. This hybrid is frequent in northern New England where the two parents frequently grow together. Plants of *Spiranthes casei* in northern Pennsylvania grow, often abundantly, along old railroad right of ways in the ballast between the railroad ties. *Thuja occidentalis*, the northern white cedar, so typical of the northern locations for the species, is locally abundant here and the ties are made from the cedars.

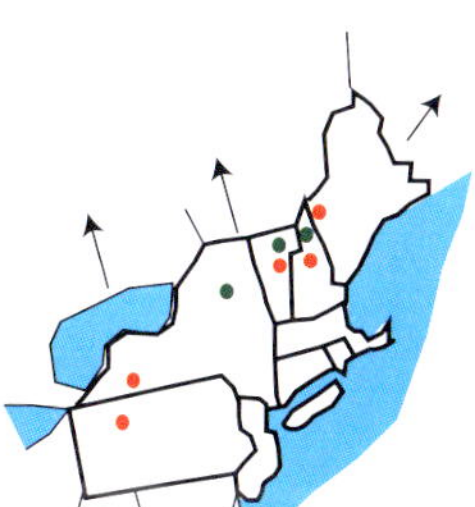

## *Spiranthes cernua* (Linnaeus) L.C. Richard

### nodding ladies'-tresses

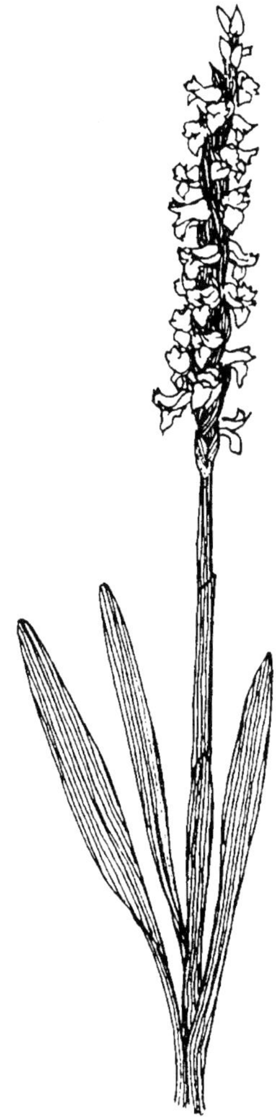

**Range:** South Dakota east to Nova Scotia, south to Texas and Florida
**In the Northeast: Maine, New Hampshire, Vermont, Massachusetts, Connecticut, Rhode Island, New York, Pennsylvania, New Jersey:** locally common
**Plant**: terrestrial, 10–50 cm tall
**Leaves**: 3–5; appearing basal or on the lower portion of the stem; linear-oblanceolate, up to 2 cm wide × 26 cm long; ascending to spreading; leaves are usually present at anthesis in most races
**Flowers**: 10–50; in a spike, tightly to loosely spiraled with 5 or more flowers per cycle, nodding from the base of the perianth or rarely ascending; bracts with a white or light green central stripe; sepals and petals similar, lanceolate; perianth white, ivory; lip oblong, broad at the apex, the central portion of the lip, in some races, creamy-yellow or green; the sepals approximate and extending forward, sometimes arching above the flower; individual flower size 0.6–10.5 mm
**Habitat**: wet to dry open sites, lightly wooded areas, moist grassy roadsides, pine flatwoods, etc.
**Flowering period:** late August to October

Of all of our native orchids in North America, *Spiranthes cernua* is the most difficult to describe simply and concisely. Because it is a compilospecies—one that has gene flow from several different similar species—plants in different geographic areas have strong resemblances to the basic diploid species contributing that area's unidirectional gene flow. In northeastern North America we are somewhat fortunate that the only basic diploid *Spiranthes* that contributes gene flow at this time is *S. ochroleuca*. That is not to say that identification of *S. cernua* plants is always easy—quite to the contrary. Because the plants are apomictic—not fertilized in the traditional sexual manner, but producing seed (actually minute plantlets) directly without fertilization—local races occur that are quite distinctive.

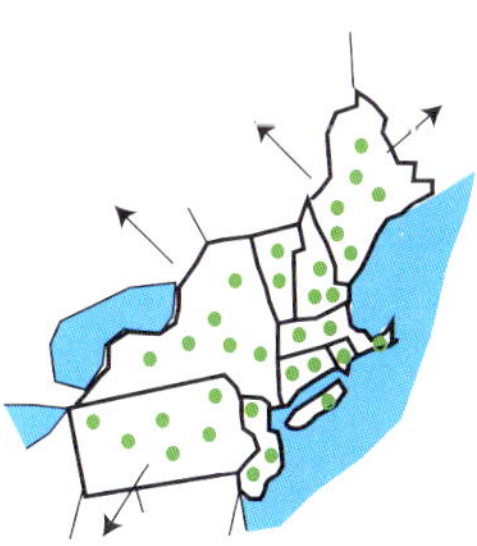

## *Spiranthes lacera* Rafinesque var. *lacera*

### northern slender ladies'-tresses

**Range:** Alberta east to Nova Scotia, south to Missouri and Virginia
**In the Northeast: Maine, New Hampshire, Vermont, Massachusetts, New York, Pennsylvania**: local
**Plant**: terrestrial, 15–65 cm tall; pubescent
**Leaves**: 2–4; ovate, dark green, 1–2 cm wide × 2–5 cm long, usually present at flowering time
**Flowers**: 10–35; in a single rank, in a dense spiral; sepals and petals similar, elliptic; perianth white; lip oblong, with the apex rounded; central portion green with a clearly defined crisp apron; the lower flowers spaced out from those above; individual flower size 4.0–7.5 mm
**Habitat**: dry to moist meadows, grassy roadsides, cemeteries, open sandy areas in woodlands, lawns, old fields
**Flowering period**: July to September

The differences between var. *lacera* and the more southerly var. *gracilis* are not great, but the more northern of the two has the lower flowers well spaced out on the inflorescence and they appear to be much smaller because of the position of the sepals. Disjunct populations occur on Long Island and in central Pennsylvania.

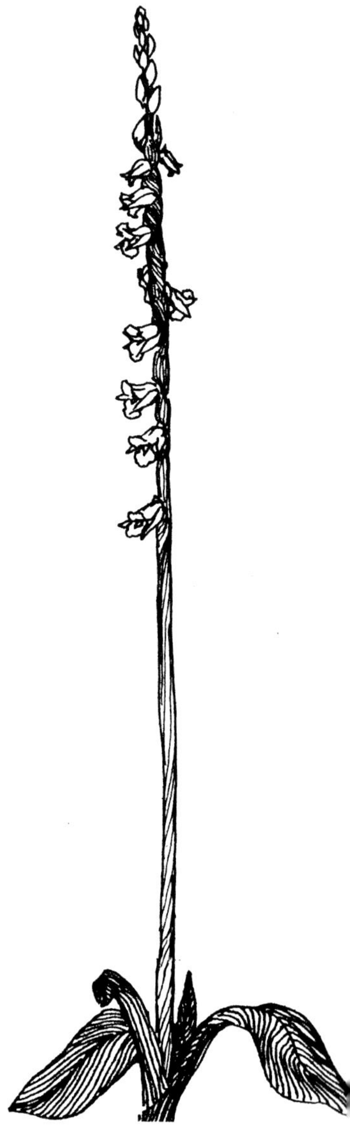

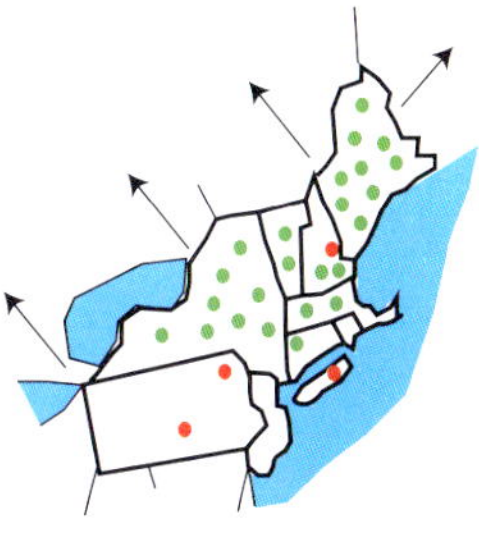

## *Spiranthes lacera* (Rafinesque) Rafinesque var. *gracilis* (Bigelow) Luer

### southern slender ladies'-tresses

**Range:** Michigan east to Nova Scotia and Maine, south to Kansas, Texas, and Georgia
**In the Northeast: Maine, New Hampshire, Massachusetts, Connecticut, Rhode Island, New York, Pennsylvania, New Jersey**: locally common, especially southward
**Plant**: terrestrial, 15–65 cm tall; glabrous to sparsely pubescent
**Leaves**: 2–4; ovate, dark green, 1–2 cm wide × 2–5 cm long, usually absent at flowering time
**Flowers**: 10–35; in a single rank, spiraled or secund; sepals and petals similar, elliptic; perianth white; lip oblong, with the apex rounded; central portion green with a clearly defined crisp apron; individual flower size 4.0–7.5 mm
**Habitat**: dry to moist meadows, grassy roadsides, cemeteries, open sandy areas in woodlands, lawns, old fields
**Flowering period**: July to September

*Spiranthes lacera* var. *gracilis* is the more southerly of the two varieties and found in nearly every state in the central and eastern United States. The small, white, green-throated flowers are very distinctive and the dense spiral of the inflorescence quite eye-catching. Plants are often encountered in lawns, and local cemeteries are usually a good place to search as well. Hybrids with *Spiranthes tuberosa* are known as *S.* ×*eamesii*, and with *S. vernalis* as *S.* ×*intermedia*.

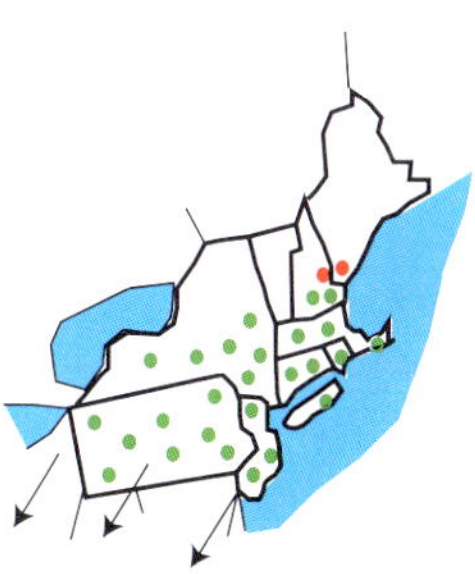

## *Spiranthes laciniata* (Small) Ames

**lace-lipped ladies'-tresses**

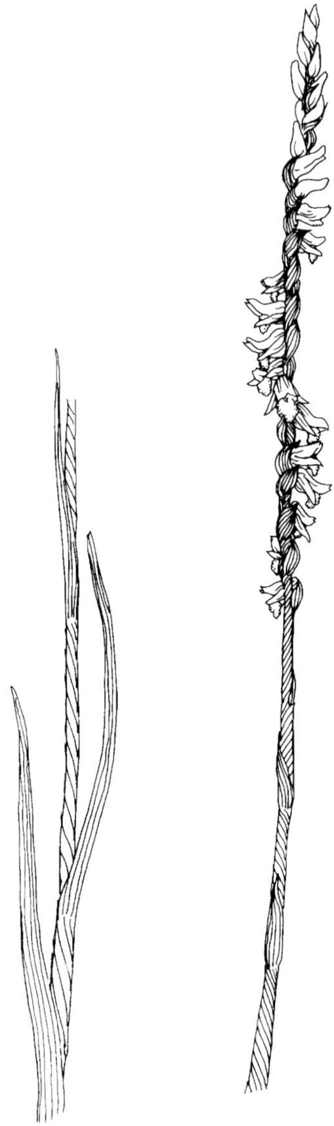

**Range:** eastern Texas east through all of Florida and north to southern New Jersey, primarily on the Coastal Plain
**In the Northeast: New Jersey**
**Plant**: terrestrial, 20–95 cm tall, densely pubescent with capitate hairs
**Leaves**: 3–5; lanceolate, 1.0–1.7 cm wide × 5.0–40.0 cm long
**Flowers**: 10–50; in a single rank, spiraled or secund; sepals and petals similar, elliptic; perianth white to ivory; lip oblong, with the apex undulate-lacerate, the central portion of the lip yellow; individual flower size ca. 1 cm
**Habitat**: wet, grassy roadsides, ditches, swamps, and shallow open water
**Flowering period**: May to July

The **lace-lipped ladies'-tresses** is easily distinguished from the **grass-leaved ladies'-tresses**, *Spiranthes vernalis*, which it superficially resembles, by its ball-tipped hairs, in contrast to the pointed articulate hairs found on *S. vernalis*. In southern New Jersey it may flower at the same time or just a bit later than *S. vernalis*. Almost always in a wetland habitat, the tall, creamy white spikes with a diagnostic yellowish lip help to separate it from any other autumn flowering ladies'-tresses. It is very rare in New Jersey and many specimens previously identified as *S. laciniata* have proven to be *S. vernalis*.

## *Spiranthes lucida* (H.H. Eaton) Ames

### shining ladies'-tresses

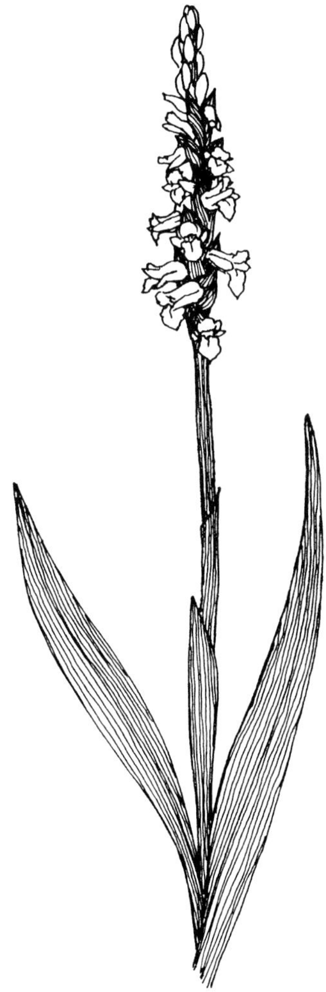

**Range:** Wisconsin east to Nova Scotia, south to Kansas, Alabama, and West Virginia
**In the Northeast: Maine, New Hampshire, Vermont, Massachusetts, Connecticut, Rhode Island, New York, Pennsylvania, New Jersey**: rare to local; primarily in calcareous wetlands
**Plant**: terrestrial, 10–38 cm tall
**Leaves**: 3–4; basal, elliptic-lanceolate, 0.5–1.5 cm wide × 3.0–12.0 cm long; the surface shiny; present at flowering time and long beyond
**Flowers**: 10–20; in an open spiral; nearly horizontal to nodding; sepals and petals similar, white, lanceolate; lateral sepals appressed to the petals and lip forming a tube; the lip oblong, bright yellow with the central portion yellow to orange or green, the margin crenulate; individual flower size 0.6–0.9 mm
**Habitat**: rocky riverbanks, seeps, fens; usually calcareous
**Flowering period**: mid-June to early July

The **shining ladies'-tresses**, *Spiranthes lucida*, is unlike any other in the genus in North America. The broad, shining leaves and tubular yellow-lipped flowers set it apart. Here in the northern portion of its range *S. lucida* is often accompanied by plants of *S. romanzoffiana*, the **hooded ladies'-tresses**, a species that flowers later in the summer or early autumn. Calcareous rocky riverbanks and seeps seem to be the preferred habitat and it is the earliest flowering *Spiranthes* species and the only one to be in flower in our region at that time.

## *Spiranthes magnicamporum* Sheviak

### Great Plains ladies'-tresses

**Range:** Manitoba east to southern Ontario, south to New Mexico, Texas, Pennsylvania, and Georgia
**In the Northeast: Pennsylvania**: based upon herbarium records from two southern counties
**Plant**: terrestrial, 10–63 cm tall
**Leaves**: 2–4; appearing basal or on the lower portion of the stem; linear-oblanceolate, up to 1.5 cm wide × 16 cm long; ascending to spreading; leaves usually absent or withering at anthesis
**Flowers**: 12–54; in a spike, tightly to loosely spiraled with 3–4 flowers per cycle, abruptly nodding from the base; lateral sepals wide-spreading and usually arched above the flower, petals linear-lanceolate; perianth white, ivory, or cream; lip ovate to oblong, the apex crenulate, the central portion of the lip usually yellow; individual flower size 0.4–1.2 cm
**Habitat**: wet to dry alkaline prairies, bluffs, and fens
**Flowering period**: September through November southward

The **Great Plains ladies'-tresses**, *Spiranthes magnicamporum*, a typical prairie species, is reaching the eastern limit of its range in disjunct sites in Pennsylvania. The **Great Plains ladies'-tresses** is one of several species of *Spiranthes* that contribute gene flow to the **nodding ladies'-tresses**, *S. cernua*. Several of these eastern prairie sites contain mixed populations of both *S. magnicamporum* and *S. cernua*, so the plants and, if absolutely necessary, the seeds need to be carefully examined to determine the correct species. Seeds from the basic diploid species *S. magnicamporum*, *S. ochroleuca*, *S. odorata*, and *S. ovalis* are monoembryonic whereas those of *S. cernua*, usually a polyploid species, are polyembryonic. This type of examination goes beyond the scope of this field guide and requires more sophisticated techniques. A compound microscope and the skills to use it are required.

The Pennsylvania records are based upon collections (*fide* Sheviak) from Lancaster County, 1892, and Lebanon County, 1889. The species has not been vouchered in Pennsylvania since then.

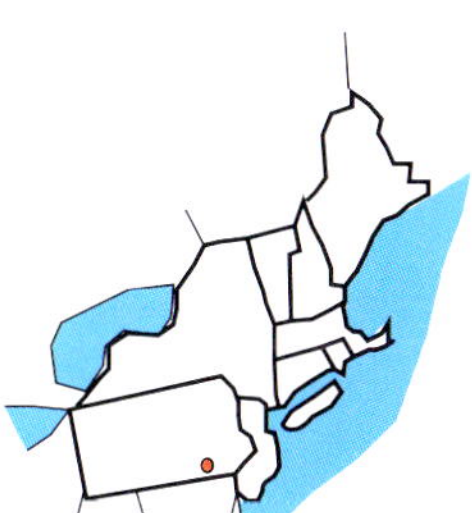

## *Spiranthes ochroleuca* (Rydberg) Rydberg

### yellow ladies'-tresses

forma *foliobracteata* P.M. Brown
*North American Native Orchid Journal* 13: 8. 2007, type: New Hampshire

**Range:** Michigan east to Nova Scotia, south to Kentucky and South Carolina
**In the Northeast: Maine, New Hampshire, Vermont, Massachusetts, Connecticut, Rhode Island, New York, Pennsylvania, New Jersey**: occasional
**Plant**: terrestrial, 10–55 cm tall
**Leaves**: 3–5; appearing basal or on the lower portion of the stem; linear-lanceolate, up to 2 cm wide × 21 cm long; ascending to spreading; the leaves are present at anthesis
**Flowers**: 10–50; in a spike, tight to loosely spiraled with 3–4(5) flowers per cycle, ascending; sepals and petals similar, lanceolate; lateral sepals appressed to petals and lip, straight; perianth white to cream-colored; lip oblong to ovate, the central portion of the lip a deeper creamy yellow or butterscotch color, individual flower size 0.7–1.2 cm, or in the forma *foliobracteata*, leaves and bracts replacing the flowers
**Habitat**: dry to somewhat moist open sites, ledges, barrens, slightly wooded areas, grassy roadsides
**Flowering period**: late August to September

Typically, *Spiranthes ochroleuca* has a distinct butterscotch-colored trough in the center of the lip, something that is very visible if one looks at the bottom side of the lip. Perhaps the very best areas to look for the **yellow ladies'-tresses** are roadside scrapes and borrow pits. The plants often colonize such areas. They usually occupy the drier portions while **nodding ladies'-tresses**, *S. cernua*, are often found in the wetter areas. Such combinations are very helpful in comparing the species.

S. *cernua* and *S. ochroleuca*

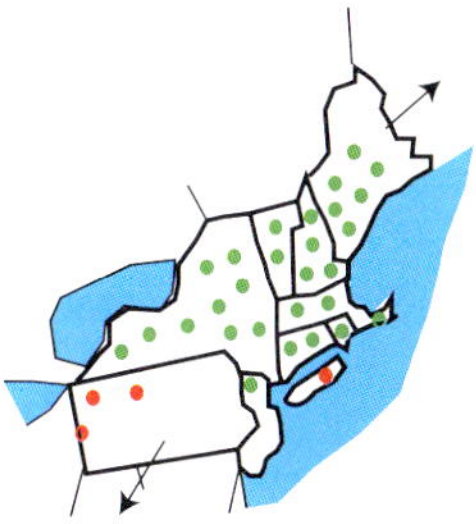

## *Spiranthes ovalis* Lindley var. *erostellata* Catling

### northern oval ladies'-tresses

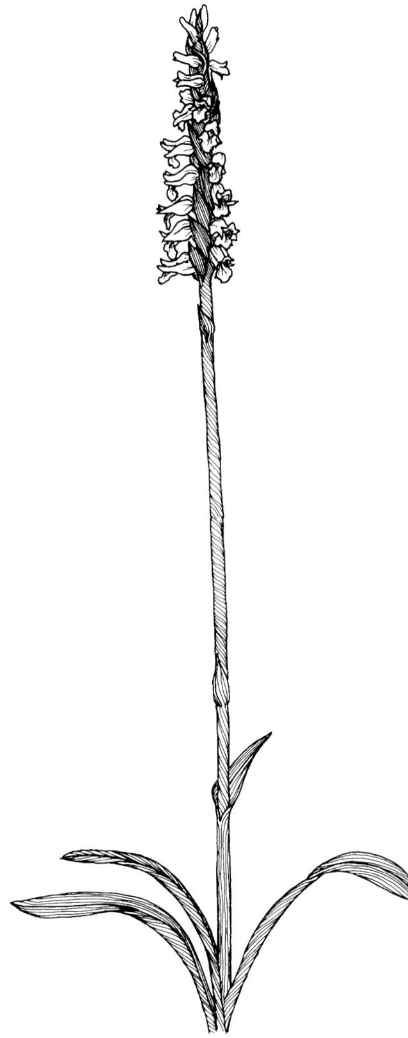

**Range:** Ontario south to Illinois and Arkansas, east to Ohio and western Pennsylvania and south to northern Florida
**In the Northeast: Pennsylvania**: rare in the central and western counties
**Plant**: terrestrial, 20–40 cm tall, pubescent
**Leaves**: 2–4; basal and on the lower half of the stem, oblanceolate, 0.5–1.5 cm wide × 3–15 long, present at flowering time
**Flowers**: 10–50; in 3 tight ranks; sepals and petals similar, lanceolate; perianth white; lip oblong, tapering to the apex with a delicate undulate margin; the sepals extending forward; individual flower size 3.5–5.0 mm; rostellum lacking, therefore the plants self-pollinating; flowers not always fully open
**Habitat**: rich, damp woodlands and floodplains
**Flowering period**: September to early November

In most plants of **northern oval ladies'-tresses**, *S. ovalis* var. *erostellata*, the flowers are never quite fully open, or in many individuals they are tiny cleistogamous flowers, and the ovaries are simultaneously swollen on each flower within the inflorescence. Primarily a Midwestern plant, this orchid is found in Pennsylvania in scattered sites in a variety of habitats. Plants of the southern *S. ovalis* var. *ovalis* have fully open flowers and the ovaries swell progressively.

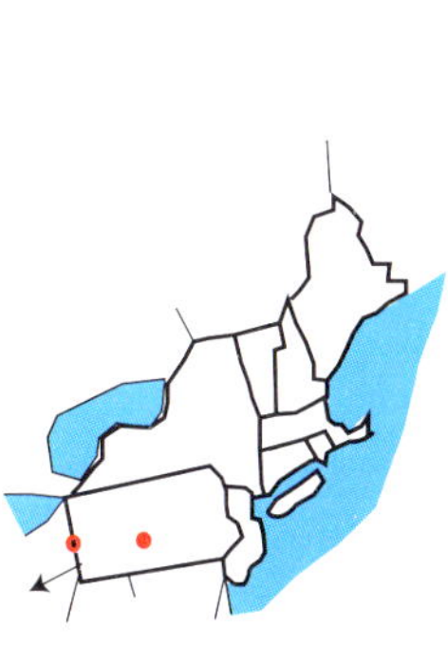

## *Spiranthes romanzoffiana* Chamisso

### hooded ladies'-tresses

**Range:** Alaska east to Newfoundland; south to California, northern New Mexico, Indiana, Pennsylvania; Northern Ireland, Great Britain
**In the Northeast: Maine, New Hampshire, Vermont, Massachusetts, Connecticut, Rhode Island, New York, Pennsylvania, New Jersey**: locally common in northern calcareous habitats; very rare southward
**Plant**: terrestrial, 10–50 cm tall
**Leaves**: 3–6; basal and extending up the lower quarter of the stem, linear-lanceolate, up to 1.5 cm wide × 25 cm long, passing into a few slender bracts; present at flowering time
**Flowers**: 10–60; in a dense spiral; nearly horizontal to ascending; sepals and petals similar, creamy white to greenish-white to creamy-yellow, lanceolate, acuminate; lateral sepals appressed to the petals and lip forming an ascending hood; the lip oblong, panduriform, the broadened margin recurved and finely lacerate; individual flower size 0.9–1.2 cm
**Habitat**: rocky riverbanks, seeps, fens; usually calcareous
**Flowering period**: mid-July through August and into early September

*Spiranthes romanzoffiana*, the **hooded ladies'-tresses**, is the most widespread *Spiranthes* in northern North America. Starting to flower in midsummer in the far north, it continues flowering until late August further south. The almond-scented flowers and arching hood are distinctive among our eastern *Spiranthes* and could not possibly be mistaken for any other species. In a few areas it has hybridized with *Spiranthes lacera* var. *lacera* to produce *Spiranthes ×simpsonii.*

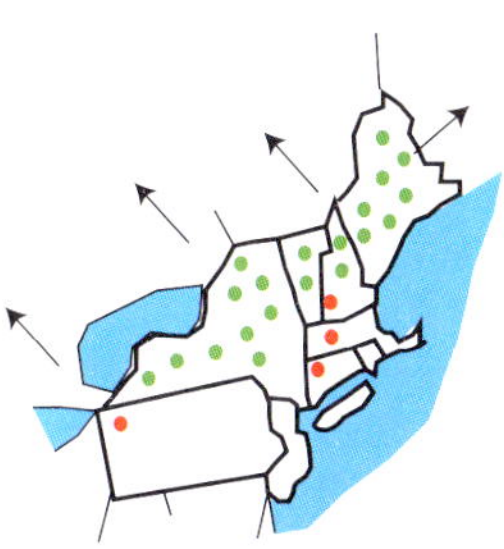

## *Spiranthes tuberosa* Rafinesque

### little ladies'-tresses

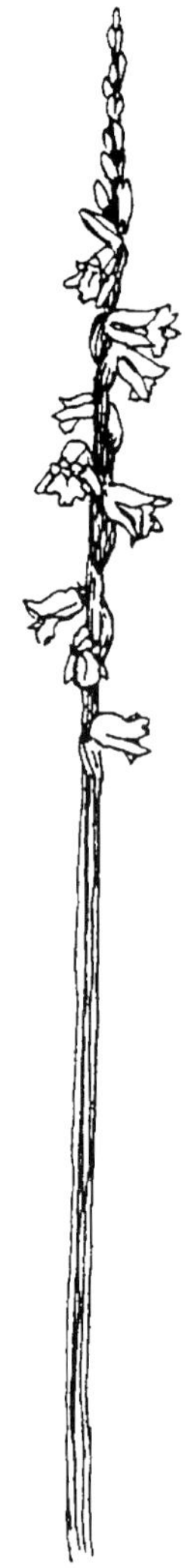

**Range:** Arkansas east to southern Michigan and Massachusetts, south to Florida and west to Texas
**In the Northeast: Massachusetts, Connecticut, Rhode Island, New York, Pennsylvania, New Jersey**: an occasional summer-flowering species along the Coastal Plain; very rare inland
**Plant**: terrestrial, 10–30 cm tall, glabrous
**Leaves**: 2–4; ovate, dark green, 1–2 cm wide × 2–5 cm long, absent at flowering time
**Flowers**: 10–35; in a single rank, spiraled or secund; sepals and petals similar, elliptic; perianth crystalline white; lip oblong, with the apex undulate-lacerate, exceeding the sepals; individual flower size ca. 3–4 mm
**Habitat**: grassy roadsides, cemeteries, open sandy areas in woodlands
**Flowering period**: late June to early September

*Spiranthes tuberosa*, the **little ladies'-tresses**, is the only pure white *Spiranthes* to flower in midsummer. One of its favorite habitats is old, dry cemeteries and abandoned fields. The nomenclatural history of this plant is rather complex, and among the names applied to it are *Spiranthes beckii* and *Spiranthes grayi*. See Correll (1950) for a discussion. This species is easily recognized by its pure white flowers, broad crisped lip, and absence of leaves at flowering time. The **little ladies'-tresses** was considered extirpated in Connecticut and was recently found by Eleanor Saulys. Hybrids with *Spiranthes lacera* var. *gracilis* are known as *S.* ×*eamesii*.

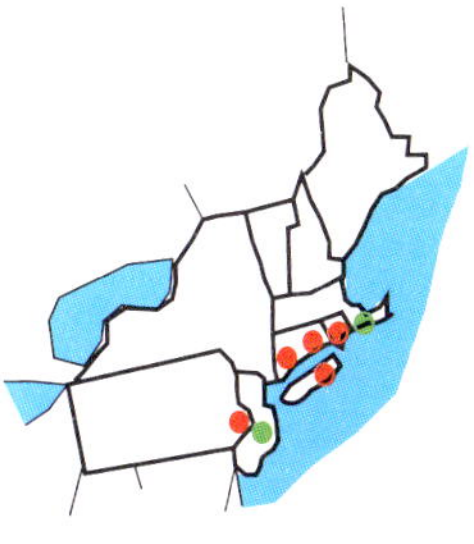

## *Spiranthes vernalis* Englemann & Gray

### grass-leaved ladies'-tresses

**Range:** Nebraska south to Texas, east to Florida, north to southern New Hampshire
**In the Northeast: New Hampshire, Massachusetts, Connecticut, Rhode Island, New York, Pennsylvania, New Jersey**: primarily along the Coastal Plain, but not unusual in isolated areas further inland
**Plant**: terrestrial, 10–85 cm tall, pubescent with sharp-pointed hairs
**Leaves**: 2–7; basal and on the lower third of the stem, linear-lanceolate, 1–2 cm wide × 5–25 cm long, present at flowering time
**Flowers**: 10–50; in either a single or multiple rank; sepals and petals similar, lanceolate; perianth typically creamy-white; lip ovate-oblong, rounded to the apex with a delicate undulate margins, usually a deeper creamy-yellow; the sepals wide-spreading; individual flower size 6–9mm
**Habitat**: roadsides, meadows, prairies, cultivated lawns—just about anywhere that is sunny
**Flowering period**: late July to early September

*Spiranthes vernalis,* the **grass-leaved ladies'-tresses**, is perhaps our most variable *Spiranthes* in habit, although the flowers remain surprisingly consistent. Plants may vary greatly in size and vigor as well as degree of spiraling, resulting in plants that are essentially secund to those that appear to be multiple-ranked. Plants are not consistent in habit from year to year. Color is somewhat variable from nearly pure white to cream with a contrasting, yellower lip, and some individuals have two brown or orange spots on the lip. The most consistent diagnostic character is the presence in the inflorescence of copious articulate, pointed hairs, which readily distinguish *S. vernalis* from other species.

Unusual form with brown-spotted lips

**Hybrids:**

*Spiranthes* ×*borealis* P.M. Brown
**northern hybrid ladies'-tresses**
(*S. casei* var. *casei* × *S. ochroleuca*)

Brown, P. M. 1995. *North American Native Orchid Journal* 1(4): 290.

Known primarily from northern New England; there are few places where both parents are found within the range of this guide. It appears as a small-flowered *S. ochroleuca* or a large-flowered *S. casei* and may be either single or multiple ranked. *Spiranthes* ×*borealis* was erroneously reported in *Flora of North America* as the hybrid between *S. casei* var. *novaescotiae* and *S. ochroleuca*.

*Spiranthes* ×*eamesii* P.M. Brown
Eames' hybrid ladies'-tresses
(*S. lacera* var. *gracilis* × *S. tuberosa*)

*North American Native Orchid Journal* 12: 60. 2006, type: Connecticut

The hybrid is rare because *S. tuberosa* is relatively rare, but when the two parents occur together it is almost always found. The type specimen was collected in 1895 in Bridgeport, Connecticut.

*Spiranthes* ×*intermedia* Ames
**intermediate hybrid ladies'-tresses**
(*S. lacera* var. *gracilis* × *S. vernalis*)

*Rhodora* 5: 262, pl. 47. 1903, type: Massachusetts

One of the first *Spiranthes* hybrids to be described, it occurs in only a few places, primarily north of the Southeast, where both parents flower at the same time.

*Spiranthes* ×*simpsonii* Catling & Sheviak
**Simpson's hybrid ladies'-tresses**
(*S. lacera* var. *lacera* × *S. romanzoffiana*)

Catling, P. M., & C. J. Sheviak. 1993. *Lindleyana* 8(2): 78–80.

Although the two parents often grow in proximity the hybrid is known from only a few collections and perhaps has been overlooked in the past.

## *Tipularia*

*Tipularia* is a small genus of only two species known from the Himalayas and the eastern United States. The species are very similar to each other but differ in the shape of the lip. The genus is characterized by a series of tubers from which arise, first, a single, annual leaf that remains green throughout the winter, then in the summer a leafless spike of flowers that has the sepals and petals all drawn to one side. A single species in the Northeast is the **crane-fly orchid**, *Tipularia discolor*.

## *Tipularia discolor* (Pursh) Nuttall

### crane-fly orchis

forma *viridifolia* P.M. Brown—green-leaved form
*North American Native Orchid Journal* (4): 336–337. 2000, type: Florida

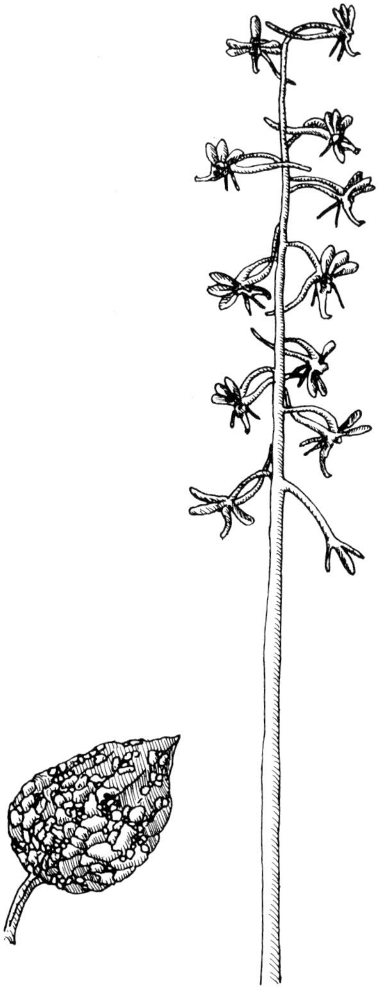

**Range:** eastern Texas northeastward to southern Michigan and east to southeastern Massachusetts and south to Florida
**In the Northeast: Massachusetts, Connecticut, Rhode Island, New York, Pennsylvania, New Jersey**: rare and local at the northern limit of its range
**Plant**: terrestrial, 25–60 cm tall
**Leaves**: 1; basal, ovate, typically dark green above with raised purple spots and dark purple beneath or, in the forma *viridifolia*, green on both sides; 6–7 cm wide × 8–10 cm, the long petiole ca. 5 cm; leaf withering in the spring and absent at flowering time
**Flowers**: 20–40; in a loose raceme; sepals and petals similar, oblanceolate; perianth greenish-yellow, tinged and mottled with pale purple; lip three-lobed, the central lobe slender, blunt, with a few shallow teeth; the sepals and petals asymmetrical and all drawn to one side; spur to 2.5–3.0 cm; individual flower size 2.0–3.0 × 3.0–3.5 cm not including spur
**Habitat**: deciduous and mixed woodlands
**Flowering period**: late June to mid-August

This very distinctive species is most easily found during the winter months when not in flower, when the single leaf is most apparent. The dark green leaf has a seersucker look with raised purple spots on the upper surface. If one turns over the leaf the satiny purple underside can be seen—hence the name *discolor*, two colors. Plants with no purple present, forma *viridifolia*, have been seen in scattered locations. The flower spike appears in midsummer and the coloring of the stem and flowers makes it most difficult to see in the woodlands, although the spike and flowers are not at all small. Spikes usually grow to 45–50+ cm tall.

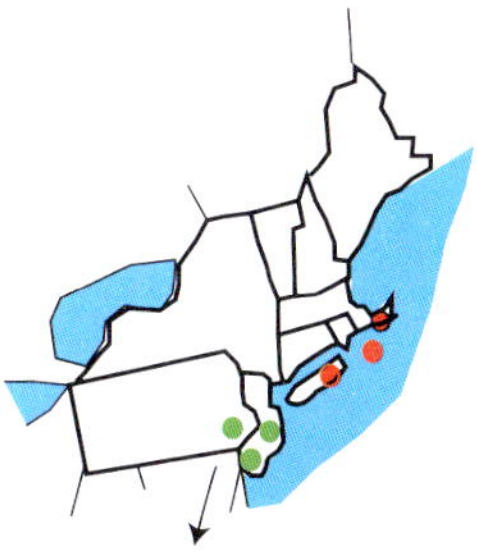

## *Triphora*

Consisting of about twenty species in North America, the West Indies, Mexico, and Central America, *Triphora* is a genus of small, delicate herbs, including many that may be largely mycotrophic. They all arise from swollen tuberoids and some produce very colorful, although small, flowers. Several species have flowers that do not fully open.

## *Triphora trianthophora* (Swartz) Rydberg var. *trianthophora*

### three birds orchid

forma *albidoflava* Keenan—white-flowered form
*Rhodora* 94: 38–39. 1992, type: New Hampshire

forma *caerulea* P.M. Brown—blue-flowered form
*North American Native Orchid Journal* 7(1): 94–95. 2001, type: Florida

forma rossii P.M. Brown—multi-colored form
*North American Native Orchid Journal* 5(1): 5. 1999, type: Florida

**Range:** Texas north to Minnesota east to Maine south to Florida
**In the Northeast: Maine, New Hampshire, Vermont, Massachusetts, Connecticut, New York, Pennsylvania, New Jersey**: rare and local throughout
**Plant**: terrestrial, 8–25 cm tall
**Leaves**: 2–8; broadly ovate-cordate, with smooth margins, dark green often with a purple cast or, in the forma *rossii*, the stem and leaves white, pink, and yellow; 10–15 × 2–15 mm
**Flowers**: 1–8 (12), nodding; from the axils of the upper leaves; sepals and petals similar, oblanceolate; perianth white to pink; lip three-lobed, the central lobe with the margin sinuate and three parallel green crests or, in the forma *albidoflava*, the perianth pure white and the crests yellow or, in the forma *caerulea*, lilac-blue; individual flower size ca. 1–2 cm
**Habitat**: deciduous and mixed woodlands, often with partridgeberry
**Flowering period:** late July to mid-September

**Three birds orchid** is the largest flowered and showiest species in the genus *Triphora*. The plants are quite elusive and appear for only a few days most years. The stunning little flowers open in mid-morning and usually close by mid-afternoon, leaving only a few hours for the eager eye to observe them. Colonies are not at all consistent in their flowering habits from year to year and it often takes a great deal of persistence on the part of the observer to catch them in prime condition. The three birds orchid was thought to be extirpated in Connecticut but was recently found by Eleanor Saulys. *Triphora trianthophora* var. *mexicana* has occasionally been reported from Florida but no vouchers could be found. It is restricted to Mexico.

forma *albidoflava*

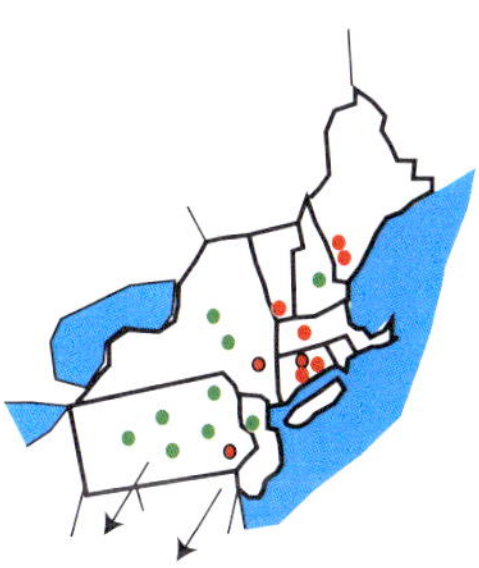

## *Gymnadenia conopsea* (Linnaeus) R. Brown

### fragrant orchis

Known from a single collection in Litchfield, Connecticut, in 1887 and has not persisted; native to Europe.

*Epipactis palustris*, a showy European species, is mapped on the NYFA atlas (NYFA, 2005) and the record is based upon a garden plant growing near Albany, New York. Although not yet an escape, it is spreading sufficiently that in the future it may be found apart from the horticultural setting.

## Bordering Species

*Hexalectris spicata* (Walter) Barnhardt
**crested coralroot**
Found in northern Maryland not far from Pennsylvania.

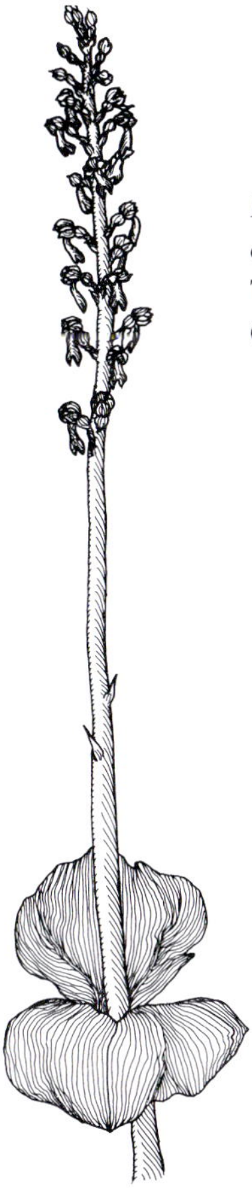

*Listera ovata* (Linnaeus) R. Brown ex W. Aiton & W.T. Aiton
**common twayblade**
This European native has become well established in southern Ontario not far from westernmost New York.

*Piperia unalascensis* (Sprengel) Rydberg
**Alaskan piperia**
Also found in southern Ontario and elsewhere on the Niagara escarpment; it would not be surprising to have it appear in western New York State as well.

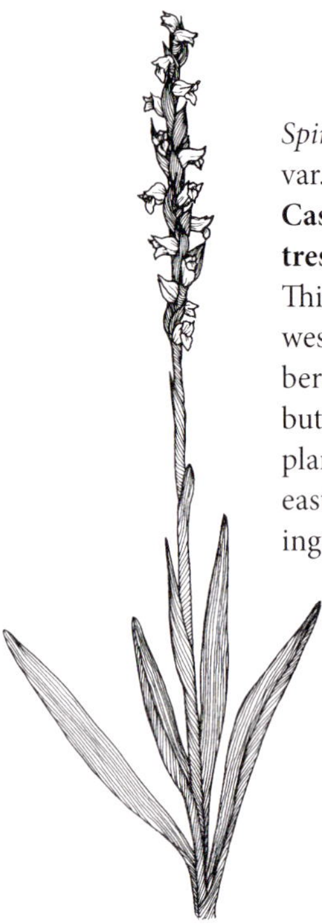

*Spiranthes casei* Catling & Cruise var. *novaescotiae* Catling
**Case's Nova Scotian ladies'-tresses**
This plant is endemic to southwestern Nova Scotia in the blueberry barrens and sandy roadsides, but abundant habitat with similar plant associations exists in northeastern Maine, especially in Washington County.

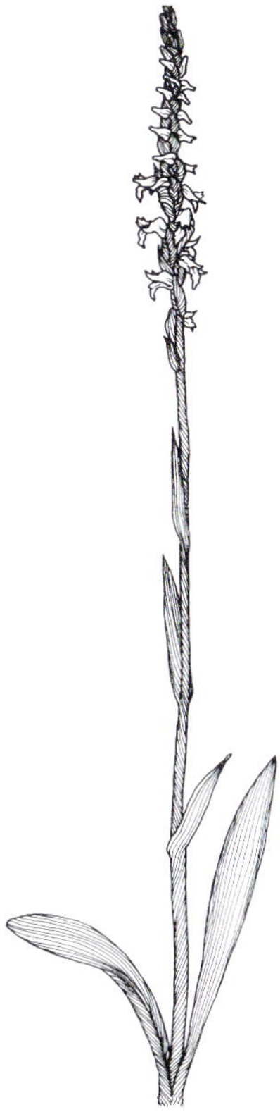

*Spiranthes odorata* (Nuttall) Lindley
**fragrant ladies'-tresses**
The range northward from eastern Virginia into Delaware and New Jersey is imprecise; plants referred to this species are usually *S. cernua* exhibiting gene flow from *S. odorata*; see Sheviak, 1991.

*Spiranthes praecox* (Walter) S. Watson
**giant ladies'-tresses**
Although many reports exist for this species in New Jersey and even eastern Long Island (Brown, 1997), reassessment of the plants and confirmation of identification is needed; if typical plants have a green-veined lip, identification is simplified, but if plants with white lips are found they may be confused with other similar *Spiranthes* species.

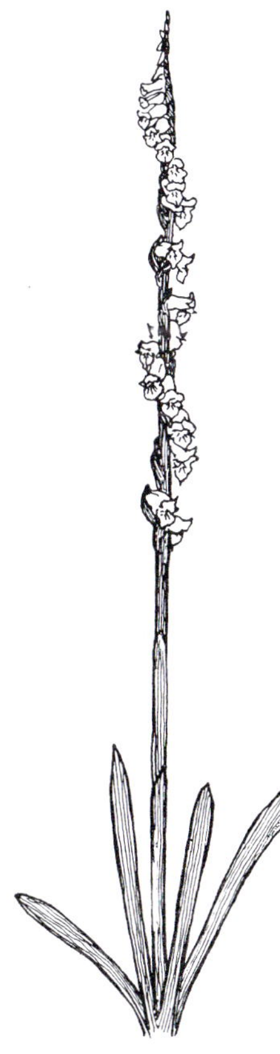

## Unvouchered and Discounted Reports

*Cleistes divaricata*—New York; Lamont (1996) hypothesizes the possibility on Long Island, but no further information has been forthcoming
*Corallorhiza striata*—Vermont; as a report in *Flora of Vermont* (Dole, 1936)
*Cypripedium candidum*—erroneously shown for Connecticut in Luer (1975)
*Goodyera oblongifolia*—Vermont, Massachusetts, New York; usually hybrids between *G. pubescens* and *G. tesselata* with large, unmarked leaves
*Platanthera blephariglottis* var. *conspicua*—southern New England and New York; erroneous report (Brown, 1993, 1997, 2004)
*Platanthera ciliaris*—New Hampshire (1872) (Brackley, 1985); Vermont (Niles, 1904)
*Platanthera leucophaea*—scattered reports throughout; most likely white-flowered forms of the large purple fringed orchis
*Platanthera peramoena*—reported in Correll (1950) and erroneously shown for New York in Luer (1975)
*Spiranthes odorata*—Rhode Island, Connecticut, New York; large coastal forms of *S. cernua* exhibit gene flow from *S. odorata*
*Spiranthes praecox*—Rhode Island, New York, New Jersey; erroneous reports (Brown, 1993, 1997; Correll, 1950) over many years that need current documentation
*Tipularia discolor*—Vermont; as a report in *Flora of Vermont* (Dole, 1936)

# *Part 3*

## References and Resources

# *Checklist of the Wild Orchids of the Northeast*

*Amerorchis rotundifolia* (Banks) Hultén
small round-leaf orchis
forma *angustifolia* (Rousseau) P.M. Brown—narrow-leafed form
forma *beckettiae* (Boivin) Hultén—white-flowered form
forma *immaculata* Mazurski & L.P. Johnson—white-lipped form
forma *lineata* (Mousley) Hultén—lined-lip form
forma *rosea* P.M. Brown—pink-flowered form
forma *wardii* P.M. Brown—pink/white/green form

*Aplectrum hyemale* (Mühlenberg *ex* Willdenow) Nuttall
putty-root; Adam-and-Eve
forma *pallidum* House—yellow-flowered form

*Arethusa bulbosa* Linnaeus
dragon's-mouth
forma *albiflora* Rand & Redfield—white-flowered form
forma *subcaerulea* Rand & Redfield—lilac-blue flowered form

*Calopogon tuberosus* (Linnaeus) Britton, Sterns, & Poggenberg
common grass-pink
forma *albiflorus* Britton—white flowered form

*Calypso bulbosa* (Linnaeus) Oakes var. *americana* (R. Brown) Luer
eastern fairy-slipper
forma *albiflora* P.M. Brown—white-flowered form
forma *biflora* P.M. Brown—two-flowered form
forma *rosea* P.M. Brown—pink-flowered form

*Cleistes divaricata* (Linnaeus) Ames
large spreading pogonia
forma *leucantha* P.M. Brown—white-flowered form

*Coeloglossum viride* (Linnaeus) Hartman var. *virescens* (Mühlenberg) Luer
long-bracted green orchis

*Corallorhiza maculata* (Rafinesque) Rafinesque var. *maculata*
spotted coralroot
forma *flavida* (Peck) Farwell—yellow-stemmed form
forma *rubra* P.M. Brown—red-stemmed form
*Corallorhiza maculata* (Rafinesque) Rafinesque var. *occidentalis* (Lindley) Ames
western spotted coralroot
forma *aurea* P.M. Brown—golden yellow/spotted form
forma *immaculata* (Peck) Howell—yellow spotless form
forma *intermedia* Farwell—brown-stemmed form
forma *punicea* (Bartholomew) Weatherby & Adams—red-stemmed form

*Corallorhiza odontorhiza* (Willdenow) Poiret var. *odontorhiza*
autumn coralroot
forma *flavida* Wherry—yellow-flowered form
*Corallorhiza odontorhiza* (Willdenow) Nuttall var. *pringlei* (Greenman) Freudenstein
Pringle's autumn coralroot

*Corallorhiza striata* Lindley var. *striata*
striped coralroot
forma *eburnea* P.M. Brown—yellow/white form
forma *fulva* Fernald—dusky tan-colored form

*Corallorhiza trifida* Chatelain
early coralroot
forma *verna* (Nuttall) P.M. Brown—yellow stemmed/white lipped form

*Corallorhiza wisteriana* Conrad
Wister's coralroot
forma *albolabia* P.M. Brown—white-lipped form
forma *cooperi* P.M. Brown—cranberry-pink colored form
forma *rubra* P.M. Brown—red-stemmed form

*Cypripedium acaule* Aiton
pink lady's-slipper; moccasin flower
forma *albiflorum* Rand & Redfield—white-flowered form
forma *biflorum* P.M. Brown—two-flowered form
forma *lancifolium* House—narrow-leaved form

*Cypripedium arietinum* R. Brown
ram's-head lady's-slipper
forma *albiflorum* House—white-flowered form
forma *biflorum* P.M. Brown—two-flowered form

*Cypripedium candidum* Mühlenberg *ex* Willdenow
small white lady's-slipper

*Cypripedium parviflorum* Salisbury var. *parviflorum*
southern small yellow lady's-slipper
forma *albolabium* Magrath & Norman—white-lipped form
*Cypripedium parviflorum* Salisbury var. *makasin* (Farwell) Sheviak
northern small yellow lady's-slipper
*Cypripedium parviflorum* Salisbury var. *pubescens* (Willdenow) Knight
large yellow lady's-slipper

*Cypripedium reginae* Walter
showy lady's-slipper
forma *albolabium* Fernald & Schubert—white-flowered form

Hybrids:
*Cypripedium* ×*andrewsii* Fuller nm *andrewsii*
Andrews' hybrid lady's-slipper

*Cypripedium* ×*andrewsii* Fuller nm *favillianum* (Curtis) Boivin
Faville's hybrid lady's-slipper

*Cypripedium* ×*andrewsii* Fuller nm *landonii* (Garay) Boivin
Landon's hybrid lady's-slipper

*Epipactis atrorubens* (Hoffmann *ex* Bernhardii) Besser
red helleborine*

*Epipactis helleborine* (Linnaeus) Cranz
broad-leaved helleborine*
forma *alba* (Webster) Boivin—white-flowered form
forma *luteola* P.M. Brown—yellow-flowered form
forma *monotropoides* (Mousley) Scoggin—albino form
forma *variegata* (Webster) Boivin—variegated form
forma *viridens* A. Gray—green-flowered form

*Galearis spectabilis* (Linnaeus) Rafinesque
showy orchis
forma *gordinierii* (House) Whiting & Catling—white-flowered form
forma *willeyi* (Seymour) P.M. Brown—pink-flowered form

*Goodyera oblongifolia* Rafinesque
giant rattlesnake orchis
forma *reticulata* (Boivin) P.M. Brown—reticulated leaved form

*Goodyera pubescens* (Willdenow) R. Brown
downy rattlesnake orchis

*Goodyera repens* (Linnaeus) R. Brown
lesser rattlesnake orchis
forma *ophioides* (Fernald) P.M. Brown—white-veined leaved form

*Goodyera tesselata* Loddiges
checkered rattlesnake orchis

*Gymnadeniopsis clavellata* (Michaux) Rydberg var. *clavellata*
little club-spur orchis
forma *slaughteri* (P.M. Brown) P.M. Brown—white-flowered form
forma *wrightii* (Olive) P.M. Brown—spurless form
*Gymnadeniopsis clavellata* (Michaux) Rydberg var. *ophioglossoides* (Fernald) W.J. Schrenk
northern club-spur orchis

*Gymnadeniopsis integra* (Nuttall) Rydberg
yellow fringeless orchis

*Gymnadeniopsis nivea* (Nuttall) Rydberg
snowy orchis

*Isotria medeoloides* (Pursh) Rafinesque
small whorled pogonia

*Isotria verticillata* (Mühlenberg *ex* Willdenow) Rafinesque
large whorled pogonia

*Liparis liliifolia* (Linnaeus) Richard *ex* Lindley
lily-leaved twayblade
forma *viridiflora* Wadmond—green-flowered form

*Liparis loeselii* (Linnaeus) Richard
Loesel's twayblade; fen orchis

Hybrid:
*Liparis ×jonesii* S. Bentley
Jones's hybrid twayblade

*Listera auriculata* Wiegand
auricled twayblade
forma *trifolia* (Lepage) Lepage—three-leaved form

*Listera australis* Lindley
southern twayblade
forma *scottii* P.M. Brown—many-leaved form
forma *trifolia* P.M. Brown—three-leaved form
forma *viridis* P.M. Brown—green-flowered form

*Listera convallarioides* (Swartz) Nuttall
broad-lipped twayblade
forma *trifolia* P.M. Brown—three-leaved form

*Listera cordata* (Linnaeus) R. Brown var. *cordata*
heart-leaved twayblade
forma *disjuncta* Lepage—alternate-leaved form
forma *tetraphylla* Lavoie—four-leaved form
forma *trifolia* P.M. Brown—three-leaved form
forma *variegata* P.M. Brown—variegated-leaved form
forma *viridens* P.M. Brown—green-flowered form

*Listera smallii* Wiegand
Small's twayblade
forma *variegata* P.M. Brown—variegated-leaved form

Hybrid:
*Listera ×veltmanii* Case
Veltman's hybrid twayblade

*Malaxis bayardii* Fernald
Bayard's adder's-mouth
forma *kelloggiae* P.M. Brown—albino form

*Malaxis brachypoda* (Gray) Fernald
white adder's-mouth
forma *bifolia* (Mousley) Fernald—two-leaved form

*Malaxis unifolia* Michaux
green adder's-mouth
forma *bifolia* Mousley—two-leaved form
forma *variegata* Mousley—variegated-leaf form

*Platanthera aquilonis* Sheviak
northern green bog orchis
forma *alba* (Light) P.M. Brown—albino form

*Platanthera blephariglottis* (Willdenow) Lindley
northern white fringed orchis
forma *holopetala* (Lindley) P.M. Brown—entire-lip form

*Platanthera ciliaris* (Linnaeus) Lindley
orange fringed orchis

*Platanthera cristata* (Michaux) Lindley
orange crested orchis
forma *straminea* P.M. Brown—pale yellow-flowered form

*Platanthera dilatata* (Pursh) Lindley
white bog orchis; bog candles

*Platanthera flava* (Linnaeus) Lindley var. *flava*
southern tubercled orchis
*Platanthera flava* (Linnaeus) Lindley var. *herbiola* (R. Brown) Luer
northern tubercled orchis
forma *lutea* (Boivin) Whiting & Catling—yellow-flowered form

*Platanthera grandiflora* (Bigelow) Lindley
large purple fringed orchis
forma *albiflora* (Rand & Redfield) Catling—white-flowered form
forma *bicolor* P.M. Brown—bicolor-flowered form
forma *carnea* P.M. Brown—pink-flowered form
forma *mentotonsa* (Fernald) P.M. Brown—entire-lip form

*Platanthera hookeri* (Torrey) Lindley
Hooker's orchis
forma *abbreviata* (Fernald) P.M. Brown—dwarfed form
forma *oblongifolia* (J.A. Paine) P.M. Brown—narrow-leaved form

*Platanthera huronensis* (Nuttall) Lindley
green bog orchis

*Platanthera lacera* (Michaux) G. Don
green fringed orchis; ragged orchis

*Platanthera leucophaea* (Nuttall) Lindley
eastern prairie fringed orchis

*Platanthera macrophylla* (Goldie) P.M. Brown
Goldie's pad-leaved orchis

*Platanthera obtusata* (Banks *ex* Pursh) Lindley
blunt-leafed rein orchis
  forma *collectanea* (Fernald) P.M. Brown—dwarfed form
  forma *foliosa* P.M. Brown—multiple-leaved form

*Platanthera orbiculata* (Pursh) Lindley
pad-leaved orchis
  forma *lehorsii* (Fernald) P.M. Brown—dwarfed form
  forma *longifolia* (Clute) P.M. Brown—narrow-leaved form
  forma *pauciflora* (Jennings) P.M. Brown—few-flowered form
  forma *trifolia* (Mousley) P.M. Brown—three-leaved form

*Platanthera pallida* P.M. Brown
pale fringed orchis

*Platanthera peramoena* (A. Gray) A. Gray
purple fringeless orchis
  forma *doddsiae*—white-flowered form

*Platanthera psycodes* (Linnaeus) Lindley
small purple fringed orchis
  forma *albiflora* (R. Hoffman) Whiting & Catling—white-flowered form
  forma *ecalcarata* (Bryan) P.M. Brown—spurless form
  forma *fernaldii* (Rousseau & Rouleau) P.M. Brown—dwarf form
  forma *rosea* P.M. Brown—pink-flowered form
  forma *varians* (Bryan) P.M. Brown—entire-lip form

Hybrids:
*Platanthera ×andrewsii* (Niles) Luer
Andrew's hybrid fringed orchis

*Platanthera ×bicolor* (Rafinesque) Luer
Bicolor hybrid fringed orchis

*Platanthera ×canbyi* (Ames) Luer
Canby's hybrid fringed orchis

*Platanthera ×channellii* Folsom
Channell's hybrid fringed orchis

*Platanthera ×keenanii* P.M. Brown
Keenan's hybrid fringed orchis

×*Platanthopsis vossii* (Case) P.M. Brown
Voss's hybrid rein orchis

*Pogonia ophioglossoides* (Linnaeus) Ker-Gawler
rose pogonia; snakemouth orchid
forma *albiflora* Rand & Redfield—white-flowered form
forma *brachypogon* (Fernald) P.M. Brown—short-bearded form

*Spiranthes casei* Catling & Cruise var. *casei*
Case's ladies'-tresses

*Spiranthes cernua* (Linnaeus) L.C. Richard
nodding ladies'-tresses

*Spiranthes lacera* Rafinesque var. *lacera*
northern slender ladies'-tresses
*Spiranthes lacera* Rafinesque var. *gracilis* (Bigelow) Luer
southern slender ladies'-tresses

*Spiranthes laciniata* (Small) Ames
lace-lipped ladies'-tresses

*Spiranthes lucida* (H.H. Eaton) Ames
shining ladies'-tresses

*Spiranthes magnicamporum* Sheviak
Great Plains ladies'-tresses

*Spiranthes ochroleuca* (Rydberg) Rydberg
yellow ladies'-tresses
forma *foliobracteata* P.M. Brown

*Spiranthes ovalis* Lindley var. *erostellata* Catling
northern oval ladies'-tresses

*Spiranthes romanzoffiana* Chamisso
hooded ladies'-tresses

*Spiranthes tuberosa* Rafinesque
little ladies'-tresses

*Spiranthes vernalis* Engelmann & Gray
grass-leaved ladies'-tresses

Hybrids:
*Spiranthes ×borealis* P.M. Brown
northern hybrid ladies'-tresses

*Spiranthes ×eamesii* P.M. Brown
Eames' hybrid ladies'-tresses

*Spiranthes ×intermedia* Ames
intermediate hybrid ladies'-tresses

*Spiranthes ×simpsonii* Catling & Sheviak
Simpson's hybrid ladies'-tresses

*Tipularia discolor* (Pursh) Nuttall
crane-fly orchis
  forma *viridifolia* P.M. Brown—green-leaved form

*Triphora trianthophora* (Swartz) Rydberg
three birds orchid
  forma *albidoflava* Keenan—white-flowered form
  forma *caerulea* P.M. Brown—blue-flowered form
  forma *rossii* P.M. Brown—multi-colored form

Waif:
*Gymnadenia conopsea* (Linnaeus) R. Brown
fragrant orchis

# *State Checklists*

Note: H = historical, [] = unvouchered reports

## Maine

53 species and varieties
*Amerorchis rotundifolia*, small round-leaf orchis
*Arethusa bulbosa*, dragon's-mouth
*Calopogon tuberosus*, common grass-pink
*Calypso bulbosa* var. *americana*, eastern fairy-slipper
*Coeloglossum viride* var. *virescens*, long-bracted green orchis
*Corallorhiza maculata* var. *maculata*, spotted coralroot
*Corallorhiza maculata* var. *occidentalis*, western spotted coralroot
*Corallorhiza odontorhiza* var. *odontorhiza*, autumn coralroot
*Corallorhiza odontorhiza* var. *pringlei*, Pringle's autumn coralroot
*Corallorhiza trifida*, early coralroot
*Cypripedium acaule*, pink lady's-slipper
*Cypripedium arietinum*, ram's-head lady's-slipper
*Cypripedium parviflorum* var. *makasin*, northern small yellow lady's-slipper
*Cypripedium parviflorum* var. *pubescens*, large yellow lady's-slipper
*Cypripedium reginae*, showy lady's-slipper
*Epipactis helleborine*, broad-leaved helleborine*
*Galearis spectabilis*, showy orchis
*Goodyera oblongifolia*, giant rattlesnake orchis
*Goodyera pubescens*, downy rattlesnake orchis
*Goodyera repens*, lesser rattlesnake orchis
*Goodyera tesselata*, checkered rattlesnake orchis
*Gymnadeniopsis clavellata* var. *clavellata*, little club-spur orchis
*Gymnadeniopsis clavellata* var. *ophioglossoides*, northern club-spur orchis
*Isotria medeoloides*, small whorled pogonia
*Isotria verticillata*, large whorled pogonia
*Liparis loeselii*, Loesel's twayblade
*Listera auriculata*, auricled twayblade
*Listera convallarioides*, broad-lipped twayblade
*Listera cordata*, heart-leaved twayblade
*Malaxis brachypoda*, white adder's-mouth
*Malaxis unifolia*, green adder's-mouth
*Platanthera aquilonis*, northern green bog orchis

*Platanthera blephariglottis*, northern white fringed orchis
*Platanthera dilatata*, white bog orchis; bog candles
*Platanthera flava* var. *herbiola*, northern tubercled orchis
*Platanthera grandiflora*, large purple fringed orchis
*Platanthera hookeri*, Hooker's orchis
*Platanthera huronensis*, green bog orchis
*Platanthera lacera*, green fringed orchis; ragged orchis
*Platanthera leucophaea*, eastern prairie fringed orchis
*Platanthera macrophylla*, Goldie's pad-leaved orchis
*Platanthera obtusata*, blunt-leafed rein orchis
*Platanthera orbiculata*, pad-leaved orchis
*Platanthera psycodes*, small purple fringed orchis
*Pogonia ophioglossoides*, rose pogonia
*Spiranthes casei* var. *casei*, Case's ladies'-tresses
*Spiranthes cernua*, nodding ladies'-tresses
*Spiranthes lacera* var. *lacera*, northern slender ladies'-tresses
*Spiranthes lacera* var. *gracilis*, southern slender ladies'-tresses
*Spiranthes lucida*, shining ladies'-tresses
*Spiranthes ochroleuca*, yellow ladies'-tresses
*Spiranthes romanzoffiana*, hooded ladies'-tresses
*Triphora trianthophora*, three birds orchid

## New Hampshire

54 species and varieties including 1 discounted record and 1 unvouchered report
*Amerorchis rotundifolia*, small round-leaf orchis H
[*Aplectrum hyemale*, putty-root]
*Arethusa bulbosa*, dragon's-mouth
*Calopogon tuberosus*, common grass-pink
*Calypso bulbosa* var. *americana*, eastern fairy-slipper H
*Coeloglossum viride* var. *virescens*, long-bracted green orchis
*Corallorhiza maculata* var. *maculata*, spotted coralroot
*Corallorhiza maculata* var. *occidentalis*, western spotted coralroot
*Corallorhiza odontorhiza* var. *odontorhiza*, autumn coralroot
*Corallorhiza trifida*, early coralroot
*Cypripedium acaule*, pink lady's-slipper
*Cypripedium arietinum*, ram's-head lady's-slipper
*Cypripedium parviflorum* var. *makasin*, northern small yellow lady's-slipper
*Cypripedium parviflorum* var. *pubescens*, large yellow lady's-slipper
*Cypripedium reginae*, showy lady's-slipper
*Epipactis helleborine*, broad-leaved helleborine*
*Galearis spectabilis*, showy orchis
*Goodyera pubescens*, downy rattlesnake orchis
*Goodyera repens*, lesser rattlesnake orchis

*Goodyera tesselata,* checkered rattlesnake orchis
*Gymnadeniopsis clavellata* var. *clavellata*, little club-spur orchis
*Gymnadeniopsis clavellata* var. *ophioglossoides*, northern club-spur orchis
*Isotria medeoloides*, small whorled pogonia
*Isotria verticillata*, large whorled pogonia
*Liparis liliifolia*, lily-leaved twayblade H
*Liparis loeselii*, Loesel's twayblade
*Listera auriculata*, auricled twayblade
*Listera convallarioides*, broad-lipped twayblade
*Listera cordata,* heart-leaved twayblade
*Malaxis brachypoda,* white adder's-mouth
*Malaxis unifolia*, green adder's-mouth
*Platanthera aquilonis*, northern green bog orchis
*Platanthera blephariglottis*, northern white fringed orchis
[*Platanthera ciliaris*, orange fringed orchis]
*Platanthera dilatata*, white bog orchis; bog candles
*Platanthera flava* var. *herbiola*, northern tubercled orchis
*Platanthera grandiflora*, large purple fringed orchis
*Platanthera hookeri*, Hooker's orchis
*Platanthera huronensis*, green bog orchis
*Platanthera lacera*, green fringed orchis; ragged orchis
*Platanthera macrophylla*, Goldie's pad-leaved orchis
*Platanthera obtusata*, blunt-leafed rein orchis
*Platanthera orbiculata*, pad-leaved orchis
*Platanthera psycodes*, small purple fringed orchis
*Pogonia ophioglossoides*, rose pogonia
*Spiranthes casei* var. *casei*, Case's ladies'-tresses
*Spiranthes cernua*, nodding ladies'-tresses
*Spiranthes lacera* var. *lacera*, northern slender ladies'-tresses
*Spiranthes lacera* var. *gracilis*, southern slender ladies'-tresses
*Spiranthes lucida*, shining ladies'-tresses
*Spiranthes ochroleuca*, yellow ladies'-tresses
*Spiranthes romanzoffiana*, hooded ladies'-tresses
*Spiranthes vernalis*, grass-leaved ladies'-tresses H
*Triphora trianthophora*, three birds orchid

## Vermont

57 species and varieties including 3 unvouchered reports
*Amerorchis rotundifolia*, small round-leaf orchis H
*Aplectrum hyemale*, putty-root
*Arethusa bulbosa*, dragon's-mouth
*Calopogon tuberosus*, common grass-pink
*Calypso bulbosa* var. *americana,* eastern fairy-slipper

*Coeloglossum viride* var. *virescens*, long-bracted green orchis
*Corallorhiza maculata* var. *maculata*, spotted coralroot
*Corallorhiza maculata* var. *occidentalis*, western spotted coralroot
*Corallorhiza odontorhiza* var. *odontorhiza*, autumn coralroot
[*Corallorhiza striata*, striped coralroot]
*Corallorhiza trifida*, early coralroot
*Cypripedium acaule*, pink lady's-slipper
*Cypripedium arietinum*, ram's-head lady's-slipper
*Cypripedium parviflorum* var. *makasin*, northern small yellow lady's-slipper
*Cypripedium parviflorum* var. *pubescens*, large yellow lady's-slipper
*Cypripedium reginae*, showy lady's-slipper
*Epipactis atrorubens*, red helleborine*
*Epipactis helleborine*, broad-leaved helleborine*
*Galearis spectabilis*, showy orchis
*Goodyera pubescens*, downy rattlesnake orchis
*Goodyera repens*, lesser rattlesnake orchis
*Goodyera tesselata*, checkered rattlesnake orchis
*Gymnadeniopsis clavellata* var. *clavellata*, little club-spur orchis
*Gymnadeniopsis clavellata* var. *ophioglossoides*, northern club-spur orchis
*Isotria medeoloides*, small whorled pogonia H
*Isotria verticillata*, large whorled pogonia
*Liparis liliifolia*, lily-leaved twayblade
*Liparis loeselii*, Loesel's twayblade
*Listera auriculata*, auricled twayblade
*Listera australis*, southern twayblade
*Listera convallarioides*, broad-lipped twayblade
*Listera cordata*, heart-leaved twayblade
*Malaxis bayardii*, Bayard's adders-mouth
*Malaxis brachypoda*, white adder's-mouth
*Malaxis unifolia*, green adder's-mouth
*Platanthera aquilonis*, northern green bog orchis
*Platanthera blephariglottis*, northern white fringed orchis
[*Platanthera ciliaris*, orange fringed orchis]
*Platanthera dilatata*, white bog orchis; bog candles
*Platanthera flava* var. *herbiola*, northern tubercled orchis
*Platanthera grandiflora*, large purple fringed orchis
*Platanthera hookeri*, Hooker's orchis
*Platanthera huronensis*, green bog orchis
*Platanthera lacera*, green fringed orchis; ragged orchis
*Platanthera macrophylla*, Goldie's pad-leaved orchis
*Platanthera obtusata*, blunt-leafed rein orchis
*Platanthera orbiculata*, pad-leaved orchis
*Platanthera psycodes*, small purple fringed orchis
*Pogonia ophioglossoides*, rose pogonia
*Spiranthes casei* var. *casei*, Case's ladies'-tresses

*Spiranthes cernua*, nodding ladies'-tresses
*Spiranthes lacera* var. *lacera*, northern slender ladies'-tresses
*Spiranthes lucida*, shining ladies'-tresses
*Spiranthes ochroleuca*, yellow ladies'-tresses
*Spiranthes romanzoffiana*, hooded ladies'-tresses
[*Tipularia discolor*, crane-fly orchis]
*Triphora trianthophora*, three birds orchid

## Massachusetts

54 species and varieties
*Aplectrum hyemale*, putty-root
*Arethusa bulbosa*, dragon's-mouth
*Calopogon tuberosus*, common grass-pink
*Coeloglossum viride* var. *virescens*, long-bracted green orchis
*Corallorhiza maculata* var. *maculata*, spotted coralroot
*Corallorhiza maculata* var. *occidentalis*, western spotted coralroot
*Corallorhiza odontorhiza* var. *odontorhiza*, autumn coralroot
*Corallorhiza odontorhiza* var. *pringlei*, Pringle's autumn coralroot
*Corallorhiza trifida*, early coralroot
*Cypripedium acaule*, pink lady's-slipper
*Cypripedium arietinum*, ram's-head lady's-slipper
*Cypripedium parviflorum* var. *parviflorum*, southern small yellow lady's-slipper
*Cypripedium parviflorum* var. *makasin*, northern small yellow lady's-slipper
*Cypripedium parviflorum* var. *pubescens*, large yellow lady's-slipper
*Cypripedium reginae*, showy lady's-slipper
*Epipactis helleborine*, broad-leaved helleborine*
*Galearis spectabilis*, showy orchis
*Goodyera pubescens*, downy rattlesnake orchis
*Goodyera repens*, lesser rattlesnake orchis
*Goodyera tesselata*, checkered rattlesnake orchis
*Gymnadeniopsis clavellata* var. *clavellata*, little club-spur orchis
*Gymnadeniopsis clavellata* var. *ophioglossoides*, northern club-spur orchis
*Isotria medeoloides*, small whorled pogonia
*Isotria verticillata*, large whorled pogonia
*Liparis liliifolia*, lily-leaved twayblade
*Liparis loeselii*, Loesel's twayblade
*Listera cordata*, heart-leaved twayblade H?
*Malaxis bayardii*, Bayard's adder's-mouth
*Malaxis brachypoda*, white adder's-mouth
*Malaxis unifolia*, green adder's-mouth
*Platanthera aquilonis*, northern green bog orchis
*Platanthera blephariglottis*, northern white fringed orchis

*Platanthera ciliaris*, orange fringed orchis H
*Platanthera cristata*, orange crested orchis
*Platanthera dilatata*, white bog orchis; bog candles
*Platanthera flava* var. *herbiola*, northern tubercled orchis
*Platanthera grandiflora*, large purple fringed orchis
*Platanthera hookeri*, Hooker's orchis
*Platanthera huronensis*, green bog orchis
*Platanthera lacera*, green fringed orchis; ragged orchis
*Platanthera macrophylla*, Goldie's pad-leaved orchis
*Platanthera obtusata*, blunt-leafed rein orchis H
*Platanthera orbiculata*, pad-leaved orchis
*Platanthera psycodes*, small purple fringed orchis
*Pogonia ophioglossoides*, rose pogonia
*Spiranthes cernua*, nodding ladies'-tresses
*Spiranthes lacera* var. *lacera*, northern slender ladies'-tresses
*Spiranthes lacera* var. *gracilis*, southern slender ladies'-tresses
*Spiranthes lucida*, shining ladies'-tresses
*Spiranthes ochroleuca*, yellow ladies'-tresses
*Spiranthes romanzoffiana*, hooded ladies'-tresses
*Spiranthes tuberosa*, little ladies'-tresses
*Spiranthes vernalis*, grass-leaved ladies'-tresses
*Tipularia discolor*, crane-fly orchis
*Triphora trianthophora*, three birds orchid

## Connecticut

55 species and varieties including 1 unvouchered literature report
*Aplectrum hyemale*, putty-root H
*Arethusa bulbosa*, dragon's-mouth H
*Calopogon tuberosus*, common grass-pink
*Coeloglossum viride* var. *virescens*, long-bracted green orchis
*Corallorhiza maculata* var. *maculata*, spotted coralroot
*Corallorhiza maculata* var. *occidentalis*, western spotted coralroot
*Corallorhiza odontorhiza* var. *odontorhiza*, autumn coralroot
*Corallorhiza odontorhiza* var. *pringlei*, Pringle's autumn coralroot H
*Corallorhiza trifida*, early coralroot
*Cypripedium acaule*, pink lady's-slipper
*Cypripedium arietinum*, ram's-head lady's-slipper H
[*Cypripedium candidum*, small white lady's-slipper]
*Cypripedium parviflorum* var. *parviflorum*, southern small yellow lady's-slipper
*Cypripedium parviflorum* var. *makasin*, northern small yellow lady's-slipper
*Cypripedium parviflorum* var. *pubescens*, large yellow lady's-slipper
*Cypripedium reginae*, showy lady's-slipper
*Epipactis helleborine*, broad-leaved helleborine*

*Galearis spectabilis*, showy orchis
*Goodyera pubescens*, downy rattlesnake orchis
*Goodyera repens*, lesser rattlesnake orchis H
*Goodyera tesselata,* checkered rattlesnake orchis
*Gymnadenia conopsea*, fragrant orchis* (waif)
*Gymnadeniopsis clavellata* var. *clavellata*, little club-spur orchis
*Gymnadeniopsis clavellata* var. *ophioglossoides*, northern club-spur orchis
*Isotria medeoloides*, small whorled pogonia
*Isotria verticillata*, large whorled pogonia
*Liparis liliifolia*, lily-leaved twayblade
*Liparis loeselii*, Loesel's twayblade
*Listera cordata*, heart-leaved twayblade H
*Malaxis bayardii*, Bayard's adder's-mouth H
*Malaxis brachypoda*, white adder's-mouth
*Malaxis unifolia*, green adder's-mouth
*Platanthera aquilonis*, northern green bog orchis
*Platanthera blephariglottis*, northern white fringed orchis
*Platanthera ciliaris*, orange fringed orchis
*Platanthera dilatata*, white bog orchis; bog candles H
*Platanthera flava* var. *herbiola*, northern tubercled orchis
*Platanthera grandiflora*, large purple fringed orchis
*Platanthera hookeri*, Hooker's orchis H
*Platanthera huronensis*, green bog orchis
*Platanthera lacera*, green fringed orchis; ragged orchis
*Platanthera macrophylla*, Goldie's pad-leaved orchis H
*Platanthera obtusata*, blunt-leafed rein orchis H
*Platanthera orbiculata*, pad-leaved orchis
*Platanthera psycodes*, small purple fringed orchis
*Pogonia ophioglossoides*, rose pogonia
*Spiranthes cernua*, nodding ladies'-tresses
*Spiranthes lacera* var. *lacera*, northern slender ladies'-tresses
*Spiranthes lacera* var. *gracilis*, southern slender ladies'-tresses
*Spiranthes lucida*, shining ladies'-tresses
*Spiranthes ochroleuca*, yellow ladies'-tresses
*Spiranthes romanzoffiana*, hooded ladies'-tresses
*Spiranthes tuberosa*, little ladies'-tresses
*Spiranthes vernalis*, grass-leaved ladies'-tresses
*Triphora trianthophora*, three birds orchid

## Rhode Island

39 species and varieties
*Arethusa bulbosa*, dragon's-mouth
*Calopogon tuberosus*, common grass-pink

*Coeloglossum viride* var. *virescens*, long-bracted green orchis
*Corallorhiza maculata* var. *maculata*, spotted coralroot
*Corallorhiza odontorhiza* var. *odontorhiza*, autumn coralroot
*Corallorhiza trifida*, early coralroot
*Cypripedium acaule*, pink lady's-slipper
*Cypripedium parviflorum* var. *parviflorum*, southern small yellow lady's-slipper
*Cypripedium parviflorum* var. *pubescens*, large yellow lady's-slipper
*Epipactis helleborine*, broad-leaved helleborine*
*Galearis spectabilis*, showy orchis H?
*Goodyera pubescens*, downy rattlesnake orchis
*Goodyera tesselata*, checkered rattlesnake orchis
*Gymnadeniopsis clavellata* var. *clavellata*, little club-spur orchis
*Isotria medeoloides*, small whorled pogonia
*Isotria verticillata*, large whorled pogonia
*Liparis liliifolia*, lily-leaved twayblade H?
*Liparis loeselii*, Loesel's twayblade
*Listera cordata*, heart-leaved twayblade H
*Malaxis bayardii*, Bayard's adder's-mouth H?
*Malaxis unifolia*, green adder's-mouth
*Platanthera aquilonis*, northern green bog orchis
*Platanthera blephariglottis*, northern white fringed orchis
*Platanthera ciliaris*, orange fringed orchis
*Platanthera dilatata*, white bog orchis; bog candles
*Platanthera flava* var. *herbiola*, northern tubercled orchis
*Platanthera grandiflora*, large purple fringed orchis
*Platanthera hookeri*, Hooker's orchis H?
*Platanthera huronensis*, green bog orchis
*Platanthera lacera*, green fringed orchis; ragged orchis
*Platanthera orbiculata*, pad-leaved orchis H?
*Platanthera psycodes*, small purple fringed orchis
*Pogonia ophioglossoides*, rose pogonia
*Spiranthes cernua*, nodding ladies'-tresses
*Spiranthes lacera* var. *gracilis*, southern slender ladies'-tresses
*Spiranthes lucida*, shining ladies'-tresses H?
*Spiranthes ochroleuca*, yellow ladies'-tresses
*Spiranthes tuberosa*, little ladies'-tresses
*Spiranthes vernalis*, grass-leaved ladies'-tresses

## New York

65 species and varieties
*Amerorchis rotundifolia*, small round-leaf orchis H
*Aplectrum hyemale*, putty-root
*Arethusa bulbosa*, dragon's-mouth

*Calopogon tuberosus*, common grass-pink
*Calypso bulbosa* var. *americana*, eastern fairy-slipper H
*Coeloglossum viride* var. *virescens*, long-bracted green orchis
*Corallorhiza maculata* var. *maculata*, spotted coralroot
*Corallorhiza maculata* var. *occidentalis*, western spotted coralroot
*Corallorhiza odontorhiza* var. *odontorhiza*, autumn coralroot
*Corallorhiza odontorhiza* var. *pringlei*, Pringle's autumn coralroot
*Corallorhiza striata*, striped coralroot
*Corallorhiza trifida*, early coralroot
*Cypripedium acaule*, pink lady's-slipper
*Cypripedium arietinum*, ram's-head lady's-slipper
*Cypripedium candidum*, small white lady's-slipper
*Cypripedium parviflorum* var. *parviflorum*, southern small yellow lady's-slipper
*Cypripedium parviflorum* var. *makasin*, northern small yellow lady's-slipper
*Cypripedium parviflorum* var. *pubescens*, large yellow lady's-slipper
*Cypripedium reginae*, showy lady's-slipper
*Epipactis helleborine*, broad-leaved helleborine*
*Galearis spectabilis*, showy orchis
*Goodyera pubescens*, downy rattlesnake orchis
*Goodyera repens*, lesser rattlesnake orchis
*Goodyera tesselata*, checkered rattlesnake orchis
*Gymnadeniopsis clavellata* var. *clavellata*, little club-spur orchis
*Gymnadeniopsis clavellata* var. *ophioglossoides*, northern club-spur orchis
*Isotria medeoloides*, small whorled pogonia H
*Isotria verticillata*, large whorled pogonia
*Liparis liliifolia*, lily-leaved twayblade
*Liparis loeselii*, Loesel's twayblade
*Listera auriculata*, auricled twayblade
*Listera australis*, southern twayblade
*Listera convallarioides*, broad-lipped twayblade
*Listera cordata*, heart-leaved twayblade
*Malaxis bayardii*, Bayard's adder's-mouth
*Malaxis brachypoda*, white adder's-mouth
*Malaxis unifolia*, green adder's-mouth
*Platanthera aquilonis*, northern green bog orchis
*Platanthera blephariglottis*, northern white fringed orchis
*Platanthera ciliaris*, orange fringed orchis
*Platanthera cristata*, orange crested orchis
*Platanthera dilatata*, white bog orchis; bog candles
*Platanthera flava* var. *herbiola*, northern tubercled orchis
*Platanthera grandiflora*, large purple fringed orchis
*Platanthera hookeri*, Hooker's orchis
*Platanthera huronensis*, green bog orchis
*Platanthera lacera*, green fringed orchis; ragged orchis
*Platanthera leucophaea*, eastern prairie fringed orchis H

*Platanthera macrophylla*, Goldie's pad-leaved orchis
*Platanthera obtusata*, blunt-leafed rein orchis
*Platanthera orbiculata*, pad-leaved orchis
*Platanthera pallida*, pale fringed orchis
*Platanthera psycodes*, small purple fringed orchis
*Pogonia ophioglossoides*, rose pogonia
*Spiranthes casei* var. *casei*, Case's ladies'-tresses
*Spiranthes cernua*, nodding ladies'-tresses
*Spiranthes lacera* var. *lacera*, northern slender ladies'-tresses
*Spiranthes lacera* var. *gracilis*, southern slender ladies'-tresses
*Spiranthes lucida*, shining ladies'-tresses
*Spiranthes ochroleuca*, yellow ladies'-tresses
*Spiranthes romanzoffiana*, hooded ladies'-tresses
*Spiranthes tuberosa*, little ladies'-tresses
*Spiranthes vernalis*, grass-leaved ladies'-tresses
*Tipularia discolor*, crane-fly orchis
*Triphora trianthophora*, three birds orchid

## Pennsylvania

60 species and varieties
*Aplectrum hyemale*, putty-root
*Arethusa bulbosa*, dragon's-mouth
*Calopogon tuberosus*, common grass-pink
*Coeloglossum viride* var. *virescens*, long-bracted green orchis
*Corallorhiza maculata* var. *maculata*, spotted coralroot
*Corallorhiza maculata* var. *occidentalis*, western spotted coralroot
*Corallorhiza odontorhiza* var. *odontorhiza*, autumn coralroot
*Corallorhiza odontorhiza* var. *pringlei*, Pringle's autumn coralroot
*Corallorhiza trifida*, early coralroot
*Corallorhiza wisteriana*, Wister's coralroot
*Cypripedium acaule*, pink lady's-slipper
*Cypripedium candidum*, small white lady's-slipper H
*Cypripedium parviflorum* var. *parviflorum*, southern small yellow lady's-slipper
*Cypripedium parviflorum* var. *makasin*, northern small yellow lady's-slipper
*Cypripedium parviflorum* var. *pubescens*, large yellow lady's-slipper
*Cypripedium reginae*, showy lady's-slipper
*Epipactis helleborine*, broad-leaved helleborine*
*Galearis spectabilis*, showy orchis
*Goodyera pubescens*, downy rattlesnake orchis
*Goodyera tesselata*, checkered rattlesnake orchis
*Gymnadeniopsis clavellata* var. *clavellata*, little club-spur orchis
*Isotria medeoloides*, small whorled pogonia
*Isotria verticillata*, large whorled pogonia

*Liparis liliifolia*, lily-leaved twayblade
*Liparis loeselii*, Loesel's twayblade
*Listera australis*, southern twayblade
*Listera cordata*, heart-leaved twayblade
*Listera smallii*, Small's twayblade
*Malaxis bayardii*, Bayard's adder's-mouth
*Malaxis brachypoda*, white adder's-mouth
*Malaxis unifolia*, green adder's-mouth
*Platanthera aquilonis*, northern green bog orchis
*Platanthera blephariglottis*, northern white fringed orchis
*Platanthera ciliaris*, orange fringed orchis
*Platanthera cristata*, orange crested orchis H
*Platanthera dilatata*, white bog orchis; bog candles
*Platanthera flava* var. *herbiola*, northern tubercled orchis
*Platanthera grandiflora*, large purple fringed orchis
*Platanthera hookeri*, Hooker's orchis
*Platanthera huronensis*, green bog orchis
*Platanthera lacera*, green fringed orchis; ragged orchis
*Platanthera leucophaea*, eastern prairie fringed orchis H
*Platanthera macrophylla*, Goldie's pad-leaved orchis
*Platanthera orbiculata*, pad-leaved orchis
*Platanthera peramoena*, purple fringeless orchis
*Platanthera psycodes*, small purple fringed orchis
*Pogonia ophioglossoides*, rose pogonia
*Spiranthes casei* var. *casei*, Case's ladies'-tresses
*Spiranthes cernua*, nodding ladies'-tresses
*Spiranthes lacera* var. *lacera*, northern slender ladies'-tresses
*Spiranthes lacera* var. *gracilis*, southern slender ladies'-tresses
*Spiranthes lucida*, shining ladies'-tresses
*Spiranthes magnicamporum*, Great Plains ladies'-tresses H
*Spiranthes ochroleuca*, yellow ladies'-tresses
*Spiranthes ovalis* var. *erostellata*, northern oval ladies'-tresses
*Spiranthes romanzoffiana*, hooded ladies'-tresses
*Spiranthes tuberosa*, little ladies'-tresses
*Spiranthes vernalis*, grass-leaved ladies'-tresses
*Tipularia discolor*, crane-fly orchis
*Triphora trianthophora*, three birds orchid

## New Jersey

57 species and varieties including 2 unvouchered reports
*Arethusa bulbosa*, dragon's-mouth
*Calopogon tuberosus*, common grass-pink
*Cleistes divaricata*, large spreading pogonia

*Coeloglossum viride* var. *virescens*, long-bracted green orchis
*Corallorhiza maculata* var. *maculata*, spotted coralroot
*Corallorhiza odontorhiza* var. *odontorhiza*, autumn coralroot
*Corallorhiza trifida*, early coralroot
*Corallorhiza wisteriana*, Wister's coralroot H
*Cypripedium acaule*, pink lady's-slipper
*Cypripedium candidum*, small white lady's-slipper
*Cypripedium parviflorum* var. *parviflorum*, southern small yellow lady's-slipper
*Cypripedium parviflorum* var. *makasin*, northern small yellow lady's-slipper
*Cypripedium parviflorum* var. *pubescens*, large yellow lady's-slipper
*Cypripedium reginae*, showy lady's-slipper
*Epipactis helleborine*, broad-leaved helleborine*
*Galearis spectabilis*, showy orchis
*Goodyera pubescens*, downy rattlesnake orchis
*Goodyera tesselata*, checkered rattlesnake orchis
*Gymnadeniopsis clavellata* var. *clavellata*, little club-spur orchis
*Gymnadeniopsis integra*, yellow fringeless orchis
*Gymnadeniopsis nivea*, snowy orchis H?
*Isotria medeoloides*, small whorled pogonia
*Isotria verticillata*, large whorled pogonia
*Liparis liliifolia*, lily-leaved twayblade
*Liparis loeselii*, Loesel's twayblade
*Listera australis*, southern twayblade
*Listera smallii*, Small's twayblade
*Malaxis bayardii*, Bayard's adder's-mouth H?
*Malaxis brachypoda*, white adder's-mouth
*Malaxis unifolia*, green adder's-mouth
*Platanthera aquilonis*, northern green bog orchis
*Platanthera blephariglottis*, northern white fringed orchis
*Platanthera ciliaris*, orange fringed orchis
*Platanthera cristata*, orange crested orchis
*Platanthera dilatata*, white bog orchis; bog candles
*Platanthera flava* var. *flava*, southern tubercled orchis
*Platanthera flava* var. *herbiola*, northern tubercled orchis
*Platanthera grandiflora*, large purple fringed orchis
*Platanthera hookeri*, Hooker's orchis H?
*Platanthera huronensis*, green bog orchis
*Platanthera lacera*, green fringed orchis
*Platanthera orbiculata*, pad-leaved orchis
*Platanthera peramoena*, purple fringeless orchis
*Platanthera psycodes*, small purple fringed orchis
*Pogonia ophioglossoides*, rose pogonia
*Spiranthes cernua*, nodding ladies'-tresses
*Spiranthes lacera* var. *gracilis*, southern slender ladies'-tresses
*Spiranthes laciniata*, lace-lipped ladies'-tresses

*Spiranthes lucida*, shining ladies'-tresses
*Spiranthes ochroleuca*, yellow ladies'-tresses
[*Spiranthes odorata*, fragrant ladies'-tresses]
[*Spiranthes praecox*, giant ladies'-tresses]
*Spiranthes romanzoffiana*, hooded ladies'-tresses
*Spiranthes tuberosa*, little ladies'-tresses
*Spiranthes vernalis*, grass-leaved ladies'-tresses
*Tipularia discolor*, crane-fly orchis
*Triphora trianthophora*, three birds orchid

# *Some Regional Orchid Statistics*

Ten species and varieties are found within only one state in the Northeast
*Cleistes divaricata*, large spreading pogonia—New Jersey
*Corallorhiza striata*, striped coralroot—New York
*Epipactis atrorubens*, red helleborine—Vermont
*Goodyera oblongifolia*, giant rattlesnake orchis—Maine
*Gymnadeniopsis integra*, yellow fringeless orchis—New Jersey
*Gymnadeniopsis nivea*, snowy orchis—New Jersey
*Platanthera flava* var. *flava*, southern tubercled orchis—New Jersey
*Platanthera pallida*, pale fringed orchis—New York
*Spiranthes laciniata*, lace-lipped ladies'-tresses—New Jersey
*Spiranthes magnicamporum*, Great Plains ladies'-tresses—Pennsylvania
*Spiranthes ovalis* var. *erostellata*, northern oval ladies'-tresses—Pennsylvania

Three species are found within two states in the Northeast
*Corallorhiza wisteriana*, Wister's coralroot—New Jersey, Pennsylvania
*Listera smallii*, Small's twayblade—New Jersey, Pennsylvania
*Platanthera peramoena*, purple fringeless orchis—New Jersey, Pennsylvania

Two species have been found in only three states in the Northeast
*Cypripedium candidum*, small white lady's-slipper—New York, New Jersey, Pennsylvania
*Platanthera leucophaea*, eastern prairie fringed orchis—Maine, New York, Pennsylvania

Four species and varieties are found in only four states in the Northeast
*Listera auriculata*, auricled twayblade—Maine, New Hampshire, Vermont, New York
*Listera australis*, southern twayblade—Vermont, New York, Pennsylvania, New Jersey
*Listera convallarioides*, broad-lipped twayblade—Maine, New Hampshire, Vermont, New York
*Platanthera cristata*, orange crested orchis—Vermont, New York, Pennsylvania, New Jersey

One species is considered historical or extirpated from the Northeast
*Spiranthes magnicamporum*, Great Plains ladies'-tresses—Pennsylvania

One species is endemic to the Northeast
*Platanthera pallida*, pale fringed orchis—New York

Twelve species and varieties are typically northern or boreal in their distribution, many reaching the southern limit of their range in the Northeast
*Amerorchis rotundifolia*, small round-leaf orchis
*Calypso bulbosa* var. *americana*, eastern fairy-slipper
*Corallorhiza striata* var. *striata*, striped coralroot
*Cypripedium arietinum*, ram's-head lady's-slipper
*Goodyera oblongifolia*, giant rattlesnake orchis
*Goodyera repens*, lesser rattlesnake orchis
*Gymnadeniopsis clavellata* var. *ophioglossoides*, northern club-spur orchis
*Listera auriculata*, auricled twayblade
*Listera convallarioides*, broad-lipped twayblade
*Malaxis brachypoda*, white adder's-mouth
*Spiranthes casei* var. *casei*, Case's ladies'-tresses
*Spiranthes romanzoffiana*, hooded ladies'-tresses

Eighteen species and varieties are typically southern or southeastern in their distribution and reach the northern limit of their distribution in the Northeast
*Cleistes divaricata*, large spreading pogonia
*Corallorhiza wisteriana*, Wister's coralroot
*Cypripedium parviflorum* var. *parviflorum*, southern small yellow lady's-slipper
*Gymnadeniopsis integra*, yellow fringeless orchis
*Gymnadeniopsis nivea*, snowy orchis
*Isotria verticillata*, large whorled pogonia
*Liparis liliifolia*, lily-leaved twayblade
*Listera smallii*, Small's twayblade
*Platanthera ciliaris*, orange fringed orchis
*Platanthera cristata*, orange crested orchis
*Platanthera flava* var. *flava*, southern tubercled orchis
*Platanthera peramoena*, purple fringeless orchis
*Spiranthes laciniata*, lace-lipped ladies'-tresses
*Spiranthes odorata*, fragrant ladies'-tresses
*Spiranthes ovalis* var. *erostellata*, northern oval ladies'-tresses
*Spiranthes praecox*, giant ladies'-tresses
*Spiranthes tuberosa*, little ladies'-tresses
*Spiranthes vernalis*, grass-leaved ladies'-tresses
*Tipularia discolor*, crane-fly orchis

Three species are typically prairie species
occurring in specialized prairie-like or fen habitats in the Northeast
*Cypripedium candidum*, small white lady's-slipper

*Platanthera leucophaea*, eastern prairie fringed orchis
*Spiranthes magnicamporum*, Great Plains ladies'-tresses

Two species are listed as federally threatened by the Endangered Species Act
*Isotria medeoloides*, small whorled pogonia
*Platanthera leucophaea*, eastern prairie fringed orchis

Five species, although not listed by the Endangered Species Act, may be equally as rare globally as to be considered threatened
*Cypripedium candidum*, small white lady's-slipper
*Listera auriculata*, auricled twayblade
*Listera smallii*, Small's twayblade
*Malaxis bayardii*, Bayard's adder's-mouth
*Platanthera pallida*, pale fringed orchis

Five species and varieties have recently been described or revalidated
*Corallorhiza maculata* var. *occidentalis*, western spotted coralroot 1997
*Corallorhiza odontorhiza* var. *pringlei*, Pringle's autumn coralroot 1997
*Cypripedium parviflorum* var. *parviflorum*, southern small yellow lady's-slipper 1994
*Cypripedium parviflorum* var. *makasin*, northern small yellow lady's-slipper 1994
*Malaxis bayardii*, Bayard's adder's-mouth 1993
*Platanthera pallida*, pale fringed orchis 1993
*Spiranthes ovalis* var. *erostellata*, northern oval ladies'-tresses 1983

In most states, except for Maine, a few to several species that were documented from those states are considered historical/extirpated or have not been seen in recent years.

## New Hampshire

*Amerorchis rotundifolia*, small round-leaf orchis
*Calypso bulbosa* var. *americana*, eastern fairy-slipper
*Liparis liliifolia*, lily-leaved twayblade
*Spiranthes vernalis*, grass-leaved ladies'-tresses

## Vermont

*Amerorchis rotundifolia*, small round-leaf orchis
*Isotria medeoloides*, small whorled pogonia
*Malaxis bayardii*, Bayard's adders-mouth

### Massachusetts

*Listera cordata*, heart-leaved twayblade
*Platanthera ciliaris*, orange fringed orchis
*Platanthera obtusata*, blunt-leafed rein orchis

### Connecticut

*Aplectrum hyemale*, putty-root
*Arethusa bulbosa*, dragon's-mouth
*Corallorhiza odontorhiza* var. *pringlei*, Pringle's autumn coralroot
*Cypripedium arietinum*, ram's-head lady's-slipper
*Goodyera repens*, lesser rattlesnake orchis
*Listera cordata*, heart-leaved twayblade
*Malaxis bayardii*, Bayard's adder's-mouth
*Platanthera dilatata*, white bog orchis; bog candles
*Platanthera hookeri*, Hooker's orchis
*Platanthera macrophylla*, Goldie's pad-leaved orchis

### Rhode Island

*Galearis spectabilis*, showy orchis
*Liparis liliifolia*, lily-leaved twayblade
*Listera cordata*, heart-leaved twayblade
*Malaxis bayardii*, Bayard's adder's-mouth
*Platanthera hookeri*, Hooker's orchis
*Platanthera orbiculata*, pad-leaved orchis
*Spiranthes lucida*, shining ladies'-tresses

### New York

*Amerorchis rotundifolia*, small round-leaf orchis
*Isotria medeoloides*, small whorled pogonia
*Platanthera leucophaea*, eastern prairie fringed orchis
*Calypso bulbosa* var. *americana*, eastern fairy-slipper

### Pennsylvania

*Cypripedium candidum*, small white lady's-slipper
*Platanthera cristata*, orange crested orchis
*Platanthera leucophaea*, eastern prairie fringed orchis
*Spiranthes magnicamporum*, Great Plains ladies'-tresses

## New Jersey

*Corallorhiza wisteriana*, Wister's coralroot
*Gymnadeniopsis nivea*, snowy orchis
*Malaxis bayardii*, Bayard's adder's-mouth
*Platanthera hookeri*, Hooker's orchis

Two species are not native (and indicated throughout the text with an asterisk)
*Epipactis atrorubens*, red helleborine*
*Epipactis helleborine*, broad-leaved helleborine*

One species is considered a waif
*Gymnadenia conopsea*, fragrant orchis*—Connecticut 1887

# *Rare, Threatened, and Endangered Species*

In the United States each state has a somewhat different system for listing and ranking rare plants, whereas the Natural Heritage Programs and NatureServe have a uniform system for ranking species. The list of orchids for each state may also be influenced by the presence, or lack thereof, of persons with a particular interest in the Orchidaceae. The following rankings and their definitions should enable the reader to understand the current status of the listed species. This information is taken from information provided by credited sources and printed exactly as they list the species, with current synonyms in parentheses.

S1 or SE Extremely rare throughout its range in the state or province (typically 5 or fewer occurrences or very few remaining individuals). May be especially vulnerable to extirpation.

S2 or ST Rare throughout its range in the state or province (6–20 occurrences or few remaining individuals). May be vulnerable to extirpation because of rarity or other factors.

S3 or SR Uncommon throughout its range in the state or province or found only in a restricted range even if abundant at some locations (21–100 occurrences).

S#S# Numeric range rank: a range between two consecutive numeric ranks. Denotes uncertainty about the exact rarity of the species (e.g., S1S2).

SH Historical: species occurred historically throughout its range in the state or province (with expectation that it may be rediscovered), perhaps not verified in the past 20–70 years (depending on the species) and suspected to be still extant.

State rankings indicate the relative rarity of the species within the province or state only. National and global rankings indicate the rarity within a larger area. Most species within the scope of this field guide are ranked as G4 or G5, indicating that globally they are considered secure. Only 4 species are ranked otherwise.

Sources: NatureServe
http://www.natureserve.org
Committee on the Status of Endangered Wildlife in Canada
http://www.cosewic.gc.ca

SU Unconfirmed record; usually from the out-of-area literature. Unrankable: Possibly in peril throughout its range in the state or province but status uncertain; need more information.

SX Extinct/Extirpated: Species is believed to be extirpated within the state or province.

S? Unranked: Species is not yet ranked.
GH Of historical occurrence throughout its range; may be rediscovered.
GX Believed to be extinct throughout its range.

Additional ranks are used for those species whose populations are ample and secure and not noted here.

Note: Because of recent taxonomic work involving *Corallorhiza maculata* var. *maculata*, *C. maculata* var. *occidentalis*, *Platanthera aquilonis*, and *P. huronensis*, their precise distributional information is still not complete. None of these species or varieties is exceptionally rare, but they do need to be sorted out to determine relative rarity within each state. *Malaxis bayardii*, although vouchered from several states, is not listed in some states because of incomplete data. Occasionally species are listed as historical or extirpated but are currently known from extant populations. This would reflect the date of the available data and publication of the state lists. Not all states update their lists annually. Certain states do not list species considered extirpated (historical). Choice of names and their spelling are as presented by the various states.

### MAINE

*Amerorchis rotundifolia*, Small round-leaved orchis S2? G5 T
*Corallorhiza odontorhiza*, Autumn coral-root S1 G5 E
*Cypripedium arietinum*, Ram's-head lady's-slipper S1 G3 E
*Cypripedium reginae*, Showy lady's-slipper S3 G4 T
*Goodyera oblongifolia*, Giant rattlesnake-plantain S2 G5? E
*Isotria medeoloides*, Small whorled pogonia S2 G2 LT E
*Isotria verticillata*, Large whorled pogonia SX G5 PE
*Malaxis monophyllos*, White adder's-mouth S1 G5 E
(syn. *Malaxis brachypoda*)
*Platanthera flava*, Pale green orchis S2 G4T4Q SC
*Platanthera leucophaea*, Prairie white-fringed orchid S1 G2 LT E
*Spiranthes lacera* var. *gracilis*, Southern Slender ladies' tresses SH G5T4T5 PE
*Spiranthes lucida*, Shining ladies'-tresses S1 G5 T
*Triphora trianthophora*, Nodding pogonia S1 G3G4 T
Source: Maine Natural Areas Program
Rare Threatened and Endangered Plant Taxa
http://www.mainenaturalareas.org/docs/rare_plants/links/plant_list.pdf

### NEW HAMPSHIRE

*Amerorchis rotundifolia*, One-leaf Orchis E
*Arethusa bulbosa*, Arethusa T
*Calypso bulbosa* var. *americana*, Fairy Slipper E
*Corallorhiza odontorhiza*, Autumn Coralroot E
*Cypripedium arietinum*, Ram's-head Lady's Slipper E
*Cypripedium parviflorum* var. *makasin*, Yellow Lady's Slipper E
*Cypripedium parviflorum* var. *pubescens*, Large Yellow Lady's Slipper T

*Cypripedium reginae*, Showy Lady's Slipper E
*Galearis spectabilis*, Showy Orchis T
*Isotria medeoloides*, Small Whorled Pogonia T
*Isotria verticillata*, Large Whorled Pogonia E
*Liparis liliifolia*, Large Twayblade SX
*Liparis loeselii*, Loesel's Twayblade T
*Listera auriculata*, Auricled Twayblade E
*Listera convallarioides*, Lily-leaved Twayblade T
*Listera cordata*, Heart-leaved Twayblade T
*Malaxis monophyllos* ssp. *Brachypoda*, White Adder's Mouth E
(syn. *Malaxis brachypoda*)
*Malaxis unifolia*, Green Adder's Mouth T
*Platanthera flava* var. *herbiola*, Pale Green Orchid T
*Spiranthes casei*, Case's Ladies' Tresses E
*Spiranthes lucida*, Shining Ladies' Tresses T
*Triphora trianthophora*, Three-birds Orchid T
Source: NH Division of Forests and Lands
http://www.dred.state.nh.us/divisions/forestandlands/bureaus/naturalheritage/RarePlants.htm

VERMONT

*Amerorchis rotundifolia* E/PX
*Aplectrum hyemale*, Putty-root T
*Arethusa bulbosa*, Arethusa T
*Calypso bulbosa*, Fairy slipper T
*Corallorhiza odontorhiza*, Autumn coral-root T
*Cypripedium arietinum*, Ram's head lady's-slipper T
*Isotria medeoloides*, Small whorled pogonia E/PX LT
*Isotria verticillata*, Large whorled pogonia T
*Liparis liliifolia*, Lily-leaved twayblade T
*Listera auriculata*, Auricled twayblade E
*Listera australis*, Southern twayblade E
*Malaxis bayardii*, Bayard's adders-mouth E/PX
*Malaxis brachypoda*, White adder's mouth T
*Platanthera flava*, Tubercled orchis T
*Platanthera hookeri*, Hooker's orchis T
*Triphora trianthophora*, Three-bird orchid T
Source: Endangered and Threatened Plants of Vermont
Vermont Department of Fish and Wildlife
Nongame and Natural Heritage Program April 23, 2005
http://www.vtfishandwildlife.com/library/Reports_and_Documents/NonGame_and_Natural_Heritage/Rare_Threatened_and_Endangered_Species/Endangered%20_and_Threatened_Plants_of_Vermont-April_2005.pdf

MASSACHUSETTS

*Aplectrum hyemale,* putty-root E
*Arethusa bulbosa*, Arethusa T
*Corallorrhiza odontorhiza*, Autumn Coralroot SC
*Cypripedium arietinum*, Ram's-head Lady's-slipper E
*Cypripedium parviflorum* var. *makasin*, Small Yellow Lady's-slipper E
*Cypripedium reginae*, Showy Lady's-slipper SC
*Goodyera repens*, Dwarf Rattlesnake-plantain E
*Isotria medeoloides*, Small Whorled Pogonia E LT
*Liparis liliifolia*, Lily-leaf Twayblade T
*Listera cordata*, Heartleaf Twayblade E
*Malaxis bayardii*, Bayard's Green Adder's-mouth E
*Malaxis monophyllos* var. *brachypoda*, White Adder's-mouth E
(syn. *Malaxis brachypoda*)
*Platanthera cristata*, Crested Fringed Orchis E
*Platanthera dilatata*, Leafy White Orchis E
*Platanthera flava* var. *herbiola*, Pale Green Orchis E
*Spiranthes romanzoffiana*, Hooded Ladies'-tresses E
*Spiranthes vernalis*, Grass-leaved Ladies'-tresses E
*Tipularia discolor*, Cranefly Orchid E
*Triphora trianthophora*, Nodding Pogonia E
Source: Massachusetts List of Endangered, Threatened, and Special Concern Species
http://www.mass.gov/dfwele/dfw/nhesp/nhrare.htm

CONNECTICUT

*Aplectrum hyemale*, Puttyroot SC PE
*Arethusa bulbosa*, Arethusa SC PE
*Coeloglossum viride* var. *virescens*, Long-bracted green orchid SC
*Corallorhiza trifida*, Early coralroot SC
*Cypripedium arietinum*, Ram's-head lady's-slipper SC PE
*Cypripedium parviflorum*, Yellow lady's-slipper SC
*Cypripedium reginae*, Showy lady's-slipper E
*Goodyera repens* var. *ophioides*, Dwarf rattlesnake plantain SC PE
*Isotria medeoloides*, Small whorled pogonia E FT
*Malaxis monophyllos*, White adder's-mouth E
(syn. *Malaxis brachypoda*)
*Malaxis unifolia*, Green adder's-mouth E
*Platanthera blephariglottis*, White-fringed orchid E
*Platanthera ciliaris*, Yellow-fringed orchid T
*Platanthera dilatata*, Tall white bog orchid SC PE
*Platanthera flava*, Pale green orchid SC
*Platanthera hookeri*, Hooker's orchid SC PE
*Platanthera orbiculata*, Large round-leaved orchid SC PE
*Spiranthes tuberosa* var. *grayi*, Little ladies'-tresses SC

(syn. *Spiranthes tuberosa*)
*Triphora trianthophora*, Nodding pogonia SC
Source: Connecticut Department of Environmental Protection http://dep.state.ct.us/cgnhs/nddb/plants.htm

RHODE ISLAND

*Arethusa bulbosa*, arethusa swamp-pink dragon's mouth S1
*Calopogon tuberosus*, grass-pink swamp-pink S2
*Corallorhiza maculata*, spotted coral-root S1
*Corallorhiza odontorhiza*, late or autumn coral-root S1 PE
*Corallorhiza trifida*, early pale or northern coral-root S1
*Cypripedium calceolus* var. *parviflorum*, small yellow lady's-slipper S1
(syn. *Cypripedium parviflorum* var. *parviflorum*)
*Cypripedium calceolus* var. *pubescens*, large yellow lady's-slipper moccasin-flower or golden slipper; whip-poor-will shoes S1
(syn. *Cypripedium parviflorum* var. *pubescens*)
*Isotria medeoloides*, small whorled pogonia little five-leaves S1
*Liparis liliifolia*, lily-leaved or large twayblade S1
*Liparis loeselii*, yellow bog or Loesel's twayblade; fen- orchid S1
*Listera cordata*, heart-leaved or heartleaf twayblade SH
*Malaxis unifolia*, green adder's mouth S1
*Orchis spectabilis*, showy orchis S1
(syn. *Galearis spectabilis*)
*Platanthera blephariglottis*, white-fringed orchid S1
*Platanthera ciliaris*, yellow fringed orchid or orchis; orange-plume S1
*Platanthera flava* var. *herbiola*, tubercled or pale green orchis/orchid S1
*Platanthera hookeri*, Hooker's orchid or orchis S1
*Platanthera hyperborea*, leafy northern green orchis tall northern bog-orchid S1
(including both *P. aquilonis* and *P. huronensis*)
*Platanthera orbiculata*, round-leaved orchid S1
*Platanthera orbiculata* var. *macrophylla*, large round-leaved orchis S1
(syn. *Platanthera macrophylla*)
*Platanthera psycodes*, small purple fringed orchid S2
*Spiranthes lucida*, shining or wide-leaved ladies'-tresses SH
*Spiranthes tuberosa*, little ladies'-tresses S1
*Spiranthes vernalis*, spring ladies'-tresses S2
Rhode Island Natural History Survey http://www.uri.edu/ce/rinhs/database/db_rinhp_plants.htm

NEW YORK

*Amerorchis rotundifolia*, Round-leaved Orchis G5 SX U
*Aplectrum hyemale*, Puttyroot G5 S1 E
*Arethusa bulbosa*, Dragon's Mouth Orchid G4 S2 T
*Calypso bulbosa* var. *americana*, Calypso G5T5? SH E

*Corallorhiza striata* var. *striata*, Striped Coralroot G5T4T5 S1 E
*Cypripedium arietinum*, Ram's-head Ladyslipper G3 S2 T
*Cypripedium candidum*, Small White Ladyslipper G4 S1 E
*Cypripedium parviflorum* var. *parviflorum*, Small Yellow Ladyslipper G5T3T5 SH E
*Isotria medeoloides*, Small Whorled Pogonia G2 SH E
*Liparis liliifolia*, Large Twayblade G5 S1 E
*Listera auriculata*, Auricled Twayblade G3G4 S1 E
*Listera australis*, Southern Twayblade G4 S1S2 E
*Listera convallarioides*, Broad-lipped Twayblade G5 S1 E
*Malaxis bayardii*, Bayard's Adder's-mouth Orchid G2 S1 E
*Platanthera ciliaris*, Orange Fringed Orchid G5 S1 E
*Platanthera cristata*, Crested Fringed Orchis G5 S1 E
*Platanthera hookeri*, Hooker's Orchid G4 S1 E
*Platanthera leucophaea*, Eastern Prairie Fringed Orchid G2 SH E
*Spiranthes vernalis*, Spring Ladies'-tresses G5 S1 E
*Tipularia discolor*, Cranefly Orchid G4G5 S1 E
*Triphora trianthophora*, Nodding Pogonia G3G4 S2 E
New York Natural Heritage Program
Rare Plant Status List
http://www.nynhp.org/

NEW JERSEY

*Aplectrum hyemale*, Puttyroot S1 G5
*Arethusa bulbosa*, Dragon Mouth S2 G4
*Cleistes divaricata*, Spreading Pogonia S1 G4
*Corallorhiza trifida*, Early Coralroot S2 G5
*Corallorhiza wisteriana*, Spring Coralroot SX G5
*Cypripedium candidum*, Small White Lady's-slipper S1 G4
*Cypripedium parviflorum* var. *makasin*, Fen Small Yellow Lady's-slipper S2 G5
*Cypripedium reginae*, Showy Lady's-slipper S1 G4
*Isotria medeoloides*, Small Whorled Pogonia S1 G2 LT
*Listera cordata*, Heartleaf Twayblade S1 G5T5 LP
*Listera smallii*, Appalachian Twayblade S1.1 G4
*Malaxis bayardii*, Bayard Long's Adder's-mouth SH G2
*Malaxis monophyllos*, White Adder's-mouth SH G4Q LP
(syn. *Malaxis brachypoda*)
*Malaxis unifolia*, Green Adder's-mouth S2 G5
*Platanthera ciliaris*, Yellow Fringed Orchid S2 G5
*Platanthera cristata*, Crested Yellow Orchid S3 G5
*Platanthera flava* var. *flava*, Southern Rein Orchid S1 G4
*Platanthera flava* var. *herbiola*, Tubercled Rein Orchid S2 G4
*Platanthera grandiflora*, Large Purple Fringed Orchid S2 G5
*Platanthera hookeri*, Hooker's Orchid SH G5

*Platanthera hyperborea* var. *hyperborea*, Leafy Northern Green Orchid SX G5
(misapplied name for *P. huronensis*)
*Platanthera integra*, Yellow Fringeless Orchid S1 G3G4
(syn. *Gymnadeniopsis integra*)
*Platanthera nivea*, Snowy Orchid SH G5
(syn. *Gymnadeniopsis nivea*)
*Platanthera orbiculata*, Round-leaf Orchid S1 G5?
*Platanthera peramoena*, Purple Fringeless Orchid S1 G5
*Platanthera psycodes*, Purple Fringed Orchid S2 G5
*Spiranthes laciniata*, Lace-lip Ladies'-tresses S1 G4G5
*Spiranthes lucida*, Shining Ladies'-tresses S2 G5
*Spiranthes ochroleuca*, Yellowish Nodding Ladies'-tresses S3 G4
*Spiranthes odorata*, Fragrant Ladies'-tresses S2 G5
*Spiranthes tuberosa*, Little Ladies'-tresses S3 G5
*Tipularia discolor*, Cranefly Orchid S3 G4G5
*Triphora trianthophora*, Three Birds Orchid S1 G3G4
Source: List of Endangered Plant Species and Plant Species of Concern
http://www.state.nj.us/dep/parksandforests/natural/heritage/june2005plantlist.p

PENNSYLVANIA

*Aplectrum hyemale*, Puttyroot G5 S3
*Cypripedium calceolus* var. *parviflorum*, Small Yellow Lady's- slipper G5 S1
(syn. *Cypripedium parviflorum* var. *parviflorum)*
*Cypripedium candidum*, Small White Lady's-slipper G4 SX
*Cypripedium reginae*, Showy Lady's-slipper G4 S2
*Goodyera repens*, Lesser Rattlesnake-plantain G5 S2
*Goodyera tesselata*, Checkered Rattlesnake-plantain G5 S1
*Isotria medeoloides,* Small Whorled Pogonia S1 G2 FT
*Listera australis*, Southern Twayblade G4 S1
*Listera cordata*, Heart-leaved Twayblade G5 S1
*Listera smallii*, Kidney-leaved Twayblade G4 S1
*Malaxis bayardii*, Bayard's Malaxis G1G2 S1
*Malaxis monophyllos* var. *brachypoda*, White Adder's-mouth G4 S1
(syn. *Malaxis brachypoda*)
*Platanthera blephariglottis*, White Fringed-orchid G4G5 S2S3
*Platanthera ciliaris*, Yellow-fringed Orchid G5 S2
*Platanthera cristata*, Crested Yellow Orchid G5 SX
*Platanthera dilatata*, Leafy White Orchid G5 S1
*Platanthera hookeri*, Hooker's Orchid G4 S1
*Platanthera hyperborea*, Leafy Northern Green Orchid G5 S1
(misapplied name for *P. huronensis* and/or *P. aquilonis*)
*Platanthera leucophaea*, Prairie White-fringed Orchid G3 SX
*Platanthera peramoena*, Purple-fringeless Orchid G5 S2
*Spiranthes casei*, Case's Ladies'-tresses G4 S1

*Spiranthes lucida*, Shining Ladies'-tresses G5 S3
*Spiranthes magnicamporum*, Ladies'-tresses G4 SX
*Spiranthes ovalis*, October Ladies'-tresses G5? S1
*Spiranthes romanzoffiana*, Hooded Ladies'-tresses G5 S1
*Spiranthes tuberosa*, Little Ladies'-tresses G5 S1
*Spiranthes vernalis*, Spring Ladies'-tresses G5 S1
*Tipularia discolor*, Cranefly Orchid G4G5 S3
*Triphora trianthophora*, Nodding Pogonia G3G4 SH
Source: Pennsylvania Natural Heritage Program http://www.naturalheritage.state.pa.us/PlantsPage.aspx

# *Recent Literature References for New Taxa, Combinations, and Additions to the Orchid Flora of the Northeast*

Note: references for recently described forms are found within the species treatments.

Additional information may be found in volume 26 of the *Flora of North America* (FNA, 1993).

*Corallorhiza maculata* (Rafinesque) Rafinesque var. *occidentalis* (Lindley) Ames
western spotted coralroot
Freudenstein, J. V. 1986. *Contributions from the University of Michigan Herbarium* 16: 145–153.
———. 1997. *Harvard Papers in Botany* 10: 5–51.

*Corallorhiza odontorhiza* (Willdenow) Nuttall var. *pringlei* (Greenman) Freudenstein
Pringle's autumn coralroot
Freudenstein, J. V. 1993. Dissertation. Cornell University.
———. 1997. *Harvard Papers in Botany* 10: 5–51.

*Cypripedium parviflorum* Salisbury var. *parviflorum*
southern small yellow lady's-slipper
Sheviak, C. J. 1994. *AOS Bulletin* 63(6): 664–669.
———. 1995. *AOS Bulletin* 64(6): 606–612.
———. 1996. *NANOJ* 2(4): 319–343.

*Cypripedium parviflorum* Salisbury var. *makasin* (Farwell) Sheviak
northern small yellow lady's-slipper
Sheviak, C. J. 1993. *AOS Bulletin* 62(4): 403.
———. 1994. *AOS Bulletin* 63(6): 664–669.
———. 1995. *AOS Bulletin* 64(6): 606–612.
———. 1996. *NANOJ* 2(4): 319–343.

*Cypripedium parviflorum* Salisbury var. *pubescens*
large yellow lady's-slipper
Sheviak, C. J. 1994. *AOS Bulletin* 63(6): 664–669.
———. 1995. *AOS Bulletin* 64(6): 606–612.

———. 1996. *NANOJ* 2(4): 319–343.

*Gymnadeniopsis clavellata* (Michaux) Rydberg
*Gymnadeniopsis integra* (Nuttall) Rydberg
*Gymnadeniopsis nivea* (Nuttall) Rydberg
Brown, P. M. 2002. *NANOJ* 8: 32–40.

*Platanthera aquilonis* Sheviak
northern green bog orchis
Sheviak, C. J. 1999. *Lindleyana* 14(4): 193–203.
Wallace, L. E. 2004. *Canadian Journal of Botany* 82: 244–252.

*Platanthera huronensis* (Nuttall) Lindley
green bog orchis
Wallace, L. E. 2003. *International Journal of Plant Science.* 164(6): 907–16.
———. 2004. *Canadian Journal of Botany* 82:244–52.

*Platanthera leucophaea* (Nuttall) Lindley
eastern prairie fringed orchis
Sheviak, C. J., and M. Bowles. 1986. *Rhodora* 88: 267–290.

*Platanthera peramoena* (A. Gray) A. Gray
purple fringeless orchis
Spooner, D. M., and J. S. Shelly. 1983. *Rhodora* 85: 55–64.

*Platanthera psycodes* (Linnaeus) Lindley
small purple fringed orchis
Stoutamire, W. P. 1974. *Brittonia* 26: 42–58.

*Spiranthes casei* Catling and Cruise var. *casei*
Case's ladies'-tresses
Catling, P. M., and J. E. Cruise. 1974. *Rhodora* 76: 256–536.

*Spiranthes cernua* (Linnaeus) L.C. Richard
nodding ladies'-tresses
Sheviak, C. J. 1991. *Lindleyana* 6(4): 228–234.

*Spiranthes magnicamporum* Sheviak
Great Plains ladies'-tresses
Sheviak, C. J. 1973. *Botanical Museum Leaflet of Harvard University* 23: 285–297.

*Spiranthes ovalis* Lindley var. *erostellata* Catling
northern oval ladies'-tresses
Catling, P. M. 1983. *Brittonia* 35: 120–125.

# *Synonyms and Misapplied Names*

Synonyms and misapplied names are both often confused and confusing in the literature and in the understanding of orchid enthusiasts. A synonym is simply an alternate name for a previously published plant name. From among the synonyms each author must select a name that he or she feels best suits the currently accepted genus and specific epithet for a given plant. Although the genus may vary, the specific epithet may often be the same. In such large groups as the spiranthoid orchids (*Spiranthes* and its allied genera) many synonyms may exist for the same species—all within different genera.

The rules of priority as set forth in the *International Code of Botanical Nomenclature* (2000) dictate that the earliest validly published species name within the chosen genus must be used. A good example would be that of the common grass-pink *Calopogon tuberosus* (Linnaeus) Britton, Sterns, & Poggenberg, which was originally published by Linnaeus in 1753 as *Limodorum tuberosum*, then as a new combination by Britton, et al. in 1888. *Calopogon pulchellus* (Salisbury) R. Brown (1853) was based upon *Limodorum pulchellum* Salisbury (1796). Although the latter name as *Calopogon pulchellus* was in widespread usage for many years priority indicates that the former is the valid name. It rarely comes down to months and usually the year of publication is sufficient for determining the valid name.

*Orchis spectabilis* would be a synonym for *Galearis spectabilis*, *Galearis* being the currently accepted genus for the North American species. *Habenaria* is another group that has undergone a great deal of scrutiny in the past twenty-five years. Several groups of species formerly included within *Habenaria* are now treated as distinct genera. This is not always so much a case of correct or incorrect names but that of the preference of the author for one genus over another. The recent trend for molecular, i.e., DNA, analysis of species has resulted in the placement of several species or groups of species within other genera. Although this is tempting to accept as the end-all and be-all of taxonomy it is still only one tool to help in formulating an opinion.

A misapplied name is an incorrect name for a given plant that may have resulted from a reassessment of the genus or species, resulting in two or more species being described from within the original species, or it may simply be a wrong name assigned to the plants. This is especially common in geographic areas at the edge of a group's range. The most frequently encountered example would be *Cypripedium calceolus*. For many years our North American yellow lady's-slippers have been treated as a geographic variant of the Eurasian species. Many years of work by Sheviak have demonstrated that this is not the case and that the North American plants are a distinct species—*Cypripedium parviflorum*. Therefore the name *C. calceolus* is a misapplied name for the North American plants. The term *auct.* (*auctorum*, i.e., of authors) is used to indicate a misapplied name and occasionally an author will incorrectly append the phrase "in part" after a name listed under synonymy. Misapplied names are not synonyms and refer only to the specific geographic area being treated—in this case the northeastern United States.

An issue can arise as to whether a name is a synonym or misapplied and that depends on a broad or narrow view of the taxonomy—the lumpers vs. the splitters. Such a situation would best be described thus: if *Platanthera huronensis* is considered to be synonymous with or the same species as *Platanthera hyperborea*, *Platanthera huronensis* becomes a synonym of *Platanthera hyperborea*; but if *Platanthera huronensis* is considered a good species on its own *Platanthera hyperborea* becomes a misapplied name for *Platanthera huronensis*. At times this appears to be an endless argument and each author must make his or her own decision as to synonymy and misapplied names. In the northeastern United States there are very few misapplied names. Cross-references to all taxa with synonyms and misapplied names can be found at the end of this chapter.

Synonyms and misapplied names are given for taxa in specific journal articles, referenced in the species accounts, and in the following texts:

Brown, P. M., and S. N. Folsom. 2003. *The Wild Orchids of North America, North of Mexico*.

———. 2004. *Wild Orchids of the Southeastern United States, North of Peninsular Florida*.

———. 2006. *Wild Orchids of the Canadian Maritimes and Northern Great Lakes Region*.

Case, F. W. 1987. *Orchids of the Western Great Lakes Region*.

Chapman, W. 1997. *Orchids of the Northeast*.

Correll, D. S. 1950. *Native Orchids of North America*.

*Flora of North America*. 2002. Vol. 26, *Orchidaceae*.

Luer, C. A. 1975. *The Native Orchids of the United States and Canada excluding Florida*.

Williams, J. G., A. E. Williams, and N. Arlott. 1983. *A Field Guide to the Orchids of North America*.

## Segregate Genera

Three genera within the range of this book have been historically treated within the genus *Habenaria* and are currently treated differently by various authors. Those are:

*Coeloglossum*
*Gymnadeniopsis*
*Platanthera*

## Synonyms

Most current taxonomic treatments recognize the numerous segregate genera of the spiranthoid orchids (Garay 1980). References given are for recent taxonomic treatments, not necessarily the taxonomic work that first designated the new combination. Volume 26 of the *Flora of North America* (FNA, 2002) treats many of the following taxa as well.

*Amerorchis rotundifolia* (Banks *ex* Pursh) Hultén
SYNONYM
*Orchis rotundifolia* Banks *ex* Pursh

*Calypso bulbosa* (Linnaeus) Oakes var. *americana* (R. Brown) Luer
SYNONYM
*Cytherea bulbosa* (Linnaeus) House *p.p.*

*Coeloglossum viride* (Linnaeus) Hartman var. *virescens* (Mühlenberg) Luer
SYNONYMS
*Coeloglossum bracteatum* (Mühlenberg *ex* Willdenow) Parlin
*Coeloglossum viride* subsp. *bracteatum* (Mühlenberg *ex* Willdenow) Hultén
*Dactylorhiza viridis* R.M. Bateman, A. Pridgeon & M.W. Chase
*Habenaria bracteata* (Mühlenberg *ex* Willdenow) R. Brown *ex* Aiton *f.*
*Habenaria viridis* Linnaeus var. *bracteata* (Mühlenberg *ex* Willdenow) Reichenbach *ex* Gray

*Corallorhiza maculata* (Rafinesque) Rafinesque var. *maculata*
SYNONYM
*Corallorhiza multiflora* Nuttall

*Corallorhiza maculata* (Rafinesque) Rafinesque var. *occidentalis* (Lindley) Ames
SYNONYM
*Corallorhiza maculata* (Rafinesque) Rafinesque subsp. *occidentalis* (Lindley) Cockerell

*Corallorhiza odontorhiza* (Willdenow) Nuttall var. *pringlei* (Greenman) Freudenstein
SYNONYM
*Corallorhiza pringlei* Greenman

*Corallorhiza trifida* Chatelain
SYNONYMS
*Corallorhiza trifida* Chatelain var. *verna* (Nuttall) Fernald
*Corallorhiza corallorhiza* (Linnaeus) Karsten

*Cypripedium acaule* Aiton
SYNONYM
*Fissipes acaulis* (Aiton) Small

*Cypripedium arietinum* R. Brown
SYNONYM
*Criosanthes arietina* (Aiton *f.*) House

*Cypripedium parviflorum* Salisbury var. *parviflorum*
SYNONYM
*Cypripedium calceolus* Linnaeus var. *parviflorum* (Salisbury) Fernald *p.p.*

*Cypripedium parviflorum* Salisbury var. *pubescens* (Willdenow) Knight
SYNONYMS
*Cypripedium pubescens* Willdenow
*Cypripedium calceolus* Linnaeus var. *planipetalum* (Fernald) Victorin & Rousseau
*Cypripedium calceolus* Linnaeus var. *pubescens* (Willdenow) Correll
*Cypripedium parviflorum* var. *planipetalum* Fernald
*Cypripedium flavescens* de Candolle
*Cypripedium veganum* Cockerell & Barber
MISAPPLIED
*Cypripedium calceolus* Linnaeus

*Cypripedium reginae* Walter
SYNONYM
*Cypripedium spectabile* Salisbury

*Epipactis helleborine* (Linnaeus) Cranz*
SYNONYM
*Epipactis latifolia* (Linnaeus) Allioni*

*Goodyera oblongifolia* Rafinesque
SYNONYM
*Goodyera decipiens* (Hooker) F.T. Hubbard

*Gymnadeniopsis clavellata* (Michaux) Rydberg *ex* Britton
SYNONYMS
*Habenaria clavellata* (Michaux) Sprengel
*Platanthera clavellata* (Michaux) Luer

*Gymnadeniopsis integra* (Nuttall) Rydberg
SYNONYMS
*Habenaria integra* (Nuttall) Sprengel
*Platanthera integra* (Nuttall) Luer

*Gymnadeniopsis nivea* (Nuttall) Rydberg
SYNONYMS
*Habenaria nivea* (Nuttall) Sprengel
*Platanthera nivea* (Nuttall) Luer

*Isotria medeoloides* (Pursh) Rafinesque
SYNONYMS
*Pogonia affinis* Austin *ex* A. Gray
*Isotria affinis* (Austin *ex* A. Gray) Rydberg

*Isotria verticillata* (Mühlenberg *ex* Willdenow) Rafinesque
SYNONYM
*Pogonia verticillata* (Mühlenberg *ex* Willdenow) Nuttall

*Listera auriculata* Wiegand
SYNONYM
*Neottia auriculata* (Wiegand) Szlachetko

*Listera australis* Lindley
SYNONYM
*Neottia australis* (Lindley) Szlachetko

*Malaxis brachypoda* (Gray) Fernald
SYNONYM
*Malaxis monophyllos* (Linnaeus) Swartz var. *brachypoda* (A. Gray) Morris & Eames

*Platanthera aquilonis* Sheviak
MISAPPLIED
*Habenaria hyperborea* (Linnaeus) R. Brown *ex* Aiton
*Platanthera hyperborea* (Linnaeus) Lindley

*Platanthera blephariglottis* (Willdenow) Lindley
SYNONYMS
*Blephariglottis blephariglottis* (Willdenow) Rydberg
*Habenaria blephariglottis* (Willdenow) Hooker

*Platanthera ciliaris* (Linnaeus) Lindley
SYNONYMS
*Blephariglottis ciliaris* (Linnaeus) Rydberg
*Habenaria ciliaris* (Linnaeus) R. Brown

*Platanthera cristata* (Michaux) Lindley
SYNONYMS
*Blephariglottis cristata* (Michaux) Rafinesque
*Habenaria cristata* (Michaux) R. Brown

*Platanthera dilatata* (Pursh) Lindley var. *dilatata*
SYNONYMS
*Habenaria dilatata* (Pursh) Hooker
*Limnorchis dilatata* (Pursh) Rydberg *ex* Britton
*Piperia dilatata* (Pursh) Szlachetko & P. Rutkowski

*Platanthera flava* (Linnaeus) Lindley var. *flava*
SYNONYM
*Habenaria flava* (Linnaeus) R. Brown

*Platanthera flava* (Linnaeus) Lindley var. *herbiola* (R. Brown) Luer
SYNONYMS
*Habenaria flava* var. *herbiola* (R. Brown *ex* Aiton) Ames & Correll
*Habenaria flava* var. *virescens sensu* Fernald
*Habenaria herbiola* R. Brown *ex* Aiton

*Platanthera grandiflora* (Bigelow) Lindley
SYNONYMS
*Blephariglottis grandiflora* (Bigelow) Rydberg
*Habenaria fimbriata* (Dryander) R. Brown *ex* Aiton
*Habenaria grandiflora* (Bigelow) Torrey
*Habenaria psycodes* (Linnaeus) Sprengel var. *grandiflora* (Bigelow) A. Gray

*Platanthera huronensis* (Nuttall) Lindley
SYNONYM
*Platanthera hyperborea* (Linnaeus) Lindley var. *huronensis* (Nuttall) Luer
*Habenaria hyperborea* Linnaeus var. *huronensis* (Nuttall) Farwell
*Habenaria ×media* (Rydberg) Niles
*Limnorchis media* Rydberg
*Platanthera ×media* (Rydberg) Luer

*Platanthera lacera* (Michaux) G. Don
SYNONYM
*Habenaria lacera* (Michaux) R. Brown

*Platanthera leucophaea* (Nuttall) Lindley
SYNONYM
*Habenaria leucophaea* (Nuttall) A. Gray

*Platanthera macrophylla* (Goldie) P.M. Brown
SYNONYMS
*Habenaria macrophylla* Goldie
*Platanthera orbiculata* (Pursh) Lindley var. *macrophylla* (Goldie) Luer

*Platanthera obtusata* (Banks *ex* Pursh) Lindley
SYNONYM
*Habenaria obtusata* (Banks *ex* Pursh) Richards

*Platanthera orbiculata* (Pursh) Lindley
SYNONYM
*Habenaria orbiculata* (Pursh) Torrey

*Platanthera peramoena* (A. Gray) A. Gray
SYNONYMS
*Blephariglottis peramoena* (Gray) Rydberg
*Habenaria peramoena* A. Gray

*Platanthera psycodes* (Linnaeus) Lindley
SYNONYMS
*Blephariglottis psycodes* (Linnaeus) Rydberg
*Habenaria psycodes* (Linnaeus) Sprengel

X*Platanthopsis vossii* (Case) P.M. Brown
SYNONYM
*Platanthera ×vossii*

*Spiranthes cernua* (Linnaeus) Richard
SYNONYM
*Ibidium cernuum* (Linnaeus) House

*Spiranthes lacera* Rafinesque var. *gracilis* (Bigelow) Luer
SYNONYMS
*Ibidium gracile* (Bigelow) House
*Ibidium beckii* (Lindley) House
*Neottia gracilis* Bigelow
*Spiranthes gracilis* (Bigelow) Beck
*Spiranthes beckii* Lindley

*Spiranthes laciniata* (Small) Ames
SYNONYM
*Ibidium laciniatum* (Small) House

*Spiranthes ochroleuca* (Rydberg) Rydberg
SYNONYMS
*Gyrostachys ochroleuca* Rydberg *ex* Britton
*Spiranthes cernua* (Linnaeus) L.C. Richard var. *ochroleuca* (Rydberg) Ames
*Spiranthes ×steigeri* Correll

*Spiranthes odorata* (Nuttall) Lindley
SYNONYMS
*Ibidium odoratum* (Nuttall) House
*Spiranthes cernua* (Linnaeus) L.C. Richard var. *odorata* (Nuttall) Correll

*Spiranthes praecox* (Walter) S. Watson
SYNONYM
*Ibidium praecox* (Walter) House

*Spiranthes tuberosa* Rafinesque
SYNONYMS
*Spiranthes beckii* Lindley
*Spiranthes grayi* Ames
*Spiranthes tuberosa* var. *grayi* (Ames) Fernald
MISAPPLIED
*Ibidium beckii* House

*Spiranthes vernalis* Engelmann & Gray
SYNONYM
*Ibidium vernale* (Engelmann & Gray) House

## Cross-references for all synonyms

The synonym is given first followed by the currently acceptable names used in this work.
= synonym
≠ misapplied name

*Blephariglottis blephariglottis* (Willdenow) Rydberg = *Platanthera blephariglottis* (Willdenow) Lindley
*Blephariglottis ciliaris* (Linnaeus) Rydberg = *Platanthera ciliaris* (Linnaeus) Lindley
*Blephariglottis cristata* (Michaux) Rafinesque = *Platanthera cristata* (Michaux) Lindley
*Blephariglottis grandiflora* (Bigelow) Rydberg = *Platanthera grandiflora* (Bigelow) Lindley
*Blephariglottis peramoena* (Gray) Rydberg = *Platanthera peramoena* (A. Gray) A. Gray
*Blephariglottis psycodes* (Linnaeus) Rydberg = *Platanthera psycodes* (Linnaeus) Lindley
*Calopogon pulchellus* var. *latifolius* (St. John) Fernald = *Calopogon tuberosus* (Linnaeus) Britton, Sterns, & Poggenberg
*Coeloglossum bracteatum* (Mühlenberg) *ex* Willdenow) Parlin = *Coeloglossum viride* (Linnaeus) Hartman var. *virescens* (Mühlenberg) Luer

*Coeloglossum viride* subsp. *bracteatum* (Mühlenberg *ex* Willdenow) Hultén = *Coeloglossum viride* (Linnaeus) Hartman var. *virescens* (Mühlenberg) Luer
*Corallorhiza corallorhiza* (Linnaeus) Karsten = *Corallorhiza trifida* Chatelain
*Corallorhiza maculata* subsp. *occidentalis* (Lindley) Cockerell = *Corallorhiza maculata* (Rafinesque) Rafinesque var. *occidentalis* (Lindley) Ames
*Corallorhiza multiflora* Nuttall = *Corallorhiza maculata* (Rafinesque) Rafinesque
*Corallorhiza pringlei* Greenman = *Corallorhiza odontorhiza* (Willdenow) Poiret var. *pringlei* (Greenman) Freudenstein
*Criosanthes arietina* (Aiton *f.*) House = *Cypripedium arietinum* R. Brown
*Cypripedium calceolus* Linnaeus ≠ *Cypripedium parviflorum* Salisbury var. *pubescens* (Willdenow) Knight
*Cypripedium calceolus* Linnaeus var. *parviflorum* (Salisbury) Fernald = *Cypripedium parviflorum* Salisbury var. *makasin* (Farwell) Sheviak
*Cypripedium calceolus* Linnaeus var. *parviflorum* (Salisbury) Fernald *p.p.* = *Cypripedium parviflorum* Salisbury var. *parviflorum*
*Cypripedium calceolus* Linnaeus var. *parviflorum* Salisbury *p.p.* = *Cypripedium parviflorum* Salisbury var. *makasin* (Farwell) Sheviak
*Cypripedium calceolus* Linnaeus var. *pubescens* (Willdenow) Correll = *Cypripedium parviflorum* Salisbury var. *pubescens* (Willdenow) Knight
*Cypripedium flavescens* de Candolle = *Cypripedium parviflorum* Salisbury var. *pubescens* (Willdenow) Knight
*Cypripedium pubescens* var. *makasin* Farwell = *Cypripedium parviflorum* Salisbury var. *makasin* (Farwell) Sheviak
*Cypripedium pubescens* Willdenow = *Cypripedium parviflorum* Salisbury var. *pubescens* (Willdenow) Knight
*Cypripedium spectabile* Salisbury = *Cypripedium reginae* Walter
*Cypripedium veganum* Cockerell & Barber = *Cypripedium parviflorum* Salisbury var. *pubescens* (Willdenow) Knight
*Cytherea bulbosa* (Linnaeus) House = *Calypso bulbosa* (Linnaeus) Oakes var. *americana* (R. Brown) Luer
*Dactylorhiza viridis* (Linnaeus) R.M. Bateman, A. Pridgeon & M.W. Chase = *Coeloglossum viride* (Linnaeus) Hartman
*Epipactis latifolia* (Linnaeus) Allioni = *Epipactis helleborine* (Linnaeus) Cranz
*Fissipes acaulis* (Aiton) Small = *Cypripedium acaule* Aiton
*Galeorchis spectabilis* (Linnaeus) Rydberg = *Galearis spectabilis* (Linnaeus) Rafinesque
*Goodyera decipiens* (Hooker) F.T. Hubbard = *Goodyera oblongifolia* Rafinesque
*Gyrostachys ochroleuca* Rydberg *ex* Britton = *Spiranthes ochroleuca* (Rydberg) Rydberg
*Gyrostachys stricta* Rydberg = *Spiranthes romanzoffiana* Chamisso
*Habenaria* ×*media* (Rydberg) Niles = *Platanthera huronensis* (Nuttall) Lindley
*Habenaria blephariglottis* (Willdenow) Hooker = *Platanthera blephariglottis* (Willdenow) Lindley
*Habenaria bracteata* (Mühlenberg *ex* Willdenow) R. Brown *ex* Aiton *f.* = *Coeloglossum viride* (Linnaeus) Hartman var. *virescens* (Mühlenberg) Luer

*Habenaria ciliaris* (Linnaeus) R. Brown = *Platanthera ciliaris* (Linnaeus) Lindley
*Habenaria clavellata* (Michaux) Sprengel = *Gymnadeniopsis clavellata* (Michaux) Rydberg
*Habenaria clavellata* var. *ophioglossoides* Fernald = *Gymnadeniopsis clavellata* (Michaux) Rydberg var. *ophioglossoides* (Fernald) W.J. Schrenk
*Habenaria cristata* (Michaux) R. Brown = *Platanthera cristata* (Michaux) Lindley
*Habenaria dilatata* (Pursh) Hooker var. *albiflora* (Chamisso) Correll = *Platanthera dilatata* (Pursh) Lindley var. *albiflora* (Chamisso) Ledebour
*Habenaria fimbriata* (Dryander) R. Brown *ex* Aiton = *Platanthera grandiflora* (Bigelow) Lindley
*Habenaria flava* (Linnaeus) R. Brown *ex* Sprengel = *Platanthera flava* (Linnaeus) Lindley var. *flava*
*Habenaria herbiola* R. Brown *ex* Aiton = *Platanthera flava* (Linnaeus) Lindley var. *flava*
*Habenaria flava* var. *herbiola* (R. Brown *ex* Aiton) Ames & Correll = *Platanthera flava* (Linnaeus) Lindley var. *herbiola* (R. Brown) Luer
*Habenaria flava* var. *virescens sensu* Fernald = *Platanthera flava* (Linnaeus) Lindley var. *herbiola* (R. Brown) Luer
*Habenaria grandiflora* (Bigelow) Torrey = *Platanthera grandiflora* (Bigelow) Lindley
*Habenaria herbiola* R. Brown *ex* Aiton = *Platanthera flava* (Linnaeus) Lindley var. *herbiola* (R. Brown) Luer
*Habenaria hookeri* Torrey = *Platanthera hookeri* (Torrey) Lindley
*Habenaria hyperborea* (Linnaeus) R. Brown *ex* Aiton ≠ *Platanthera aquilonis* Sheviak
*Habenaria hyperborea* (Linnaeus) R. Brown var. *huronensis* (Nuttall) Farwell = *Platanthera huronensis* (Nuttall) Lindley
*Habenaria integra* (Nuttall) Sprengel = *Gymnadeniopsis integra* (Nuttall) Rydberg
*Habenaria lacera* (Michaux) R. Brown = *Platanthera lacera* (Michaux) G. Don
*Habenaria leucophaea* (Nuttall) A. Gray = *Platanthera leucophaea* (Nuttall) Lindley
*Habenaria macrophylla* Goldie = *Platanthera macrophylla* (Goldie) P.M. Brown
*Habenaria nivea* (Nuttall) Sprengel = *Gymnadeniopsis nivea* Nuttall
*Habenaria obtusata* (Banks *ex* Pursh) Richards = *Platanthera obtusata* (Banks *ex* Pursh) Lindley
*Habenaria orbiculata* (Pursh) Torrey = *Platanthera orbiculata* (Pursh) Lindley
*Habenaria peramoena* A. Gray = *Platanthera peramoena* (A. Gray) A. Gray
*Habenaria psycodes* (Linnaeus) Sprengel = *Platanthera psycodes* (Linnaeus) Lindley
*Habenaria psycodes* (Linnaeus) Sprengel var. *grandiflora* (Bigelow) A. Gray = *Platanthera grandiflora* (Bigelow) Lindley
*Habenaria viridis* (Linnaeus) R. Brown *ex* Aiton *f.* = *Coeloglossum viride* (Linnaeus) Hartman var. *viride*
*Habenaria viridis* Linnaeus var. *bracteata* (Mühlenberg *ex* Willdenow) Reichenbach *ex* Gray = *Coeloglossum viride* (Linnaeus) Hartman var. *virescens* (Mühlenberg) Luer

*Ibidium beckii* (Lindley) House = *Spiranthes lacera* Rafinesque var. *gracilis* (Bigelow) Luer
*Ibidium beckii* House = *Spiranthes tuberosa* Rafinesque
*Ibidium cernuum* (Linnaeus) House = *Spiranthes cernua* (Linnaeus) L.C. Richard
*Ibidium gracile* (Bigelow) House = *Spiranthes lacera* (Rafinesque) Rafinesque var. *gracilis* (Bigelow) Luer
*Ibidium laciniatum* (Small) House = *Spiranthes laciniata* (Small) Ames
*Ibidium odoratum* (Nuttall) House = *Spiranthes odorata* (Nuttall) Lindley
*Ibidium plantagineum* (Rafinesque) House = *Spiranthes lucida* (H.H. Eaton) Ames
*Ibidium strictum* (Rydberg) House = *Spiranthes romanzoffiana* Chamisso
*Ibidium vernale* (Engelmann & A. Gray) House = *Spiranthes vernalis* Engelmann & A. Gray
*Isotria affinis* (Austin *ex* A. Gray) Rydberg = *Isotria medeoloides* (Pursh) Rafinesque
*Limnorchis dilatata* (Pursh) Rydberg *ex* Britton = *Platanthera dilatata* (Pursh) Lindley
*Limnorchis media* Rydberg = *Platanthera huronensis* (Nuttall) Lindley
*Limodorum tuberosum* Linnaeus = *Calopogon tuberosus* (Linnaeus) Britton Sterns & Poggenberg
*Malaxis unifolia* var. *bayardii* nom. nud. = *Malaxis bayardii* Fernald
*Microstylis unifolia* (Michaux) Britton, Sterns, & Poggenberg = *Malaxis unifolia* Michaux
*Neottia auriculata* (Wiegand) Szlachetko = *Listera auriculata* Wiegand
*Neottia australis* (Lindley) Szlachetko = *Listera australis* Lindley
*Neottia gracilis* Bigelow = *Spiranthes lacera* Rafinesque var. *gracilis* (Bigelow) Luer
*Neottia lacera* Rafinesque = *Spiranthes lacera* Rafinesque var. *lacera*
*Orchis rotundifolia* Banks *ex* Pursh = *Amerorchis rotundifolia* (Banks) Hultén
*Orchis spectabilis* Linnaeus = *Galearis spectabilis* (Linnaeus) Rafinesque
*Piperia dilatata* (Pursh) Szlachetko & P. Rutkowski = *Platanthera dilatata* (Pursh) Lindley var. *dilatata*
*Platanthera* ×*media* (Rydberg) Luer = *Platanthera huronensis* (Nuttall) Lindley
*Platanthera clavellata* (Michaux) Luer var. *clavellata* = *Gymnadeniopsis clavellata* (Michaux) Rydberg var. *clavellata*
*Platanthera clavellata* (Michaux) Luer var. *ophioglossoides* (Fernald) P.M. Brown = *Gymnadeniopsis clavellata* (Michaux) Rydberg var. *ophioglossoides* (Fernald) W.J. Schrenk
*Platanthera hyperborea* (Linnaeus) Lindley ≠ *Platanthera aquilonis* Sheviak
*Platanthera hyperborea* (Linnaeus) Lindley var. *huronensis* (Nuttall) Luer = *Platanthera huronensis* (Nuttall) Lindley
*Platanthera integra* (Nuttall) Luer = *Gymnadeniopsis integra* (Nuttall) Rydberg
*Platanthera nivea* (Nuttall) Luer = *Gymnadeniopsis nivea* Nuttall
*Platanthera orbiculata* var. *macrophylla* (Goldie) Luer = *Platanthera macrophylla* (Goldie) P.M. Brown
*Platanthera* ×*vossii* = X*Platanthopsis vossii* (Case) P.M. Brown

*Pogonia affinis* Austin *ex* A. Gray = *Isotria medeoloides* (Pursh) Rafinesque
*Pogonia verticillata* (Mühlenberg *ex* Willdenow) Nuttall = *Isotria verticillata* (Mühlenberg *ex* Willdenow) Rafinesque
*Spiranthes beckii* Lindley = *Spiranthes lacera* (Rafinesque) Rafinesque var. *gracilis* (Bigelow) Luer
*Spiranthes cernua* (Linnaeus) L.C. Richard var. *ochroleuca* (Rydberg) Ames = *Spiranthes ochroleuca* (Rydberg) Rydberg
*Spiranthes cernua* (Linnaeus) Richard var. *odorata* (Nuttall) Correll = *Spiranthes odorata* (Nuttall) Lindley
*Spiranthes gracilis* (Bigelow) Beck = *Spiranthes lacera* (Rafinesque) Rafinesque var. *gracilis* (Bigelow) Luer
*Spiranthes grayi* Ames = *Spiranthes tuberosa* Rafinesque
*Spiranthes intermedia* Ames ≠ *Spiranthes casei* Catling & Cruise var. *casei*
*Spiranthes plantaginea* Rafinesque = *Spiranthes lucida* (H.H. Eaton) Ames
*Spiranthes stricta* (Rydberg) A. Nelson *ex* J.M. Coulter & A. Nelson = *Spiranthes romanzoffiana* Chamisso
*Spiranthes tuberosa* var. *grayi* (Ames) Fernald = *Spiranthes tuberosa* Rafinesque
*Spiranthes vernalis* Engelmann & Gray ≠ *Spiranthes casei* Catling & Cruise
*Spiranthes ×steigeri* Correll = Spiranthes ochroleuca (Rydberg) Rydberg

# *Using Luer*

Additions, corrections, nomenclatural changes, and comments for Luer (1975), *The Native Orchids of the United States and Canada excluding Florida* as pertaining to *Wild Orchids of the Northeast*

For those fortunate enough to own or have access to a copy of Carlyle Luer's original work on the orchids of the United States and Canada, the following additions, corrections, and comments are assembled. These in no way should detract from the usefulness of this book but simply allow for more than twenty-five years of research and nomenclatural changes as well as for the addition of several species that had not been described as of the date of Luer's publication. Names of authors may be found in the text and checklist of this book. No attempt has been made to completely rework the keys or the index.

## Introduction

p. 12 for *Cypripedium calceolus* var. *planipetalum* read *Cypripedium parviflorum* var. *pubescens* extreme form; *Calopogon tuberosus* var. *latifolius* and var. *nanus* read dwarf forms; *P. hookeri* var. *abbreviata* read *P. hookeri* forma *abbreviata; P. obtusata* var. *collectanea* read *P. obtusata* forma *collectanea; P. orbiculata* var. *lehorsii* read *P. orbiculata* forma *lehorsii;* for *Cypripedium calceolus* var. *pubescens* read *Cypripedium parviflorum* var. *pubescens;* for *Malaxis monophyllos* var. *brachypoda* read *Malaxis brachypoda;* for *Platanthera hyperborea* read *Platanthera aquilonis*

## Text

p. 39, couplets 7, 8, see *Cypripedium* key in text on page 168

pp. 40–41, pl. 1:3,4, forma *albiflorum*

pp. 42–43, pl. 2:1, forma *albiflorum*

p. 44, for *Cypripedium calceolus* Linnaeus var. *pubescens* (Willdenow) Correll read *Cypripedium parviflorum* Salisbury var. *pubescens* (Willdenow) Knight

pp. 44–45, pl. 3

pp. 46–47, pl. 4, for *Cypripedium calceolus* var. *pubescens* read *Cypripedium parviflorum* var. *pubescens*

p. 48, for *Cypripedium calceolus* Linnaeus var. *parviflorum* Salisbury read *Cypripedium parviflorum* Salisbury var. *makasin* (Farwell) Sheviak

p. 49, for *Cypripedium ×andrewsii* Fuller read *Cypripedium ×andrewsii* Fuller nm *andrewsii;* for *Cypripedium ×favillianum* Curtis read C. *×andrewsii* Fuller nm *favillianum* (Curtis) Boivin; for C. *calceolus* var. *parviflorum* read *Cypripedium parviflorum* var. *makasin;* for C. *×landonii* read C. *×andrewsii* nm *landonii*

pp. 50,51, pl. 5:1,2, for *Cypripedium calceolus* var. *parviflorum* read *Cypripedium parviflorum* var. *makasin;* pl. 5:3,4,5, for *Cypripedium calceolus* Linnaeus var. *planipetalum* (Fernald) Victorin & Rousseau read C. *parviflorum* var. *pubescens* extreme expression

p. 52, map erroneously shows *Cypripedium candidum* in Connecticut

pp. 52–53, pl. 6:5, read *Cypripedium ×andrewsii* nm. *favillianum;* pl. 6:6, read *Cypripedium ×andrewsii* nm. *andrewsii*

pp. 56–57, pl. 8:5, for (*Cypripedium album*) read forma *albiflorum*

pp. 76–77, pl. 15:3, forma *viridens*

pp. 82–83, pl. 17:5, forma *viridis*

pp. 84–85, pl. 18:4, forma *viridens*

p. 99, couplet l0a, for S. *intermedia* read S. *casei*

p. 100, couplet 20, for S. *intermedia* read S. *casei*

p. l05, pl. 22:5, forma *albolabia*

p. 106, for *Spiranthes intermedia* read *Spiranthes casei* var. *casei*

p. 107, pl. 23:3–5, *Spiranthes casei* var. *casei*

p. 108, for *Spiranthes intermedia* Ames read *Spiranthes casei* Catling & Cruise var. *casei*

p. 114, read var. *ovalis*

p. 118, map incorrect; delete Newfoundland

p. 124, for *S. ×steigeri* read *S. ochroleuca*; photo is NOT *S. ochroleuca* but nonconforming *S. romanzoffiana*

p. 126, *S. ×steigeri* is a synonym for *S. ochroleuca*

pp. 144–145, pl. 35:7, forma *ophioides*

pp. 142–143, pl. 34:5, forma *reticulata*

pp. l44–145, pl. 35:7, forma *ophioides*

pp. 148–149, pl. 36:4, forma *willeyi;* 5, forma *gordinierii*; for *Cypripedium calceolus* var. *pubescens* read *Cypripedium parviflorum* var. *pubescens*

p. 178, couplet 22, for *P. orbiculata* var. *orbiculata* read *P. orbiculata*

p. 179, couplet 36, for *P. hyperborea* var. *hyperborea* read *P. aquilonis;* couplet 36a, for *P. hyperborea* var. *gracilis* read *P. huronensis;* couplet 37, for *P. hyperborea* var. *huronensis* read *P. huronensis;* couplet 37a, for *P. hyperborea* var. *viridiflora* read *P. huronensis;* couplet 34a, for *P. ×media* read *P. huronensis*

pp. 192–193, pl. 48:8,9; p. 194, for *Platanthera lacera* var. *terra-novae* read *Platanthera ×andrewsii*

pp. 196–197, pl. 49:8, forma *albiflora*

p. 200, maps erroneously show *Platanthera peramoena* in New York

pp. 215–216, pl. 57:4, for *Platanthera obtusata* var. *collectanea* read *Platanthera obtusata* forma *collectanea*

p. 218, for *Platanthera hookeri* var. *abbreviata* read forma *abbreviata*

pp. 220–221, pl. 59:1,2, for *Platanthera orbiculata* var. *orbiculata* read *Platanthera*

*orbiculata;* 3–4, for *Platanthera orbiculata* var. *macrophylla* read *Platanthera macrophylla*
pp. 220–221, pl. 59:3–6; p. 222, for *Platanthera orbiculata* var. *macrophylla* read *Platanthera macrophylla*
p. 222, for *Platanthera orbiculata* (Pursh) Lindley var. *macrophylla* (Goldie) Luer read *Platanthera macrophylla* (Goldie) P.M. Brown
p. 228, for *Platanthera hyperborea* (Linnaeus) Lindley var. *hyperborea* read *Platanthera aquilonis* Sheviak
p. 229, for *P.* ×*media* (Rydberg) Luer read *P. huronensis* (Nuttall) Lindley
pp. 230–231, for *Platanthera hyperborea* (Linnaeus) Lindley var. *huronensis* read *Platanthera huronensis* (Nuttall) Lindley; pl. 61:1,3,4, read *Platanthera aquilonis*; 5–8, read *Platanthera huronensis*
p. 232, for *Platanthera hyperborea* (Linnaeus) Lindley var. *gracilis* (Lindley) Luer read *Platanthera huronensis* (Nuttall) Lindley
p. 233, for *Platanthera hyperborea* (Linnaeus) Lindley var. *viridiflora* (Chamisso) Luer read *Platanthera huronensis* (Nuttall) Lindley
pp. 234, 235, pl. 62:1–5, read *Platanthera huronensis*
pp. 270, 271, pl. 74:1, forma *albolabia*
pp. 304, 305, pl. 85:2,3, for *Malaxis monophyllos* var. *brachypoda* read *Malaxis brachypoda*
pp. 318, 319, pl. 89:1,9, *Corallorhiza maculata* var. *occidentalis* forma *immaculata*
pp. 320–321, pl. 90:3, forma *albolabia*
pp. 324–325, pl. 92:4, forma *eburnea*
pp. 338–339, pl. 96, forma *albiflora*

The following taxa found within the Northeast are not treated in *The Native Orchids of the United States and Canada excluding Florida*:
*Corallorhiza maculata* var. *occidentalis*
*Corallorhiza odontorhiza* var. *pringlei*
*Cypripedium parviflorum* var. *parviflorum*
*Platanthera pallida*
*Platanthera* ×*keenanii*
X*Platanthopsis vossii* (Case)
*Spiranthes ovalis* var. *erostellata*
*Spiranthes* ×*borealis*
*Spiranthes* ×*simpsonii*

# *Cryptic Species, Species Pairs, and Varietal Pairs*

When two species or varieties appear to be very closely related and have a similar morphology they are often referred to as species or varietal pairs. Although not necessarily a scientific or taxonomic term the designation is often helpful in recognizing two species that are often difficult to determine whether in the field or in the herbaria. Their taxonomic history usually involves synonyms and/or recognition at different taxonomic levels, i.e., subspecies, varieties, or rarely forma. Validation of the two taxa at species level usually involves studies of pollinators, habit, habitat, range, morphology, and, in more recent years, DNA analyses. Several excellent species pairs exist for the Northeast as well as varietal pairs. Fortunately a few simple morphological characters easily separate the taxa. In each case these are characters found within the key to the species; also, range and habitat are often well separated.

*Corallorhiza maculata* var. *maculata*
**spotted coralroot**
*Corallorhiza maculata* var. *occidentalis*
**western spotted coralroot**
Differ in the shape of the lip and degree of spreading of the tepals; ranges overlap but var. *occidentalis* usually flowers earlier than var. *maculata*

*Corallorhiza odontorhiza* var. *odontorhiza*
**autumn coralroot**
*Corallorhiza odontorhiza* var. *pringlei*
**Pringle's autumn coralroot**
Differ in shape of lip and openness of flower—i.e., cleistogamous vs. chasmogamous; also, range very limited for var. *pringlei*

*Cypripedium parviflorum* var. *parviflorum*
**southern small yellow lady's-slipper**
*Cypripedium parviflorum* var. *makasin*
**northern small yellow lady's-slipper**
*Cypripedium parviflorum* var. *pubescens*
large yellow lady's-slipper
Range differences, with var. *parviflorum* basically southeastern, var. *makasin* northern, and var. *pubescens* throughout much of the United States and Canada; subtle differences in coloration of petals and sepals, shape of lip, and habitat

*Malaxis bayardii* Fernald
**Bayard's adder's-mouth**
Very rare on the east coastal states and southwestern Nova Scotia; found either in sandy Coastal Plain areas or in rocky uplands in the Appalachian foothills.
Flowers yellow-green, persistent after pollination, raceme broadly cylindrical, prominent auricles on lip
*Malaxis unifolia* Michaux
**green adder's-mouth**
Flowers mint-green, withering after pollination, inflorescence a broadened panicle, auricles not prominent on lip; wide-ranging throughout the eastern half of North America. Because of the tiny flowers on these two species of *Malaxis* the floral characters are difficult to see. The shape of the inflorescence and persistent flowers are a great aid.
See descriptions on pages 140 and 144 for details.

*Platanthera aquilonis*
**northern green bog orchis**
*Platanthera huronensis*
**green bog orchis**
Differ in lip shape and color pollination biology and somewhat in habit and habitat; ranges overlap throughout.

*Platanthera grandiflora* (Bigelow) Lindley
Synonym: *Habenaria psycodes* var. *grandiflora*
**large purple fringed orchis**
flowers eventually all open at the same time; racemes 3–5 cm in diameter, spur orifice rounded
*Platanthera psycodes* (Linnaeus) Lindley
**small purple fringed orchis**
flowers opening sequentially; racemes 1–1.5 cm in diameter, spur orifice a transverse dumbbell
Within the range of this book these two species frequently grow sympatrically in eastern Canada and form hybrid swarms often with *Platanthera lacera*. In the western and southern portions of their ranges they are much more easily distinguished. DO NOT be misled by overall size, especially height. Although the flowers of *P. psycodes* are generally smaller than those of *P. grandiflora*, be sure to check the shape of the spur opening. The more slender tapering racemes of *P. psycodes*, with the lower flowers withering before the upper flowers open, are in contrast to the stocky racemes of *P. grandiflora* with all of the flowers eventually open and in good condition.
See descriptions on pages 166 and 186 for details.

*Platanthera orbiculata* (Pursh) Lindley
**pad-leaved orchis**
average spur length less than 28 mm; petals erect
*Platanthera macrophylla* (Goldie) P.M. Brown
**Goldie's pad-leaved orchis**
*Platanthera orbiculata* (Pursh) Lindley var. *macrophylla* (Goldie) Luer
average spur length greater than 28 mm; petals nearly falcate

The superficial similarity between these two species has led many authors to simply combine them; therefore the ranges and identification criteria are merged and only continue the confusion. Perhaps the most important criterion to remember is that, except for the length of the spur, size DOES NOT count. The leaves may be larger in diameter in *P. orbiculata* and the stem may be taller in *P. macrophylla*. This is often not the case but do not be misled by overall size. The primary criteria are the length of the spur and the shape and position of the petals.

See descriptions on pages 176 and 180 for details.

*Platanthera cristata* Lindley
**orange crested orchis**
*Platanthera pallida* P.M. Brown
**pale fringed orchis**
Although viewed by others (Sheviak, FNA) as a cline of *Platanthera cristata*, *P. pallida* has many distinct characters. Apart form the coloration (and there is a pale form of *P. cristata*), the recurved lip and small spur size are distinctive. The restricted range, local abundance, and near xeric habitat are also helpful.
See descriptions on pages 158 and 182 for details.

*Spiranthes lacera* var. *lacera*
**northern slender ladies'-tresses**
*Spiranthes lacera* var. *gracilis*
**southern slender ladies'-tresses**
These two very similar varieties often overlap their ranges in southern New England and adjacent New York, with both varieties having disjunct sites north and south of their respective ranges. The well-spaced flowers on var. *lacera* contrast with the crowded flowers of var. *gracilis*. The leaves are usually present at flowering time in var. *lacera* and usually absent at flowering time in var. *gracilis*. From a floral standpoint the lip on var. *gracilis* is broader and more crisped and with a more distinctive green throat; that of var. *lacera* is narrower and therefore the green throat is not as prominent. The sepals on var. *lacera* are approximate to appressed whereas on var. *gracilis* they are nearly spreading, giving the flower a larger overall appearance.

# *Part 4*

## Orchid Hunting

# 1. The Northwoods: Bog, Fen, and Boreal Forest

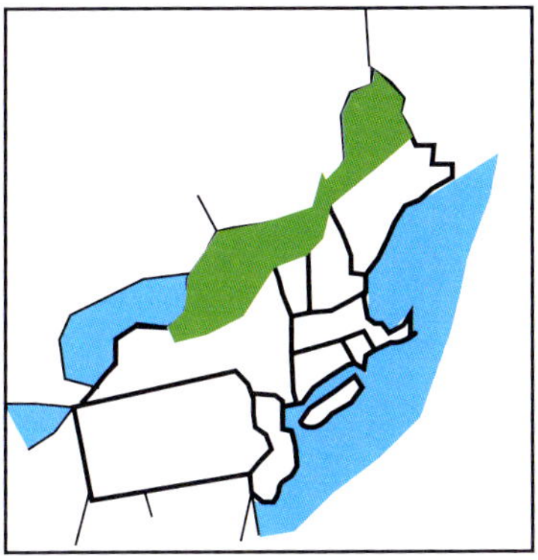

The Northwoods of northern New England and New York is rich in both animal and plant species. Although accessibility may present some problems, any effort is worthwhile and will always be rewarded. Orchid hunting here is often along roadsides and always plentiful. Much of the habitat is boreal forest, black spruce bog, and the occasional fen. In Aroostook County, Maine, Orleans County, Vermont, and much of northern New York State, limestone predominates and fens are frequent.

Species known from northern New England and New York, although several from New York are historical records, include:

*Amerorchis rotundifolia*, small round-leaved orchis
*Arethusa bulbosa*, dragon's-mouth
*Calopogon tuberosus*, common grass-pink
*Calypso bulbosa* var. *americana*, eastern fairy slipper
*Coeloglossum viride* var. *virescens*, long bracted green orchis
*Corallorhiza maculata* var. *maculata*, spotted coralroot
*Corallorhiza maculata* var. *occidentalis*, eastern spotted coralroot
*Corallorhiza striata*, striped coralroot
*Corallorhiza trifida*, early coralroot
*Cypripedium acaule*, pink lady's-slipper
*Cypripedium arietinum*, ram's-head lady's-slipper
*Cypripedium parviflorum* var. *makasin*, northern small yellow lady's-slipper
*Cypripedium parviflorum* var. *pubescens*, large yellow lady's-slipper
*Cypripedium reginae*, showy lady's-slipper
*Epipactis helleborine*, broad-leaved helleborine*
*Galearis spectabilis*, showy orchis
*Goodyera oblongifolia*, giant rattlesnake orchis
*Goodyera pubescens*, downy rattlesnake orchis
*Goodyera repens*, lesser rattlesnake orchis
*Goodyera tesselata*, checkered rattlesnake orchis

*Gymnadeniopsis clavellata* var. *clavellata*, little club-spur orchis
*Gymnadeniopsis clavellata* var. *ophioglossoides*, northern club-spur orchis
*Liparis loeselii*, Loesel's twayblade; fen orchis
*Listera auriculata*, auricled twayblade
*Listera australis*, southern twayblade
*Listera convallarioides*, broad-lipped twayblade
*Listera cordata*, heart-leaved twayblade
*Malaxis brachypoda*, white adder's-mouth
*Malaxis unifolia*, green adder's-mouth
*Platanthera aquilonis*, northern green bog orchis
*Platanthera blephariglottis*, northern white fringed orchis
*Platanthera dilatata*, tall white northern bog orchis; bog candles
*Platanthera flava* var. *herbiola*, northern tubercled orchis
*Platanthera grandiflora*, large purple fringed orchis
*Platanthera hookeri*, Hooker's orchis
*Platanthera huronensis*, green bog orchis
*Platanthera lacera*, green fringed orchis; ragged orchis
*Platanthera macrophylla*, Goldie's pad-leaved orchis
*Platanthera obtusata*, blunt-leafed orchis
*Platanthera orbiculata*, pad-leaved orchis
*Platanthera psycodes*, small purple fringed orchis
*Pogonia ophioglossoides*, rose pogonia
*Spiranthes casei* var. *casei*, Case's ladies'-tresses
*Spiranthes cernua*, nodding ladies'-tresses
*Spiranthes lacera* var. *lacera*, northern slender ladies'-tresses
*Spiranthes lacera* var. *gracilis*, southern slender ladies'-tresses
*Spiranthes lucida*, shining ladies'-tresses
*Spiranthes ochroleuca*, yellow ladies'-tresses
*Spiranthes romanzoffiana*, hooded ladies'-tresses

The premier orchid county in all of New England is Aroostook County, Maine. Forty-two species of wild orchids have been counted in this, the largest county in Maine. Two opposing areas present most of the orchids. They are the Crystal Bog region in southwestern Aroostook County and the Caribou–Fort Kent region in the northern reaches of the county. The Maine chapter of The Nature Conservancy owns much of Crystal Bog, thus it is private property. Permission to enter the portion owned by TNC must be secured in advance. There are many adjacent areas open to hiking and snowmobile trails that do provide excellent orchid habitat. In addition there are several small black spruce-tamarack bogs and a few fens nearby that are also worth exploring. Because of the size of Crystal Bog, also known locally as 10,000-Acre Bog, there are several fens present. It is in these fens that the orchids are most prolific. Northern white cedar swamps border the wettest areas and provide additional habitat.

Starting in mid-June the bogs and fens come alive with thousands of *Arethusa bulbosa*, the dragon's-mouth, and slowly progress in early July to widespread colonies of *Calopogon tuberosus*, the common grass-pink, and *Pogonia ophioglossoides*, the rose pogonia. Back in the northern white cedars late May and early June harbor a few scattered *Calypso bulbosa* var. *americana*, the eastern fairy slipper, and scattered clumps of *Corallorhiza trifida*, the early coralroot. On the sunnier edges of the cedar swamps can be found *Platanthera hookeri*, Hooker's orchis, often growing with rosettes of *Goodyera repens*, the lesser rattlesnake orchis, and flowering plants of *Corallorhiza maculata* var. *occidentalis*, the western spotted coralroot; *Cypripedium acaule*, the pink lady's-slipper, and in damp thickets large clumps of *C. parviflorum* var. *pubescens*, the large yellow lady's-slipper. By early July the first of the summer orchids are coming into flower and, in a variety of habitats, include *Coeloglossum viride* var. *virescens*, the long bracted green orchis; *Corallorhiza maculata* var. *maculata*, the spotted coralroot; *Cypripedium reginae*, the showy lady's-slipper; *Liparis loeselii*, Loesel's twayblade or fen orchis; *Platanthera aquilonis*, the northern green bog orchis; *P. dilatata*, the tall white northern bog orchis; *P. huronensis*, the green bog orchis, and *P. obtusata*, the blunt-leafed orchis.

Toward the end of July, although many of these previous species will still be in good condition, three twayblades may be found: *Listera auriculata*, the auricled twayblade, the rarest of the trio, *L. convallarioides*, the broad-lipped twayblade, and *L. cordata*, the heart-leaved twayblade, which is the most frequently encountered *Listera* in northern New England. It is just north of the main bog area that both of the rare *Listera* species grow and the even less frequently encountered hybrid, *L.* ×*veltmanii* may be found. The spectacular showy lady'-slipper, *Cypripedium reginae*, may be found at this time in scattered bogs and fens throughout much of Aroostook County.

In and around many of the local bogs *Gymnadeniopsis clavellata* var. *clavellata*, the little club-spur orchis; *Malaxis unifolia*, the green adder's-mouth; *Platanthera blephariglottis*, the northern white fringed orchis; *P. grandiflora*, the large purple fringed orchis; *P. lacera*, the green fringed or ragged orchis; *P. macrophylla*, Goldie's pad-leaved orchis; *P. orbiculata*, the pad-leaved orchis; *P. psycodes*, the small purple fringed orchis, and *Spiranthes lacera* var. *lacera*, the northern slender ladies'-tresses, will all be in fine bloom and just waiting for the observant explorer. In most of the limey woodlands the only non-native species, *Epipactis helleborine*, the broad-leaved helleborine, will just be starting to flower, coming into its best throughout August.

Early August also presents the prime attraction of Crystal Bog: *Platanthera leucophaea*, the eastern prairie fringed orchis. Known from this area for nearly a hundred years, it is sporadic and capricious. Although it has been estimated that perhaps as many as a hundred plants are growing in the Crystal Bog area, only a handful MIGHT flower in any given year. Plants are carefully monitored and precise locations confidentially mapped.

The other species-rich area is found in the northern part of Aroostook County from Caribou north to Fort Kent. Here the combination of dense, old, northern white cedar woodlands and swamps, open bogs, and secluded fens as well as the mighty Aroostook and St. John Rivers all combine to provide a delight of habitats for many species of orchids as well as several other exceedingly rare flowering plants.

About ten days later than the Crystal area, the bogs and fens of Caribou, Perham, and Woodland present a similar list. The nearby forests are alive with thousands of *Cypripedium parviflorum* var. *pubescens*, large yellow lady's-slipper, and they often line the old railroad right-of-ways. In the wetlands there are many of the same species as presented at Crystal; in addition the list includes *Amerorchis rotundifolia*, the small round-leafed orchis, much sought after by orchid enthusiasts and now known from a handful of sites in Aroostook and Penobscot counties.

Passing northward are woodlots with *Goodyera oblongifolia*, the giant rattlesnake orchis, seriously depleted in recent years so very few sites remain; *Coeloglossum viride* var. *virescens*, the long bracted green orchis; *Corallorhiza maculata* var. *occidentalis*, the western spotted coralroot, and large colonies of *Platanthera hookeri*, Hooker's orchis. The scoured riverbanks of the Aroostook River yield surprisingly resilient colonies of *P. flava* var. *herbiola*, the northern tubercled orchis; *P. grandiflora*, the large purple fringed orchis; *P. psycodes*, the small purple fringed orchis; *Spiranthes lucida*, the shining ladies'-tresses, and, a bit later in the season, *S. romanzoffiana*, the hooded ladies'-tresses. A true national treasure, Aroostook County is an orchidist's paradise.

Although not nearly as delicious as northern Maine, Coos County, New Hampshire, with its calcareous shales and damp meadows is one of the most beautiful areas in that state. North of the Presidential Range and towering Mt. Washington, it is not unusual to find both species of purple fringed orchises, *Platanthera psycodes*, the small purple fringed orchis, and *P. grandiflora*, and the large purple fringed orchis, along roadsides. In late August a quintet of fine ladies'-tresses offers themselves for examination.

*Spiranthes casei* var. *casei*, Case's ladies'-tresses; *S. cernua*, the nodding ladies'-tresses; *S. lacera* var. *lacera*, northern slender ladies'-tresses; *S. ochroleuca*, the yellow ladies'-tresses, and *S. romanzoffiana*, the hooded ladies'-tresses, may all be found in and around Colebrook, New Hampshire, often growing in genus communities that allow for careful comparison of the species. North of Colebrook in Pittsburg is one of the few places in New Hampshire where you can find *Listera auriculata* growing beside the road at a stream crossing. Just watch out for the moose!

The Northeast Kingdom of Vermont is also a mix of limestone and calcareous shales and therefore supports many of the same orchids found around Colebrook, New Hampshire. But it also offers the spectacular scenery of Lake Willoughby and the orchid-rich woodlands that form the base of Mt. Pisgah on the eastern side of the lake. These steep-sloped woodlands, complete with soaring peregrine falcons above, were known as the Garden of Eden in times past and still support a paradise of orchids, ferns, and other native plants. Easily accessible by well-used trails in the woodlands and parking areas along the lake, some of the orchids you would expect to see within a mile or two of the main parking lot at the south end of the lake are *Calypso bulbosa* var. *americana*, the eastern fairy slipper; *Coeloglossum viride* var. *virescens*, the long bracted green orchis; *Corallorhiza maculata* var. *maculata*, the spotted coralroot; *C. maculata* var. *occidentalis*, the western spotted coralroot; *C. trifida*, the early coralroot; *Cypripedium acaule*, the pink lady's-slipper; *C. arietinum*, the ram's-head lady's-slipper; *C. parviflorum* var. *makasin*, the northern small yellow lady's-slipper; *C. parviflorum* var. *pubescens*, the large yellow lady's-slipper; *C. reginae*, the showy lady's-slipper; *Epipactis helleborine*, the broad-leaved helleborine; *Goodyera tesselata*, the checkered rattlesnake orchis; *Liparis loeselii*, Loesel's twayblade or fen orchis; *Listera convallarioides*, the broad-lipped twayblade; *L. cordata*, the heart-leaved twayblade; *Malaxis brachypoda*, the white adder's-mouth; *M. unifolia*, the green adder's-mouth; *Platanthera aquilonis*, the northern green bog orchis; *P. dilatata*, the tall white northern bog orchis; *P. hookeri*, Hooker's orchis; *P. huronensis*, the green bog orchis; *P. macrophylla*, Goldie's pad-leaved orchis; *P. orbiculata*, the pad-leaved orchis; *Spiranthes casei* var. *casei*, Case's ladies'-tresses; *S. cernua*, the nodding ladies'-tresses; *S. lacera* var. *lacera*, the northern slender ladies'-tresses, and *S. romanzoffiana*, the hooded ladies'-tresses. The wet roadside ditches are especially good for the many species of *Spiranthes*. Remember that although not all of the species flower at the same time, a trip in late May–early June, one in mid-July, and another in late August–early September should find all of these orchids in flower.

The northwoods of the Adirondack Mountains and calcareous alvars and woodlands approaching Lake Ontario in northern New York State offer a more limited selection of orchids, and also have many more acres of unexplored orchid wilderness. Some of the highlights would be *Cypripedium arietinum*, the ram's-head lady's-slipper; *C. parviflorum* var. *pubescens*, the large yellow lady's-slipper; *C. reginae*, the showy lady's-slipper; *Goodyera repens*, the lesser rattlesnake orchis; *Listera auriculata*, the auricled twayblade; *L. australis*, the southern twayblade; *L. convallarioides*, the broad-lipped twayblade; *L. cordata*, the heart-leaved twayblade, and *Spiranthes casei* var. *casei*, Case's ladies'-tresses. Many of these are very local in distribution and occur as individuals or in small colonies.

Three choice species are documented as historical occurrences and have not been seen in many years: *Amerorchis rotundifolia*, the small round-leaf orchis; *Calypso bulbosa* var. *americana*, the eastern fairy slipper, and *Platanthera leucophaea*, the eastern prairie fringed orchis. Although a bit further south than we have been discussing, *Corallorhiza striata*, the striped coralroot, may still be found in a cold swamp near Cazenovia, New York. With the survival of this rare species perhaps some of the other three historical species will yet to be rediscovered.

# 2. Connecticut River Valley

The lushness and diversity of the Connecticut River Valley ranges from the northwoods and boreal forest of northernmost New Hampshire and Vermont southward through the broad floodplains and oxbows of central New Hampshire and the rich, rocky shores of Vermont, oceanward through ancient red rock and clay fossil lands of Connecticut, to the fertile farmlands of the Connecticut coast near New London. In all of these areas orchids abound and the diversity is amazing, much of it due to the varied geology of the region. The schists and shales of the north give way to basalts and limestones, especially in Vermont, and then sandstones and traprock ridges in central Connecticut. Understanding the soil requirement of the various species of orchids then helps to pinpoint the areas where the plants will be most at home. Dotted along this riverine route are many hills and mountains, most notably as we enter Massachusetts, with Toby, Tom, Holyoke, and Norwottuck in the Amherst area. Meriden Mountain, an extensive traprock ridge south of Hartford, is one of Connecticut's best orchid habitats. Another aspect of this region is the presence of the coastal plain influence in isolated islands that continue nearly to southern Vermont.

Some of the species that may be seen in various areas in the Connecticut Valley:

*Aplectrum hyemale*, putty-root
*Arethusa bulbosa*, dragon's-mouth
*Calopogon tuberosus*, common grass-pink
*Coeloglossum viride* var. *virescens*, long-bracted green orchis
*Corallorhiza maculata* var. *maculata*, spotted coralroot
*Corallorhiza maculata* var. *occidentalis*, western spotted coralroot
*Corallorhiza odontorhiza* var. *odontorhiza*, autumn coralroot
*Corallorhiza odontorhiza* var. *pringlei*, Pringle's autumn coralroot
*Corallorhiza trifida*, early coralroot
*Cypripedium acaule*, pink lady's-slipper
*Cypripedium arietinum*, ram's-head lady's-slipper
*Cypripedium parviflorum* var. *parviflorum*, southern small yellow lady's-slipper

*Cypripedium parviflorum* var. *makasin*, northern small yellow lady's-slipper
*Cypripedium parviflorum* var. *pubescens*, large yellow lady's-slipper
*Cypripedium reginae,* showy lady's-slipper
*Epipactis helleborine,* broad-leaved helleborine*
*Galearis spectabilis*, showy orchis
*Goodyera pubescens*, downy rattlesnake orchis
*Goodyera repens*, lesser rattlesnake orchis
*Goodyera tesselata*, checkered rattlesnake orchis
*Gymnadeniopsis clavellata* var. *clavellata*, little club-spur orchis
*Isotria medeoloides,* small whorled pogonia
*Isotria verticillata,* large whorled pogonia
*Liparis liliifolia*, lily-leaved twayblade
*Liparis loeselii*, Loesel's twayblade
*Listera convallarioides*, broad-lipped twayblade
*Listera cordata,* heart-leaved twayblade
*Malaxis bayardii*, Bayard's adder's-mouth
*Malaxis brachypoda,* white adder's-mouth
*Malaxis unifolia*, green adder's-mouth
*Platanthera aquilonis*, northern green bog orchis
*Platanthera blephariglottis*, northern white fringed orchis
*Platanthera ciliaris*, orange fringed orchis
*Platanthera dilatata*, white bog orchis; bog candles
*Platanthera flava* var. *herbiola*, northern tubercled orchis
*Platanthera grandiflora*, large purple fringed orchis
*Platanthera hookeri*, Hooker's orchis
*Platanthera huronensis*, green bog orchis
*Platanthera lacera*, green fringed orchis; ragged orchis
*Platanthera macrophylla*, Goldie's pad-leaved orchis
*Platanthera obtusata*, blunt-leafed rein orchis
*Platanthera orbiculata*, pad-leaved orchis
*Platanthera psycodes*, small purple fringed orchis
*Pogonia ophioglossoides*, rose pogonia
*Spiranthes casei* var. *casei*, Case's ladies'-tresses
*Spiranthes cernua*, nodding ladies'-tresses
*Spiranthes lacera* var. *lacera*, northern slender ladies'-tresses
*Spiranthes lacera* var. *gracilis*, southern slender ladies'-tresses
*Spiranthes lucida*, shining ladies'-tresses
*Spiranthes ochroleuca*, yellow ladies'-tresses
*Spiranthes romanzoffiana*, hooded ladies'-tresses
*Spiranthes vernalis*, grass-leaved ladies'-tresses
*Triphora trianthophora*, three birds orchid

In the far north the Connecticut River is just a stream originating from the Connecticut Lakes. Here in Pittsburg and just south in Colebrook, New Hampshire, excellent orchid territory may be found. The two specialties of the area are, in Pittsburg, the auricled twayblade, *Listera auriculata*, and in Colebrook, Case's ladies'-

tresses, *Spiranthes casei*. Although several other orchids may be found, including large numbers of both large and small purple fringed orchis, *Platanthera grandiflora* and *P. psycodes*; *P. obtusata*, the blunt-leafed rein orchis; *Spiranthes romanzoffiana*, the hooded ladies'-tresses, and various bog orchids and other ladies'-tresses, it is for these two specialties that many make the trek to the far north.

Working our way southward to the confluence of the White River near White River Junction and Queechee, Vermont, and Hanover, New Hampshire, large stands of showy lady's-slippers, *Cypripedium reginae*, may be seen in late June, often accompanied by tall white northern bog orchis, *Platanthera dilatata*; northern green bog orchis, *P. aquilonis*; Loesel's twayblade, *Liparis loeselii*; *Malaxis brachypoda*, white adder's-mouth; *Listera cordata*, heart-leaved twayblade, and the green adder's-mouth, *Malaxis unifolia*.

One of the more interesting orchid sites along the Connecticut River is just below the dam at North Walpole/Bellow's Falls where the shining ladies'-tresses, *Spiranthes lucida*, grows. Here, in a jumble of giant boulders, it is nestled in grassy pockets at the edge of the river.

Further south the soils become more acidic and some of the more southerly species start to appear. Not far from Brattleboro can be found the three birds orchis, *Triphora trianthophora*, and across the river in New Hampshire a disjunct site for the large whorled pogonia, *Isotria verticillata*. Rocky shorelines along the river have recently been found to host the northern tubercled orchis, *Platanthera flava* var. *herbiola*, and in many of the grassy meadows and floodplains of the oxbows along the river the common rose pogonia, *Pogonia ophioglossoides*, and small purple fringed orchis, *Platanthera psycodes*, may appear.

Just east of the Connecticut River and north of Amherst in Massachusetts lies a series of large hills known collectively as Mount Toby. The geologic formations here, including extensive limestone, coupled with great diversity in habitats, have historically brought forth a wide variety of orchids and continue to do so.

Rising south of Amherst is an area known as The Notch. It is the highest point on Route 116 as it travels south through the Holyoke Range. Several named mountains and hills dot this area, the most notable being Mount Norwottuck, which is just east of The Notch. A mixture of rich mesic forest and rocky woodlands and outcrops covers the hillsides.

Thirty-five species have been recorded from these two areas. The Mount Toby region, with 34 of those species, is by far the richer of the two. The other species have been found only in the vicinity of The Notch, which has a total of 14 species—a respectable number for a small area.

The individual species flower for the same length of time here as they do in northern Vermont, but because they are farther south the number of species in bloom at one time is not as great. As you travel farther north, or into higher elevations, the blooming times tend to overlap. Although flowering time covers a longer span here, a well-chosen day can yield several species in prime condition. The third week in May starts off the orchid season with three lady's-slippers: the large yellow, *Cypripedium parviflorum* var. *pubescens*, the pink, *C. acaule*, and the very rare ram's-head, *C. arietinum*. Large yellows are scattered throughout both areas in the richer deciduous forests typified by mature sugar maples and scattered birches and beeches. Pink lady's-slippers are more common in the acidic oak and pine woods. The only current Massachusetts site for ram's-head lady's-slipper is on Mount Toby. Historically it was reported from several sites in the region but well documented only in one area, above Roaring Brook Falls. Unfortunately, extensive searches have not revealed it there for some time. The current site is, of necessity, a well-kept secret. It is hoped that as more people search for ram's-head, additional sites for this most elusive of our slipper orchids will turn up.

Showy orchis, *Galearis spectabilis*, long bracted green orchis, *Coeloglossum viride* var. *virescens*, and Hooker's orchis, *Platanthera hookeri*, are often found growing in the company of the yellow lady's-slippers. Cooler and damper areas may also host early coralroot, *Corallorhiza trifida*. By late May and early June southern small yellow lady's-slipper, *Cypripedium parviflorum* var. *parviflorum*, and large whorled pogonia, *Isotria verticillata*, are in flower in The Notch area and on Mount Toby. The large whorled pogonia colony growing at The Notch has nearly one thousand stems. Late May and early June is also the time when the small whorled pogonia, *Isotria medeoloides*, should bloom, if we could only find it again. It was found at The Notch in the early 1900s but has not been seen there since, although it does grow in nearby Springfield. Putty-root, *Aplectrum hyemale*, was seen through the 1930s and 1940s at The Notch, but extensive searches since then have failed to turn up any plants, although the species has recently been reported from Mount Toby.

Before local flooding expanded and covered the bog at Cranberry Pond, north of Toby, dragon's-mouth, *Arethusa bulbosa*, rose pogonia, *Pogonia ophioglossoides*, and grass-pink, *Calopogon tuberosus*, could be found there. The latter two still grow near the pond and in wet, mossy pockets under a few power lines, but dragon's-mouths have yet to reappear.

Late June through midsummer brings a succession of blooms. The two pad-leaved orchises, *Platanthera macrophylla* and *P. orbiculata*, spotted coralroot, *Corallorhiza maculata* var. *maculata*, broad leaved helleborine, *Epipactis helleborine*, both downy and checkered rattlesnake orchises, *Goodyera pubescens* and *G. tesselata*, lily-leaved and Loesel's twayblades, *Liparis liliifolia* and *L. loeselii*, northern tubercled orchis, *Platanthera flava* var. *herbiola*, large and small purple fringed orchises, *P. grandiflora* and *P. psycodes*, and green fringed orchises, *P. lacera*, all grow throughout the Toby and Notch areas, and with a little background reading on habitat and time of bloom, the intrepid orchid hunter has more than a fair chance of finding them. This is one of the few areas in Massachusetts where western spotted coralroot, *Corallorhiza maculata* var. *occidentalis*, has been documented. Look for it mid-June to early July. The blooming times of this variety and spotted coralroot are usually well separated, but examine the diagnostic characters of the lip to be certain.

Autumn produces few orchids, but Mount Toby and The Notch offer a good selection of ladies'-tresses, *Spiranthes* spp., and autumn coralroot, *Corallorhiza odontorhiza* var. *odontorhiza*. Both slender ladies'-tresses, *Spiranthes lacera* var. *lacera* and S. *lacera* var. *gracilis*, have been recorded in the Toby region in August, and by September the nodding and yellow ladies'-tresses, S. *cernua* and S. *ochroleuca*, are in bloom. Autumn coralroot is an inconspicuous and elusive little orchid that favors rich woods and, at Toby, vernal streambeds. It is in no way spectacular, but it has a very special charm and delicate beauty.

Perhaps the saddest loss at Mount Toby is the extirpation of the showy lady's-slipper, *Cypripedium reginae*. The decline and eventual disappearance of this spectacular orchid can be directly attributed to gross over-collecting by the many colleges in the Connecticut Valley for herbarium specimens and for their "botanical" gardens. The Greene Swamp area, where *C. reginae* used to grow, still supports a wide variety of orchids, but careful searches have not yet found any more of this ravished queen.

Along southern Connecticut's coastal plain near New London, late May brings surprising quantities of pink lady's-slipper, *Cypripedium acaule*, in the predominant oak-pine woodlands; it is not unusual to find large colonies of several hundred plants. White-flowered forms are scattered here and there. Inland from the immediate coast these woodlands may also have stands of large whorled pogonia, *Isotria verticillata*, among the pink slippers. Connecticut records for *Malaxis bayardii*, Bayard's adder's-mouth, are not far from here as well.

By mid- to late June, rose pogonia, *Pogonia ophioglossoides*, and grass-pink, *Calopogon tuberosus*, are creating pink swaths along roadsides, in borrow pits, and in interdunal swales. Also at this time scattered sites along the coast will reveal stands of northern tubercled orchis, *Platanthera flava* var. *herbiola*, with its fragrant, greenish-yellow flowers. Large purple fringed orchis, *P. grandiflora*, is usually in bloom by July 1st, followed a month later by the small purple fringed orchis, *P. psycodes*.

Late July and early August is prime orchid time in the southern coastal plain. Within one week you may see four fringed orchises: northern white, *Platanthera blephariglottis*, orange, *P. ciliaris*, green, *P. lacera*, and small purple, *P. psycodes*; three ladies'-tresses: grass-leaved, *Spiranthes vernalis*, northern slender, *S. lacera* var. *lacera*, and southern slender, *S. lacera* var. *gracilis*; little club-spur orchis, *Gymnadeniopsis clavellata* var. *clavellata*; spotted coralroot, *Corallorhiza maculata* var. *maculata*; broad-leaved helleborine, *Epipactis helleborine*, and downy rattlesnake orchis, *Goodyera pubescens*—eleven species or varieties in a heavily populated and very accessible area. Some are more common than others, of course. The various *Spiranthes*, which are more common, seem to favor dry, grassy roadsides and cemeteries, and the assorted *Platanthera* species are often found in old cranberry bogs and in wet areas under wet power lines.

The rare orange fringed orchis, known from only a few sites in southern Rhode Island and south central Connecticut, was formerly more abundant and could be found in southeastern Massachusetts. Many of the same woodlands that hosted pink lady's-slipper in the spring now present downy rattlesnake orchis, broad-leaved helleborine, and spotted coralroot. By autumn there are only a few ladies'-tresses left, but the nodding, *Spiranthes cernua*, grows in large numbers all through this area in wet areas and brackish marshes. While you are searching for it keep an eye out for the yellow, *S. ochroleuca*, on nearby dry gravel banks and uplands.

Pringle's autumn coralroot, *Corallorhiza odontorhiza* var. *pringlei*, is a newly recognized variety documented from Old Lyme, Connecticut. This variety differs from the type in that the flowers are chasmogamous, or fully expanded, rather than cleistogamous, "hidden," or fertilized within the bud, and therefore are considerably showier. An excellent photograph appears in Case's Orchids of the Western Great Lakes Region, plate 43B.

# 3. Central New York State

Reaching from Utica to just west of Rochester and south to Corning and Binghamton, central New York State is rich in limestone and shales that often provide excellent homes for many species of orchids. The interspersed swamps and wetlands as well as remnant prairie-like areas only add to that diversity. Although much of the area to the north and west of Syracuse has long been developed there are still a few hidden spots that are worthy of exploration.

Several historical species are known from this area; some of the species that may be encountered include:

*Amerorchis rotundifolia*, small round-leaf orchis H
*Arethusa bulbosa*, dragon's-mouth
*Calopogon tuberosus*, common grass-pink
*Calypso bulbosa* var. *americana*, eastern fairy slipper H
*Coeloglossum viride* var. *virescens*, long-bracted green orchis
*Corallorhiza maculata* var. *maculata*, spotted coralroot
*Corallorhiza maculata* var. *occidentalis*, western spotted coralroot
*Corallorhiza odontorhiza* var. *odontorhiza*, autumn coralroot
*Corallorhiza striata*, striped coralroot
*Corallorhiza trifida*, early coralroot
*Cypripedium acaule*, pink lady's-slipper
*Cypripedium arietinum*, ram's-head lady's-slipper
*Cypripedium candidum*, small white lady's-slipper
*Cypripedium parviflorum* var. *parviflorum*, southern small yellow lady's-slipper
*Cypripedium parviflorum* var. *makasin*, northern small yellow lady's-slipper
*Cypripedium parviflorum* var. *pubescens*, large yellow lady's-slipper
*Cypripedium reginae*, showy lady's-slipper
*Epipactis helleborine*, broad-leaved helleborine*
*Galearis spectabilis*, showy orchis
*Goodyera pubescens*, downy rattlesnake orchis
*Goodyera repens*, lesser rattlesnake orchis

*Goodyera tesselata*, checkered rattlesnake orchis
*Gymnadeniopsis clavellata* var. *clavellata*, little club-spur orchis
*Isotria medeoloides*, small whorled pogonia
*Liparis loeselii*, Loesel's twayblade
*Listera australis*, southern twayblade
*Listera cordata*, heart-leaved twayblade
*Malaxis brachypoda*, white adder's-mouth
*Malaxis unifolia*, green adder's-mouth
*Platanthera aquilonis*, northern green bog orchis
*Platanthera blephariglottis*, northern white fringed orchis
*Platanthera dilatata*, white bog orchis; bog candles
*Platanthera flava* var. *herbiola*, northern tubercled orchis
*Platanthera grandiflora*, large purple fringed orchis
*Platanthera hookeri*, Hooker's orchis
*Platanthera huronensis*, green bog orchis
*Platanthera lacera*, green fringed orchis; ragged orchis
*Platanthera leucophaea*, eastern prairie fringed orchis H
*Platanthera macrophylla*, Goldie's pad-leaved orchis
*Platanthera obtusata*, blunt-leafed rein orchis
*Platanthera orbiculata*, pad-leaved orchis
*Platanthera psycodes*, small purple fringed orchis
*Pogonia ophioglossoides*, rose pogonia
*Spiranthes casei* var. *casei*, Case's ladies'-tresses
*Spiranthes cernua*, nodding ladies'-tresses
*Spiranthes lacera* var. *lacera*, northern slender ladies'-tresses
*Spiranthes lacera* var. *gracilis*, southern slender ladies'-tresses
*Spiranthes lucida*, shining ladies'-tresses
*Spiranthes ochroleuca*, yellow ladies'-tresses
*Spiranthes romanzoffiana*, hooded ladies'-tresses

Spring in central New York is an orchidist's paradise. Within a few hours' drive it is possible to see more than a dozen species in bloom, including two that cannot be seen elsewhere in the Northeast.

Mid- to late May is an ideal time to visit the Rochester area. Begin at the fabled Bergen Swamp on the west side of the city. Although it is not the only site in New York for small white lady's-slipper, *Cypripedium candidum*, Bergen Swamp is certainly the best known. It and several other important properties are owned by the Bergen Swamp Preservation Society, a private conservation organization whose efforts have resulted in the preservation of large tracts of valuable natural areas. A visit to the fen at Bergen Swamp reveals not only many clumps of small white lady's-slipper, but also patches of northern small yellow and large yellow lady's-slipper, *Cypripedium parviflorum* var. *makasin* and C. *parviflorum* var. *pubescens*, and their hybrids, Andrews' hybrid lady's-slipper, C. ×*andrewsii*, and Faville's hybrid lady's-slipper, C. ×*andrewsii* nm *favillianum*. On your way to the fen watch for pink lady's-slipper, *Cypripedium acaule*, early coralroot, *Corallorhiza trifida*, and long-bracted green orchis, *Coeloglossum viride* var. *virescens*, in the surrounding woodlands, and perhaps a massasauga rattlesnake. The snakes are quite rare and very shy, so don't plan your trip around them.

After feasting on the various lady's-slippers at Bergen, take a short drive to the east side of Rochester to the town of Zurich and another Bergen Swamp Preservation Society property, Zurich Bog. The large quaking bog, swamp, and extensive rich woodland offer quantities of large yellow lady's-slippers, scattered northern small yellow lady's-slippers, and, later in June, the showy lady's-slipper, *Cypripedium reginae*. The very observant may find a few colonies of the elusive southern twayblade, *Listera australis*. Both early coralroot and western spotted coralroot, *Corallorhiza maculata* var. *occidentalis*, can be found in season; and, of course, pink lady's-slippers and the various rattlesnake orchises, *Goodyera* spp., are ever present.

Later in the season, in July, long-bracted green orchis and northern club-spur orchis, *Gymnadeniopsis clavellata* var. *ophioglossoides*, flower. Search marshy meadows, damp power lines, and open wooded swamps for fringed orchises: green, *Platanthera lacera*, small purple, *P. psycodes*, and white, *P. blephariglottis*. Historically the reclusive eastern prairie fringed orchis, *P. leucophaea*, was found in this area, but it has been many years since it was last seen.

The Syracuse area offers many of the same woodland species as Rochester; in addition, the only current site in New York State for the striped coralroot, *Corallorhiza striata*, and an excellent stand of ram's-head lady's-slipper, *Cypripedium arietinum*, is just east of Syracuse. This area also supports all the other lady's-slippers with the exception of the small white, which historically was found within the edge of the city of Syracuse. Wet meadows and seepages, especially along the New York Thruway in the Utica area have offered homes to *Spiranthes lucida*, the shining ladies'-tresses, and *Malaxis brachypoda*, the white adder's-mouth.

An excellent place to search for many of the familiar species is Clark Reservation in Jamesville. The extensive limestone woodlands and outcrops are famous for ferns, notably the American hart's-tongue, *Phyllitis scolopendrium* var. *americanum*, but should be equally famous for orchids. Showy orchis, *Galearis spectabilis*, Hooker's orchis, *Platanthera hookeri*, and pad-leaved and Goldie's pad-leaved orchises, *P. orbiculata* and *P. macrophylla*, grow within these woodlands. Small whorled pogonia, *Isotria medeoloides*, has been reported from this area, and autumn coralroot, *Corallorhiza odontorhiza* var. *odontorhiza*, can be abundant.

By autumn, fen and bog and roadside ditches are resplendent with a variety of ladies'-tresses, *Spiranthes* spp. Starting in late July to mid-August watch for northern slender and southern slender ladies'-tresses, *Spiranthes lacera* var. *lacera* and *S. lacera* var. *gracilis*, on roadside banks and in cemeteries and old fields. August brings hooded ladies'-tresses, *S. romanzoffiana*, in the northern calcareous wetlands, followed by the polymorphic nodding ladies'-tresses, *S. cernua*, often accompanied in the drier areas by yellow ladies'-tresses, *S. ochroleuca*. Look carefully and you may spy autumn coralroot in the rich woodlands from late September into early October. The typically northern Case's ladies'-tresses, *S. casei*, has been found in the southern portion of this area near Olean. Search the shaley, thin-soil roadsides for this elusive ladies'-tresses.

Several species were historically found in the Rochester–Syracuse area. Eastern prairie fringed orchis, *Platanthera leucophaea,* small round-leaved orchis, *Amerorchis rotundifolia*, eastern fairy-slipper, *Calypso bulbosa* var. *americana*, and orange fringed orchis, *Platanthera ciliaris*, have all been recorded from the region. Although the landscape has changed greatly there is still abundant suitable habitat for these species and some or all may yet be found again.

# 4. *Metropolitan Boston*

Thanks to the foresight of our late nineteenth and early twentieth-century ancestors the Greater Boston area is dotted with many public lands and preserves. One need only to fly into Boston's Logan Airport to be immediately struck by this mosaic of green areas that continues from the Worcester highlands in the central part of the state right on into downtown Boston—and all of these areas still have many orchids, both rare and common, persisting within them.

Within fifty miles of Boston Common some of the orchids that may still be seen today include:

*Arethusa bulbosa*, dragon's-mouth
*Calopogon tuberosus*, common grass-pink
*Coeloglossum viride* var. *virescens*, long-bracted green orchis
*Corallorhiza maculata* var. *maculata*, spotted coralroot
*Corallorhiza odontorhiza* var. *odontorhiza*, autumn coralroot
*Corallorhiza trifida*, early coralroot
*Cypripedium acaule*, pink lady's-slipper
*Cypripedium parviflorum* var. *pubescens*, large yellow lady's-slipper
*Epipactis helleborine*, broad-leaved helleborine*
*Goodyera pubescens*, downy rattlesnake orchis
*Goodyera tesselata*, checkered rattlesnake orchis
*Gymnadeniopsis clavellata* var. *clavellata*, little club-spur orchis
*Isotria medeoloides*, small whorled pogonia
*Isotria verticillata*, large whorled pogonia
*Liparis liliifolia*, lily-leaved twayblade
*Liparis loeselii*, Loesel's twayblade
*Listera cordata*, heart-leaved twayblade
*Malaxis unifolia*, green adder's-mouth
*Platanthera blephariglottis*, northern white fringed orchis
*Platanthera flava* var. *herbiola*, northern tubercled orchis

*Platanthera grandiflora*, large purple fringed orchis
*Platanthera lacera*, green fringed orchis; ragged orchis
*Platanthera psycodes*, small purple fringed orchis
*Pogonia ophioglossoides*, rose pogonia
*Spiranthes cernua*, nodding ladies'-tresses
*Spiranthes lacera* var. *gracilis*, southern slender ladies'-tresses
*Spiranthes ochroleuca*, yellow ladies'-tresses
*Spiranthes tuberosa*, little ladies'-tresses
*Spiranthes vernalis*, grass-leaved ladies'-tresses

Only two formerly found species are considered historical:

*Platanthera ciliaris*, orange fringed orchis H
*Platanthera hookeri*, Hooker's orchis H

Sweeping in a wide arc around Boston at a distance approximating ten to fifteen miles from the city center, and servicing dozens of communities that lie within five to twenty-five miles of Boston, Route 128 commences at Gloucester on Cape Ann in the north and swings around in a broad curve to its terminus in Braintree, south of the city of Boston. In the course of its travels south it takes on the route numbers I-95, I-93, and finally Route 228. Within this great arc and adjacent to it can still be found 26 of the 34 species historically recorded from Greater Boston.

The great variety of habitat within the arc accounts for the diversity and quantity of the orchid species found here. The Metropolitan District Commission (MDC), the Massachusetts Audubon Society, local conservation commissions, and private conservation organizations own numerous properties along Route 128, and many of these habitats will be preserved.

Starting near the southern terminus of Route 128 in Quincy, Randolph, Milton, and Canton, the 8,000+ acres of the Blue Hills Reservation (MDC) present a wide array of habitats and species. This, the largest of the MDC properties, includes Great Blue Hill, the extensive Ponkapoag Pond and Bog section in Canton and Randolph, Chickatawbut Hill section in Milton and Quincy, and extensive lowlands near Hyde Park and Mattapan. Numerous wetlands of all types are widespread throughout the reservation, and twenty-two orchid species have been recorded within or adjacent to the Blue Hills over the years. Nearly all of these can still be found.

Mid- to late May starts the season in the Blue Hills with the pink lady's-slipper, *Cypripedium acaule*, large whorled pogonia, *Isotria verticillata*, and, by Memorial Day in a few of the bogs, Arethusa, or dragon's-mouth, *Arethusa bulbosa*. Another excellent area is the Stony Brook section in Hyde Park. The bogs at Turtle Pond still harbor Arethusa, and by early June the delicate rose pogonia, *Pogonia ophioglossoides*, and grass-pink, *Calopogon tuberosus*, can be found. Pink lady's-slipper and, more rarely, large whorled pogonia can also be found in the oak-pine woodlands at Stony Brook.

Cape Ann, at the other end of Route 128, offers many of these same spring-flowering species, but they bloom about a week later. Local conservation lands in many of the towns within and around the region are always good hunting areas. Often the bogs and swamps have boardwalks to make observation easier.

The first two weeks of June are prime times to search for our rarest orchid: the small whorled pogonia, *Isotria medeoloides*, a species designated Threatened by the U.S. Fish and Wildlife Service. Forests that are predominantly beech with some maple and/or hemlock on gentle slopes and along seasonal streams seem to be its favored habitat. Essex County is home to one of several stands in New England. Both areas have suitable habitat for the southern small and large yellow lady's-slippers, *Cypripedium parviflorum* var. *parviflorum* and *C. parviflorum* var. *pubescens*, but because of over-collecting they are now very rare.

By mid-June early summer has settled in and it is time to search for the lily-leaved twayblade, *Liparis liliifolia*, in the Blue Hills. There are several old records from the Hills for this, the largest of our twayblades. Its chocolate-purple flowers blend in with the surrounding forest floor, but the shiny green leaves often stand out. It favors damp hillsides and seasonal streams. In the cooler cedar swamps and bogs, the early coralroot, *Corallorhiza trifida*, may still be in good condition, and often in these areas and the adjacent red maple swamplands the large purple fringed orchis, *Platanthera grandiflora*, is starting to bloom. The small purple fringed orchis, *Platanthera psycodes*, may inhabit the same areas, but it blooms four to six weeks later. This span in blooming times plus specific identifying field marks should help you to distinguish the two species, whose color and form are similar.

In years gone by a wonderful area known as Purgatory Swamp in Norwood harbored many of the species already mentioned, including yellow lady's-slipper and several species no longer found in this region, including heart-leaved twayblade, *Listera cordata*, pad-leaved orchis, *Platanthera orbiculata*, Hooker's orchis, *P. hookeri*, and showy orchis, *Galearis spectabilis*. Purgatory Swamp is now a major industrial park, although isolated "islands" of undeveloped land are still worth exploring.

One of the most curious and often interesting habitats is the "borrow pit": a roadside area that has been scraped of its topsoil, leaving sandy or gravelly depressions that often remain seasonally wet. The term can also refer to local sand and gravel excavations. Many of the cities and towns within the region have such areas, and one near Woburn is home to a half-dozen species of orchids. Loesel's twayblade, *Liparis loeselii*, and rose pogonia start their bloom in mid-June, followed by the little club-spur orchis, *Gymnadeniopsis clavellata* var. *clavellata*, and, finally, several species of ladies'-tresses, *Spiranthes* spp. These species often occur in large numbers in this habitat.

Wet meadows and swales under power lines are another excellent orchid habitat common in most cities and towns in and around Greater Boston. These areas are kept clear of woody vegetation, so competition is at a minimum. Mid-June to early July finds the northern tubercled orchis, *Platanthera flava* var. *herbiola*, rose pogonia, grass-pink, large purple fringed orchis, Loesel's twayblade, and green fringed orchis, *P. lacera*, in such sites. In early August such areas often play host to the spectacular northern white fringed orchis, *P. blephariglottis*. A return visit later in the month and even into September might reveal small purple fringed orchis and several species of ladies'-tresses.

The summer woodlands may lack the array of blooms of springtime, but they still present a few choice gems. The rattlesnake orchises, both downy and checkered, *Goodyera pubescens* and G. *tesselata*, bloom in the summertime forests, and the ubiquitous, non-native broad-leaved helleborine, *Epipactis helleborine*, seems to pop up anywhere and everywhere. Careful searching of the richer woods should reveal spotted coralroot, *Corallorhiza maculata*, and, occasionally, small purple fringed and green fringed orchises in the wooded swamps.

Autumn is a time of fewer species, but some are widely distributed and can be found in large numbers, especially the ladies'-tresses. Examine borrow pits, wet meadows, and roadside ditches for nodding ladies'-tresses, *Spiranthes cernua*; uplands and drier gravel banks may have yellow ladies'-tresses, *S. ochroleuca*; mowed roadsides and cemeteries are good sites for slender ladies'-tresses, *S. lacera* var. *lacera* and *S. lacera* var. *gracilis*. If you were fortunate enough to find lily-leaved twayblade in June, it might well be worth a return visit in the fall to look for autumn coralroot, *Corallorhiza odontorhiza*, a small and inconspicuous plant that flowers from mid-September to early October. You have to look hard, for it's only a few inches high and, like the other coralroots, it has no green leaves or stems.

Public lands and private preserves that often have good orchid populations include the Blue Hills Reservation in Milton, Canton, Randolph, and Quincy; Stony Brook in Hyde Park; Cutler Park in Needham; Fowl Meadows in Hyde Park, Milton, and Canton; Hale Reservation in Westwood; Prospect Hill in Waltham; Beaver Brook Reservation in Belmont; the Horn Pond area in Winchester and Woburn; Middlesex Fells in Winchester, Woburn, and Stoneham; Silver Hill Bog in Lincoln; Lynnfield Marshes, in Lynnfield; Manchester Woods and Agassiz Rock, in Manchester and Essex; and Dogtown Common in Annisquam. These are among the better-known areas, but many other large and small tracts of public and quasi-public lands are havens to the many species of orchids that grow within the influence of Boston's urban sprawl.

# 5. *Cape Cod and Eastern Long Island*

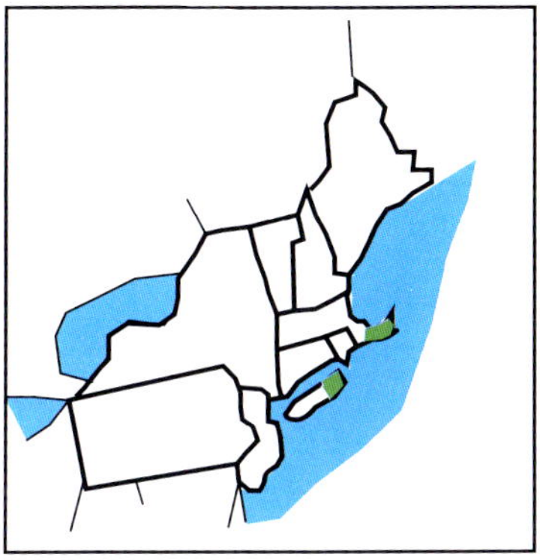

Cape Cod in Massachusetts and eastern Long Island in New York State share many botanical affinities, some linked by plant communities on Martha's Vineyard and Nantucket as well. Although each area has specialties not found in the other, orchid hunting is based a great deal upon suitable habitat and those habitats—rich beech/holly woods, interdunal swales, open dry sandplains—all yield many excellent species of wild orchids. The other common link in these areas is the overabundance of traffic, especially in the high season of summer (when most of the really good orchids flowers)! For those who have the option, weekday travel is much easier.
Species that may be found on Cape Cod and environs and Eastern Long Island:

*Arethusa bulbosa*, dragon's-mouth
*Calopogon tuberosus*, common grass-pink
*Corallorhiza maculata* var. *maculata*, spotted coralroot
*Cypripedium acaule*, pink lady's-slipper
*Epipactis helleborine*, broad-leaved helleborine*
*Goodyera pubescens*, downy rattlesnake orchis
*Gymnadeniopsis clavellata* var. *clavellata*, little club-spur orchis
*Isotria verticillata*, large whorled pogonia
*Listera cordata*, heart-leaved twayblade
*Malaxis bayardii*, Bayard's adder's-mouth
*Malaxis unifolia*, green adder's-mouth
*Platanthera blephariglottis*, northern white fringed orchis
*Platanthera ciliaris*, orange fringed orchis
*Platanthera cristata*, orange crested orchis
*Platanthera dilatata*, tall white northern bog orchis
*Platanthera flava* var. *herbiola*, northern tubercled orchis
*Platanthera lacera*, green fringed orchis; ragged orchis
*Platanthera pallida*, pale fringed orchis
*Pogonia ophioglossoides*, rose pogonia

*Spiranthes cernua*, nodding ladies'-tresses
*Spiranthes lacera* var. *lacera*, northern slender ladies'-tresses
*Spiranthes lacera* var. *gracilis*, southern slender ladies'-tresses
*Spiranthes ochroleuca*, yellow ladies'-tresses
*Spiranthes tuberosa*, little ladies'-tresses
*Spiranthes vernalis*, grass-leaved ladies'-tresses
*Tipularia discolor*, crane-fly orchis

Late May on Cape Cod brings surprising quantities of pink lady's-slipper, *Cypripedium acaule*, in the predominant oak-pine woodlands; it is not unusual to find large colonies of several hundred plants. White-flowered forma *albiflora* are scattered here and there. One of the great rarities of the Cape is the large whorled pogonia, *Isotria verticillata*. In a very small area on the mid-Cape a rich woodland supports the pink lady's-slipper, large whorled pogonia, downy rattlesnake orchis, *Goodyera pubescens*, spotted coralroot, *Corallorhiza maculata*, and, formerly, the crane-fly orchis, *Tipularia discolor*.

Also in late spring in a few scattered sites, dragon's-mouth, *Arethusa bulbosa*, is coming into bloom. It favors the sphagnum borders of sandy pond shores, interdunal swales, and quaking bogs. It was formerly more plentiful but has declined greatly since the 1960s. It is said that children sold bunches of them on street corners in Providence at the turn of the century! Historical records have been documented for *Listera cordata*, the heart-leaved twayblade, from cedar swamps within the central part of the Cape near Yarmouth and for the adventuresome and eagle eyed, this is an excellent challenge!

By mid- to late June rose pogonia, *Pogonia ophioglossoides*, and grass-pink, *Calopogon tuberosus*, are creating pink swaths along roadsides, in borrow pits, and in the interdunal swales. At the Cape Cod National Seashore in the Provincelands, both species, but especially rose pogonia, are frequent early summer wildflowers. Also at this time scattered sites along the coast will reveal stands of northern tubercled orchis, *Platanthera flava* var. *herbiola*, with its fragrant, greenish-yellow flowers. This is also the best time to search for the rare Bayard's adder's-mouth, *Malaxis bayardii*, along old cartpaths and on the edges of the oak-pine woodlands. A single site is extant in Sandwich but there are many old records for this rare species in the Falmouth area.

Late July and early August is the prime time to search for the rarest of the fringed orchises near the Cape. The orange crested orchis, *Platanthera cristata*, was found in the early 1900s near Dartmouth, Massachusetts, and was not seen again until 1987. Apparently it appears at its whim and is seen at occasional intervals. The showy northern white fringed orchis is also present in the same area. Four ladies'-tresses: the grass-leaved, *Spiranthes vernalis*, northern slender, *S. lacera* var. *lacera*, southern slender, *S. lacera* var. *gracilis*, and little, S. *tuberosa*; the aforementioned crane-fly orchis and spotted coralroot; little club-spur orchis, *Gymnadeniopsis clavellata* var. *clavellata*; broad-leaved helleborine, *Epipactis helleborine*; and downy rattlesnake orchis, *Goodyera pubescens*—so many species in a heavily populated and very accessible area. Some are more common than others, of course. The crane-fly orchis is currently known only from a few very private properties on Martha's Vineyard. The various *Spi-*

*ranthes*, which are more common, seem to favor dry, grassy roadsides and cemeteries, and the white fringed orchis is often found in wet areas under power lines.

The rare orange fringed orchis, known only from a few sites in southern Rhode Island and south central Connecticut, was formerly more abundant and could be found in southeastern Massachusetts as well. Many of the same woodlands that hosted pink lady's-slipper in the spring now present downy rattlesnake orchis, broad-leaved helleborine, and spotted coralroot. By autumn there are only a few ladies'-tresses left, but the nodding, *Spiranthes cernua*, grows in large numbers all through the Cape in wet areas, interdunal swales, and brackish marshes. While you are searching for it keep an eye out for the yellow, *S. ochroleuca*, on nearby dry gravel banks and uplands.

Although Long Island is very heavily populated, the eastern end still features an exciting array of orchids, including one endemic species and some not easily seen elsewhere in the Northeast.

In the spring, quantities of pink lady's-slipper, *Cypripedium acaule*, and an occasional stand of large whorled pogonia, *Isotria verticillata*, are familiar sights. But this area, like the southern coastal plain of New England, comes into its glory in midsummer. A single visit to the north and south forks of eastern Long Island in early August can be one of the most rewarding orchid forays of the year.

Begin in the Greenport area, where mixed beech woodlands offer the crane-fly orchis, *Tipularia discolor*, near the northern limit of its range and an occasional spotted coralroot, *Corallorhiza maculata* var. *maculata* and ever-increasing numbers of the European broad-leaved helleborine, *Epipactis helleborine*. Continuing on with two short ferry rides to the south fork, watch roadside berms and ditches for white fringed orchis, *Platanthera blephariglottis*, orange crested orchis, *P. cristata*, orange fringed orchis, *P. ciliaris*, and their various hybrids: bicolor hybrid fringed orchis, *P. ×bicolor*, Canby's hybrid fringed orchis, *P. ×canbyi*, and Channell's hybrid fringed orchis, *P. ×channellii*, along with little club-spur orchis, *Gymnadeniopsis clavellata*. The rare Bayard's adder's-mouth, *Malaxis bayardii*, occurs (and has occurred historically) in a few of the drier roadside banks, dune hollows, and cemeteries. In the past Bayard's adder's-mouth has been confused with green-adder's mouth, *Malaxis unifolia*. Some old records for green-adder's mouth from xeric sites may actually be for Bayard's adder's-mouth. You can ascertain the accuracy of the identification by comparing the field marks given in the record with those listed on p. 000 for the two species.

In the dry interdunal hollows of the Montauk region grows the pale fringed orchis, *Platanthera pallida*, New York's only endemic orchid. The plants tend to occur in fair numbers in dry interdunal hollows under mature pitch pine. Also watch for southern slender ladies'-tresses, *Spiranthes lacera* var. *gracilis*, which grows in similar habitats. Earlier in the season, in late June and early July, some of the wet interdunal swales are painted shades of pink with rose pogonia, *Pogonia ophioglossoides*, and grass-pink, *Calopogon tuberosus*. Hither Hills State Park is a particularly good spot for these two species.

The ferries may be inconvenient and the traffic heavy, but a day in early August on eastern Long Island is well worth the trouble!

# 6. The Catskills and Poconos

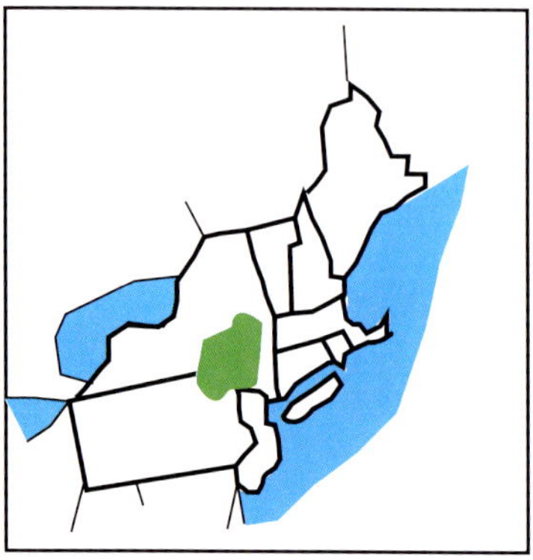

The Catskill and Pocono Mountains are a contiguous range of rolling hills and high pints dotted with more than two hundred lakes, rivers, and reservoirs. Spectacular waterfalls abound and the gentle, snaking Susquehanna River to the west contrasts with the dramatic Delaware River and Delaware Water Gap, which bisects the Poconos. In New York State the Catskills are within Delaware, Green, Sullivan, and Ulster Counties in the southeastern part of upstate New York whereas the Poconos are found within all or parts of Wayne, Pike, Monroe, Lackawanna, Carbon, Luzerne, and Wyoming Counties in much of northeastern Pennsylvania. Although major cities are few, Scranton/Wilkes-Barre being the exception, both areas abound in colorful resort towns. Access to the many state and county lands is often from these resorts that double as ski areas in the winter and hiking meccas in more favorable weather. Wild orchids abound throughout all of these counties although they have never been major botanical magnets. Many excellent orchid locations are still to be found; the elusive three birds orchid, *Triphora trianthophora*, was recently rediscovered in the Catskills.

The species list for these contiguous areas is based primarily on older herbarium records and, for the diligent orchid-hunter, inquires at various institutions that house these local herbaria would be advised before setting out. For those who prefer to just strike out and search, choose any of the public trails, pay attention to the habitat, and keep your eyes opened. A bit of reading beforehand to determine the suitability of habitat where you will be and those species that flower at the time you will be there will help to narrow your search image. But getting used to what the various species look like out of flower, in leaf or in fruit, will greatly increase your pleasure and virtually assure you of a repeat visit to a specific area.

*Aplectrum hyemale*, putty-root
*Arethusa bulbosa*, dragon's-mouth
*Calopogon tuberosus*, common grass-pink
*Coeloglossum viride* var. *virescens*, long-bracted green orchis
*Corallorhiza maculata* var. *maculata*, spotted coralroot

*Corallorhiza maculata* var. *occidentalis*, western spotted coralroot
*Corallorhiza trifida*, early coralroot
*Cypripedium acaule*, pink lady's-slipper
*Cypripedium parviflorum* var. *pubescens*, large yellow lady's-slipper
*Cypripedium reginae*, showy lady's-slipper
*Epipactis helleborine*, broad-leaved helleborine*
*Galearis spectabilis*, showy orchis
*Goodyera pubescens*, downy rattlesnake orchis
*Goodyera tesselata*, checkered rattlesnake orchis
*Gymnadeniopsis clavellata* var. *clavellata*, little club-spur orchis
*Isotria verticillata*, large whorled pogonia
*Liparis liliifolia*, lily-leaved twayblade
*Liparis loeselii*, Loesel's twayblade
*Malaxis unifolia*, green adder's-mouth
*Platanthera aquilonis*, northern green bog orchis
*Platanthera blephariglottis*, northern white fringed orchis
*Platanthera dilatata*, white bog orchis; bog candles
*Platanthera flava* var. *herbiola*, northern tubercled orchis
*Platanthera grandiflora*, large purple fringed orchis
*Platanthera hookeri*, Hooker's orchis
*Platanthera huronensis*, green bog orchis
*Platanthera lacera*, green fringed orchis; ragged orchis
*Platanthera macrophylla*, Goldie's pad-leaved orchis
*Platanthera orbiculata*, pad-leaved orchis
*Platanthera psycodes*, small purple fringed orchis
*Pogonia ophioglossoides*, rose pogonia
*Spiranthes cernua*, nodding ladies'-tresses
*Spiranthes lacera* var. *lacera*, northern slender ladies'-tresses
*Spiranthes lacera* var. *gracilis*, southern slender ladies'-tresses
*Spiranthes lucida*, shining ladies'-tresses
*Spiranthes ochroleuca*, yellow ladies'-tresses
*Spiranthes romanzoffiana*, hooded ladies'-tresses
*Triphora trianthophora*, three birds orchid

Apart from the different types of wetlands a few orchids are very habitat specific; probably the most famous of these is the three birds orchid. It is found primarily in beech/hemlock woodlands and favors the shallow bowls formed in those woodlands.

Bogs and fens occur in both the Catskills and Poconos. The species that may be found in them include:

*Arethusa bulbosa*, dragon's-mouth
*Calopogon tuberosus*, common grass-pink
*Gymnadeniopsis clavellata* var. *clavellata*, little club-spur orchis
*Platanthera aquilonis*, northern green bog orchis

*Platanthera blephariglottis*, northern white fringed orchis
*Platanthera dilatata*, white bog orchis; bog candles
*Platanthera huronensis*, green bog orchis
*Platanthera psycodes*, small purple fringed orchis
*Pogonia ophioglossoides*, rose pogonia
*Spiranthes cernua*, nodding ladies'-tresses

While the above are not particularly fussy as to soil requirements three species—*Cypripedium reginae,* the showy lady's-slipper; *Spiranthes lucida*, the shining ladies'-tresses, and *Spiranthes romanzoffiana*, the hooded ladies'-tresses—are generally found in limier areas.

Rich deciduous or even mixed woodlands may harbor *Aplectrum hyemale*, puttyroot; *Coeloglossum viride* var. *virescens*, the long-bracted green orchis; *Corallorhiza maculata* var. *maculata*, the spotted coralroot; *Corallorhiza maculata* var. *occidentalis*, the western spotted coralroot; *Cypripedium parviflorum* var. *pubescens*, the large yellow lady's-slipper; *Epipactis helleborine,* the broad-leaved helleborine*; *Galearis spectabilis*, the showy orchis; *Liparis liliifolia*, the lily-leaved twayblade; *Platanthera hookeri*, Hooker's orchis; *Platanthera macrophylla*, Goldie's pad-leaved orchis, and/or *Platanthera orbiculata*, the pad-leaved orchis.

More acidic woodlands are the typical haunts for *Corallorhiza trifida*, the early coralroot; *Cypripedium acaule*, the pink lady's-slipper; *Goodyera pubescens*, the downy rattlesnake orchis; *Goodyera tesselata*, the checkered rattlesnake orchis; *Isotria verticillata,* the large whorled pogonia, and *Malaxis unifolia*, the green adder's-mouth.

Wet woodlands, power lines, and open meadows as well as the ubiquitous roadside ditch are often suitable habitat for several orchids including *Gymnadeniopsis clavellata* var. *clavellata*, the little club-spur orchis; *Liparis loeselii*, Loesel's twayblade; *Malaxis unifolia*, the green adder's-mouth; *Platanthera aquilonis*, the northern green bog orchis; *Platanthera blephariglottis*, the northern white fringed orchis; *Platanthera dilatata*, the white bog orchis; bog candles; *Platanthera flava* var. *herbiola*, the northern tubercled orchis; *Platanthera grandiflora*, the large purple fringed orchis; *Platanthera huronensis*, the green bog orchis; *Platanthera lacera*, the green fringed orchis; *Platanthera psycodes*, the small purple fringed orchis; *Spiranthes cernua*, the nodding ladies'-tresses; *Spiranthes lacera* var. *lacera*, the northern slender ladies'-tresses; *Spiranthes lacera* var. *gracilis*, the southern slender ladies'-tresses, and *Spiranthes ochroleuca*, the yellow ladies'-tresses.

Do not be misled by these intriguing lists. They are meant only as a guide to what could be found in specific habitats. Remember that this grouping of lists is based on historical records. Much of the land has remained untouched and is perhaps more accessible now than ever before because of the recreation areas. Get out there and find more orchids!

# 7. The Pinelands of New Jersey and Cape May

Long fabled in botanical lore for both its diversity and rarity of plant life, southeastern New Jersey still boasts one of the most accessible and rewarding orchid communities in eastern North America. And the orchids are only part of it! Ferns, lilies, gentians, grasses, and sedges all have their rarities and, for many other species more common south of the area, this part of New Jersey represents the northern limit of their ranges. From meandering rivers to dry pinelands to open savannas to historic building sites and ghost towns, all have their orchid communities and many their local legends as well. The Jersey Devil has long been reputed to lurk somewhere out there, and all that remains of some of the early settlements are such names as Ong's Hat, Batsto, Martha, Lower Forge—names well-known to botanists visiting the area.

Some of the species that one might expect to find in the Pinelands and Cape May:

*Arethusa bulbosa*, dragon's-mouth
*Calopogon tuberosus*, common grass-pink
*Cleistes divaricata*, large spreading pogonia
*Coeloglossum viride* var. *virescens*, long-bracted green orchis
*Corallorhiza maculata* var. *maculata*, spotted coralroot
*Corallorhiza odontorhiza* var. *odontorhiza*, autumn coralroot
*Corallorhiza wisteriana*, Wister's coralroot
*Cypripedium acaule*, pink lady's-slipper
*Cypripedium parviflorum* var. *parviflorum*, southern small yellow lady's-slipper
*Cypripedium parviflorum* var. *pubescens*, large yellow lady's-slipper
*Epipactis helleborine*, broad-leaved helleborine*
*Goodyera pubescens*, downy rattlesnake orchis
*Gymnadeniopsis clavellata* var. *clavellata*, little club-spur orchis
*Gymnadeniopsis integra*, yellow fringeless orchis

*Gymnadeniopsis nivea*, snowy orchis
*Isotria verticillata*, large whorled pogonia
*Liparis liliifolia*, lily-leaved twayblade
*Liparis loeselii*, Loesel's twayblade
*Listera australis*, southern twayblade
*Malaxis bayardii*, Bayard's adder's-mouth
*Malaxis unifolia*, green adder's-mouth
*Platanthera blephariglottis*, northern white fringed orchis
*Platanthera ciliaris*, orange fringed orchis
*Platanthera cristata*, orange crested orchis
*Platanthera flava* var. *flava*, southern tubercled orchis
*Platanthera flava* var. *herbiola*, northern tubercled orchis
*Platanthera lacera*, green fringed orchis; ragged orchis
*Platanthera peramoena*, purple fringeless orchis
*Platanthera psycodes*, small purple fringed orchis
*Pogonia ophioglossoides*, rose pogonia
*Spiranthes cernua*, nodding ladies'-tresses
*Spiranthes lacera* var. *gracilis*, southern slender ladies'-tresses
*Spiranthes laciniata*, lace-lipped ladies'-tresses
*Spiranthes tuberosa*, little ladies'-tresses
*Spiranthes vernalis*, grass-leaved ladies'-tresses
*Tipularia discolor*, crane-fly orchis
*Triphora trianthophora*, three birds orchid

Spring comes early to the Pinelands and the cool waters flowing from the rivers and cranberry bogs flood the white-sand swamps where by late April the first orchids of the season raise their bright pink heads and *Arethusa bulbosa*, the dragon's-mouth, begins to bloom. In a few mossy woodlands *Listera australis*, the southern twayblade, will be in flower at this time as well. By early May the oak/pine woodlands are sprinkled with *Cypripedium acaule*, the pink lady's-slipper, and in a few places, especially near Folsom, *Isotria verticillata*, large whorled pogonia, is beginning to flower. By early June and then continuing on into July the wetlands are ablaze with *Calopogon tuberosus*, the common grass-pink, and *Pogonia ophioglossoides*, the rose pogonia. White-flowered forms of both are not unusual.

Perhaps the most sought-after orchid in south Jersey is *Cleistes divaricata*, the large spreading pogonia. This majestic southern beauty has had only a few records over the past 150 years and then never more than a handful of plants. Recent places where it has been found and that are certainly worth search are Bulltown and Lower Forge. Historically it was found near Quaker Bridge and near Cape May. It is a very distinctive orchid and identification certainly would not be a problem!

By early August the fringed orchises and closely related species are coming into full flower. Roadside swaths and damp meadows often near some of the commercial cranberry bogs are home to *Platanthera blephariglottis*, the northern white fringed orchis, while the deep woods of the eastern white cedar swamps near Lower Forge are especially good for not just the northern white fringed orchis, but also *P. cristata*, the orange crested orchis. The latter, growing in the company of *Gymnadeniopsis clavellata* var. *clavellata*, the little club-spur orchis, is very much at home at Quaker Bridge. It is in this area that a few of the savannas along the Batsto River still harbor small colonies of *G. integra*, the yellow fringeless orchis. The specific location of this rarest of orchids is a well-kept secret passed down personally form botanist to botanist—and good luck trying to find your way back into the myriad of savannas!

Away from the wetlands and pine forests, in some of the rich soil islands that border the Pinelands, may be found *Platanthera lacera*, the green fringed orchis; *P. psycodes*, the small purple fringed orchis and, along an old abandoned railway crossing deep within the blackberry thickets, *P. peramoena*, the purple fringeless orchis. Few sites remain for this brilliant purple beauty and New Jersey represents the northern limit of its range. The settlement at White's Bog and the blueberry fields may not seem to be the best orchid territory, but within the old concrete foundations of some of the abandoned buildings grow *Liparis loeselii*, Loesel's twayblade, *Malaxis unifolia*, the green adder's-mouth, and an uncommon fern, *Ophioglossum vulgatum*, the adder's-tongue fern. All of these are calciphiles—lime-lovers—growing in a highly acid area but within the limey confines of the old foundation!

In scattered areas along the sandy roadsides and in old fields of the Pinelands may now be found three of the ladies'-tresses: *Spiranthes lacera* var. *gracilis*, the southern slender ladies'-tresses; *S. tuberosa*, the little ladies'-tresses, and *S. vernalis*, the grass-leaved ladies'-tresses. By September, when the brilliant blue of the Pine Barrens gentian, *Gentiana pophyrio*, is at its height of bloom, the damp roadsides, savannas, and swales will host vast quantities of *Spiranthes cernua*, the nodding ladies'-tresses, and, in a very few select savannas at its northern limit, *S. laciniata*, the lace-lipped ladies'-tresses. Two other species of ladies'-tresses have been reported from this part of New Jersey and both need confirmation. *S. odorata*, the fragrant ladies'-tresses, is part of the oft- confusing *S. cernua* complex and plants that are suspect need very careful examination to confirm their identity. Despite many reports no confirmed plants have been seen. *S. praecox*, the giant ladies'-tresses, has been reported from here and the Cape May area for many years; although identification should not be a problem it apparently has been. Suspect plants would have the typical appressed sepals and (usually) green-veined lips of the species.

The area just north of Cape May is home to a wonderful natural area known as the Bennett Bogs. Owned by New Jersey Audubon Society, these series of open grass meadows surrounded by rich woodlands have long been known for their orchids. Unfortunately some of the areas have been drained and invasive grasses have moved in. Still, the area is always worth a visit. In past years the following have been found here: *Cleistes divaricata*, the large spreading pogonia; *Gymnadeniopsis nivea,* the snowy orchis; *Malaxis unifolia*, the green adder's-mouth; *Platanthera blephariglottis*, the northern white fringed orchis; *P. cristata*, the orange crested orchis; *P. flava* var. *flava*, the southern tubercled orchis; *Pogonia ophioglossoides*, the rose pogonia; *Spiranthes laciniata*, the lace-lipped ladies'-tresses; *S. vernalis*, the grass-leaved ladies'-tresses, and in the connecting woodlands hundreds of *Tipularia discolor*, the crane-fly orchis. It is here that there have also been records for many years for both *Spiranthes odorata*, the fragrant ladies'-tresses and *S. praecox*, the giant ladies'-tresses, but neither with confirming vouchers. Both the *Cleistes* and *Gymnadeniopsis* are considered historical now, although the latter was seen in the early 1990s in a large borrow pit not far from the Bennett Bogs. Along the many salt marshes, meadows, and thickets, a few have produced *Platanthera peramoena*, the purple fringeless orchis, and again, reports of the fragrant ladies'-tresses. As throughout all of south Jersey the railroad has always played an important part and along much of the right of ways one can still see both *P. ciliaris*, the orange fringed orchis, and *P. cristata*, the orange crested orchis.

A brief mention should be made of the area to the west of the southern Pinelands in the greater Glassboro area. It is here that the New Jersey records for several species have been located. This is Gloucester County and its rich woodlands did and often still do support colonies of *Aplectrum hyemale*, the putty-root; *Corallorhiza odontorhiza* var. *odontorhiza*, the autumn coralroot; *Liparis liliifolia*, the lily-leaved twayblade; *Listera australis*, the southern twayblade; *Tipularia discolor*, the crane-fly orchis, and *Triphora trianthophora*, the three birds orchid. Historically, this area was also home to New Jersey's only population of *Corallorhiza wisteriana*, Wister's coralroot.

A note should be made that, in addition, this area is home to one of the state's rarest and most spectacular members of the lily family—*Helonias bullata*, the swamp pink. The endangered species is known from so few locations now that it is no longer easy to find but it still does survive in remote swamps and along small streams in Gloucester County.

# 8. The Central Alleghenies

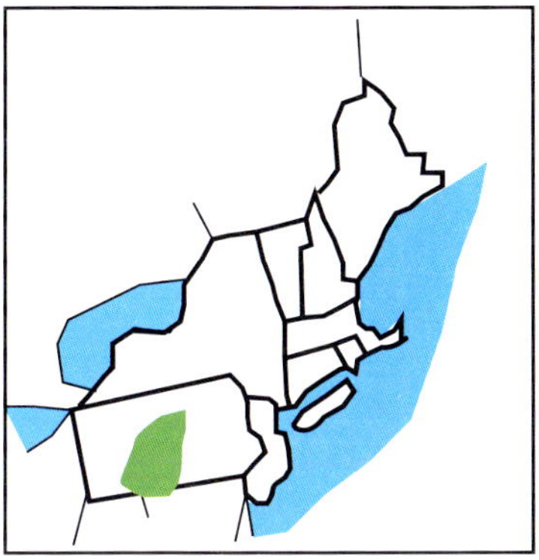

The central Allegheny Mountains, truly the heartland of the Appalachians, are the meeting place for many of Pennsylvania's orchids. Conservatively the range extends about five hundred miles from northern Pennsylvania to southwest Virginia, although some authors include both the Poconos and even the Catskills of southern New York within the range. With its cool northern-affinity forests and southern meadows this area of central Pennsylvania offers an abundance of orchid habitat. Much of the area includes state parks, state forests, and natural areas, all of which offer excellent orchid hunting.

Orchid species that may be found in the Allegheny Mountains and environs of central Pennsylvania include:

*Aplectrum hyemale*, putty root
*Coeloglossum viride* var. *virescens*, long-bracted green orchis
*Corallorhiza maculata* var. *maculata*, spotted coralroot
*Corallorhiza odontorhiza* var. *odontorhiza*, autumn coralroot
*Cypripedium acaule*, pink lady's-slipper
*Cypripedium parviflorum* var. *pubescens*, large yellow lady's-slipper
*Cypripedium reginae*, showy lady's-slipper
*Epipactis helleborine*, broad-leaved helleborine*
*Galearis spectabilis*, showy orchis
*Goodyera pubescens*, downy rattlesnake orchis
*Goodyera repens*, lesser rattlesnake orchis
*Gymnadeniopsis clavellata* var. *clavellata*, little club-spur orchis
*Isotria medeoloides*, small whorled pogonia
*Isotria verticillata*, large whorled pogonia
*Liparis liliifolia*, lily-leaved twayblade
*Listera cordata*, heart-leaved twayblade
*Listera smallii*, Small's twayblade
*Malaxis bayardii*, Bayard's adder's-mouth

*Malaxis unifolia*, green adder's-mouth
*Platanthera blephariglottis*, northern white fringed orchis
*Platanthera ciliaris*, orange fringed orchis
*Platanthera hookeri*, Hooker's orchis
*Platanthera lacera*, green fringed orchis; ragged orchis
*Platanthera orbiculata*, pad-leaved orchis
*Platanthera psycodes*, small purple fringed orchis
*Spiranthes cernua*, nodding ladies'-tresses
*Spiranthes lacera* var. *lacera*, northern slender ladies'-tresses
*Spiranthes lacera* var. *gracilis*, southern slender ladies'-tresses
*Spiranthes ochroleuca*, yellow ladies'-tresses
*Spiranthes ovalis* var. *erostellata,* northern oval ladies'-tresses

Although the central Alleghenies encompass a large area we will concentrate our efforts in the areas around and near State College. Just to the east of State College are large tracts of land comprising state forest, natural areas, and the like, all criss-crossed by excellent roadways and trails. Orchid hunting varies from surprising roadside finds to all-day hikes. Some of the specialties here include several gems of the area such as *Listera smallii*, Small's twayblade, inconspicuous and often elusively tucked under great laurel rosebays, *Rhododendron maximum*, along streams. Although a challenge to find they may not be that far from accessible parking places. Open meadows have *Platanthera ciliaris*, orange fringed orchis, and, surprisingly, large stands of *Spiranthes lacera* var. *lacera*, northern slender ladies'-tresses, can be found right along one of the forest roads! This is one of the southernmost locations for this primarily northern species.

Rich woodlands may support colonies that often include *Aplectrum hyemale*, putty-root; *Coeloglossum viride* var. *virescens*, the long-bracted green orchis; *Corallorhiza maculata* var. *maculata*, the spotted coralroot; *C. odontorhiza*, the autumn coralroot; *Cypripedium parviflorum* var. *pubescens*, the large yellow lady's-slipper; *Epipactis helleborine,* the broad-leaved helleborine; *Galearis spectabilis*, the showy orchis; *Liparis liliifolia*, the lily-leaved twayblade, and *Platanthera hookeri*, Hooker's orchis. Not that all of these will occur in the same place and some may be of only historical occurrence, but searching the rich, mesic forest is bound to turn up some of them, and perhaps even ones not seen in the area for many years.

The more acid oak/pine woodlands present a different palette of native orchids: *Cypripedium acaule*, the pink lady's-slipper; *Goodyera pubescens*, the downy rattlesnake orchis; *G. repens*, the lesser rattlesnake orchis; *Isotria verticillata,* the large whorled pogonia; *Malaxis bayardii*, Bayard's adder's-mouth, and *M. unifolia*, the green adder's-mouth. Again not all will occur everywhere and some like the lesser rattlesnake orchis and Bayard's adder's-mouth are exceedingly rare, but keep your eyes peeled and watch for suitable habitat.

Wet meadows and open swamps are often home to many of the showiest of our orchids. Here in the central Alleghenies several occur. From the rare *Cypripedium reginae*, the showy lady's-slipper, to the delightful *Gymnadeniopsis clavellata* var. *clavellata*, the little club-spur orchis, the eye may survey tantalizing delights in these habitats. Watch carefully for *Platanthera blephariglottis*, northern white fringed orchis; *P. ciliaris*, orange fringed orchis; *P. lacera*, green fringed or ragged orchis; *P. psycodes*, small purple fringed orchis, and in the autumn *Spiranthes cernua*, the nodding ladies'-tresses. Many of the fringed orchises and their kin favor the open wetlands under power lines and benefit from the periodic mowing these areas receive.

Not too far from State College there are several cedar knobs, often within pastures, a habitat favored by the very rare *Spiranthes ovalis* var. *erostellata*, the northern oval ladies'-tresses. It is here that the species reaches the northeastern limit of its range. Perhaps the rarest orchis to have been recorded from central Pennsylvania is *Isotria medeoloides*, the small whorled pogonia. Preferring mixed deciduous woodlands usually with beech, *Fagus grandifolia*, this peripatetic little orchid may appear, and disappear, at whim. It was seen in 1972 in Center County; for the avid orchid hunter this is the ultimate quest!

# *At the Limit*

Although treated to some degree in several other places in this book, a number of species reach the geographic extreme of their distribution in the northeastern states. Given that the Atlantic Ocean is a natural eastern barrier, these species in question are primarily disjuncts or do not extend their range north of our area. In addition, several species of a more southerly distribution reach their natural northern limit in the coastal southern portions of these states.

Those that represent northern extensions and/or near disjunct populations in southern New England include *Cypripedium parviflorum* var. *parviflorum*, the southern small yellow lady's-slipper; *Platanthera ciliaris*, the orange fringed orchis; *P. cristata*, the orange crested orchis; *Spiranthes tuberosa*, the little ladies'-tresses; *S. vernalis*, the grass-leaved ladies'-tresses, and *Tipularia discolor*, the crane-fly orchis.

Central and southern New Jersey, particularly the Pinelands, is the northern limit for several southern species including *Cleistes divaricata*, the large spreading pogonia; *Gymnadeniopsis integra*, the yellow fringeless orchis; *G. nivea*, the snowy orchis; *Platanthera flava* var. *flava*, the southern tubercled orchis; *P. peramoena*, the purple fringeless orchis, and *Spiranthes laciniata*, the lace-lipped ladies'-tresses. Two additional species of ladies'-tresses may also occur in this region but need to be vouchered: *Spiranthes odorata*, the fragrant ladies'-tresses and *S. praecox*, the giant ladies'-tresses.

Central Pennsylvania can boast disjunct populations for *Listera smallii*, Small's twayblade, and *Spiranthes ovalis* var. *erostellata*, the northern oval ladies'-tresses, and the historical locales for *Spiranthes magnicamporum*, the Great Plains ladies'-tresses.

Those northern or boreal species reaching the southern limit of their range include *Amerorchis rotundifolia*, the small round-leafed orchis, and *Calypso bulbosa* var. *americana*, the eastern fairy slipper, which extend only into northern New England and (formerly) northern New York; *Listera auriculata*, the auricled twayblade; *Corallorhiza striata*, the striped coralroot, *Listera convallarioides*, the broad-lipped twayblade; *Cypripedium arietinum*, the ram's-head lady's-slipper, and *Goodyera oblongifolia*, the giant rattlesnake orchis, which is restricted to northern Maine.

# Tips and Trips

Much has previously been written in this work about places to go and times to visit. Here are some tips to make your trips more pleasurable.

Orchids, as tough as they may seem at times, are vulnerable to disturbance, so tread as lightly as you are able and respect both the plants and the habitat. In many areas most orchids are protected, especially if they are in state or national parks—do not be tempted to pick or dig up the plants!

Trips in late May and early June are usually best for the spring species in much of the area, while late June and early July are best for the northern communities. The summer months in the north from July to early August are best for the fringed orchis species and on into September for the myriad of ladies'-tresses. Many of the areas are popular with tourists and require advance reservations to ensure accommodations. If you are photographing, bring twice as much film as you plan to use or ample memory cards for your digital camera. Purchasing the film you want may not always be a possibility while on the road. The weather is bound to be variable but a hat and sunscreen are almost always in order. In the wetlands insects may abound so come prepared. Enjoy the regional cuisines and customs and meet wonderful local people who are often more than happy to either grant permission to cross their lands or guide you to a special spot. Stop and talk with the local populace. They will appreciate it.

# *What Next?*

Although it may seem that all the orchids that grow in the Northeast have been found, there is still plenty of searching and discovering to be done. Apart from finding new sites for well-established species, rediscovering several species that have not been seen in many years in specific states is an opportunity for adventure:

*Amerorchis rotundifolia*, small round-leaf orchis: historical in New York, Vermont, and New Hampshire
*Calypso bulbosa* var. *americana*, eastern fairy slipper: historical in New York and New Hampshire
*Cleistes divaricata*, large spreading pogonia: sparingly present in New Jersey
*Corallorhiza striata*, striped coralroot: a single extant site in New York, several historical sites
*Corallorhiza wisteriana*, Wister's coralroot: historical in New Jersey
*Cypripedium candidum*, small white lady's-slipper: few populations in New York and New Jersey; historical in Pennsylvania
*Cypripedium parviflorum* var. *parviflorum*, southern small yellow lady's-slipper: many historical populations in southern New England and New York; all plants of yellow lady's-slippers in suitable habitat need careful examination
*Goodyera oblongifolia*, giant rattlesnake orchis: few remaining populations in Maine; abundant habitat in northern New Hampshire, Vermont, and New York
*Goodyera repens*, lesser rattlesnake orchis: historical in Connecticut
*Gymnadeniopsis nivea*, snowy orchis: historical in southern New Jersey
*Isotria medeoloides*, small whorled pogonia: many historical locations especially in New York
*Malaxis bayardii*, Bayard's adder's-mouth: many historical locations in southern New England, New York, New Jersey, and Pennsylvania; all plants of *M. unifolia* in suitable habitat need to be carefully examined
*Platanthera cristata*, orange crested orchis: single population in Massachusetts; abundant habitat exists in coastal southern New England; historical in Pennsylvania
*Platanthera leucophaea*, eastern prairie fringed orchis: historical in New York and Pennsylvania
*Spiranthes magnicamporum*, Great Plains ladies'-tresses: historical in Pennsylvania
*Spiranthes odorata*, fragrant ladies'-tresses: New Jersey? if present, needs confirmation
*Spiranthes praecox*, giant ladies'-tresses: New Jersey? if present, needs confirmation

# *Appendix 1. Distribution of the Orchids of New England, New York, Pennsylvania, New Jersey*

h= historical; ?= unsubstantiated report; *= non-native

| | Maine | N.H. | Vt. | Mass. | Conn. | R.I. | N.Y. | Pa. | N.J. |
|---|---|---|---|---|---|---|---|---|---|
| *Amerorchis rotundifolia*, small round-leaf orchis | X | Xh | Xh | | | | Xh | | |
| *Aplectrum hyemale*, putty-root | | | X | X | X | | X | X | X |
| *Arethusa bulbosa*, dragon's-mouth | X | X | X | X | X | X | X | X | X |
| *Calopogon tuberosus*, common grass-pink | X | X | X | X | X | X | X | X | X |
| *Calypso bulbosa* var. *americana*, eastern fairy slipper | X | Xh | X | | | | Xh | | |
| *Cleistes divaricata*, large spreading pogonia | | | | | | | | | X |
| *Coeloglossum viride* var. *virescens*, long-bracted green orchis | X | X | X | X | X | X | X | X | X |
| *Corallorhiza maculata* var. *maculata*, spotted coralroot | X | X | X | X | X | X | X | X | X |
| *Corallorhiza maculata* var. *occidentalis*, western spotted coralroot | X | X | X | X | | | X | | |
| *Corallorhiza odontorhiza* var. *odontorhiza*, autumn coralroot | X | X | X | X | X | Xh | X | X | X |
| *Corallorhiza odontorhiza* var. *pringlei*, Pringle's autumn coralroot | | | X | X | X | | X | | |
| *Corallorhiza striata*, striped coralroot | | | | | | | X | | |
| *Corallorhiza trifida*, early coralroot | X | X | X | X | X | | X | X | |
| *Corallorhiza wisteriana*, Wister's coralroot | | | | | | | | X | Xh |
| *Cypripedium acaule*, pink lady's-slipper | X | X | X | X | X | X | X | X | X |
| *Cypripedium arietinum*, ram's-head lady's-slipper | X | X | X | X | Xh | | X | | |
| *Cypripedium candidum*, small white lady's-slipper | | | | | | | X | Xh | X |
| *Cypripedium parviflorum* var. *parviflorum*, southern small yellow lady's-slipper | | | | X | X | X | X | | X |

*Continued*

*Continued*—Appendix 1. Distribution of the Wild Orchids of New England, New York, Pennsylvania, and New Jersey

| | Maine | N.H. | Vt. | Mass. | Conn. | R.I. | N.Y. | Pa. | N.J. |
|---|---|---|---|---|---|---|---|---|---|
| *Cypripedium parviflorum* var. *makasin*, northern small yellow lady's-slipper | X | X | X | X | | | X | X | X |
| *Cypripedium parviflorum* var. *pubescens*, large yellow lady's-slipper | X | X | X | X | X | X | X | X | X |
| *Cypripedium reginae*, showy lady's-slipper | X | X | X | X | | | X | X | X |
| *Epipactis atrorubens*, red helleborine* | | | X | | | | | | |
| *Epipactis helleborine*, broad-leaved helleborine* | X | X | X | X | X | X | X | X | X |
| *Galearis spectabilis*, showy orchis | X | X | X | X | X | Xh | X | X | X |
| *Goodyera oblongifolia*, giant rattlesnake orchis | X | | | | | | | | |
| *Goodyera pubescens*, downy rattlesnake orchis | X | X | X | X | X | X | X | X | X |
| *Goodyera repens*, lesser rattlesnake orchis | X | X | X | X | Xh | | X | X | |
| *Goodyera tesselata*, checkered rattlesnake orchis | X | X | X | X | X | X | X | X | X |
| *Gymnadeniopsis clavellata* var. *clavellata*, little club-spur orchis | X | X | X | X | X | X | X | X | X |
| *Gymnadeniopsis clavellata* var. *ophioglossoides*, northern club-spur orchis | X | X | X | | | | X | | |
| *Gymnadeniopsis integra*, yellow fringeless orchis | | | | | | | | | X |
| *Gymnadeniopsis nivea*, snowy orchis | | | | | | | | | Xh |
| *Isotria medeoloides*, small whorled pogonia | X | X | Xh | X | X | X | Xh | X | X |
| *Isotria verticillata*, large whorled pogonia | X | X | X | X | X | X | X | X | X |
| *Liparis liliifolia*, lily-leaved twayblade | | Xh | X | X | X | Xh | X | X | X |
| *Liparis loeselii*, Loesel's twayblade | X | X | X | X | X | X | X | X | X |

*Continued*—Appendix 1. Distribution of the Wild Orchids of New England, New York, Pennsylvania, and New Jersey

| | Maine | N.H. | Vt. | Mass. | Conn. | R.I. | N.Y. | Pa. | N.J. |
|---|---|---|---|---|---|---|---|---|---|
| *Listera australis*, southern twayblade | | | X | | | | X | X | X |
| *Listera convallarioides*, broad-lipped twayblade | X | X | X | | | | X | | |
| *Listera cordata*, heart-leaved twayblade | X | X | X | X | Xh | Xh | X | X | |
| *Listera smallii*, Small's twayblade | | | | | | | | X | X |
| *Malaxis bayardii*, Bayard's adder's-mouth | | | | X | Xh | Xh | X | X | Xh |
| *Malaxis brachypoda*, white adder's-mouth | X | X | X | X | | | X | X | |
| *Malaxis unifolia*, green adder's-mouth | X | X | X | X | X | X | X | X | X |
| *Platanthera aquilonis*, northern green bog orchis | X | X | X | X | X | X | X | X | X |
| *Platanthera blephariglottis*, northern white fringed orchis | X | X | X | X | X | X | X | X | X |
| *Platanthera ciliaris*, orange fringed orchis | | | | Xh | X | X | X | X | X |
| *Platanthera cristata*, orange crested orchis | | | | X | | | X | Xh | X |
| *Platanthera dilatata*, white bog orchis; bog candles | X | X | X | X | X | | X | X | X |
| *Platanthera flava* var. *flava*, southern tubercled orchis | | | | | | | | | X |
| *Platanthera flava* var. *herbiola*, northern tubercled orchis | X | X | X | X | X | X | X | X | X |
| *Platanthera grandiflora*, large purple fringed orchis | X | X | X | X | X | X | X | X | X |
| *Platanthera hookeri*, Hooker's orchis | X | X | X | X | X | Xh | X | X | X |
| *Platanthera huronensis*, green bog orchis | X | X | X | X | X | X | X | X | X |
| *Platanthera lacera*, green fringed orchis; ragged orchis | X | X | X | X | X | X | X | X | X |
| *Platanthera leucophaea*, eastern prairie fringed orchis | X | | | | | | Xh | Xh | |
| *Platanthera macrophylla*, Goldie's pad-leaved orchis | X | X | X | X | | Xh | X | X | |
| *Platanthera obtusata*, blunt-leafed rein orchis | X | X | X | Xh | | | X | | |

*Continued*

*Continued*—Appendix 1. Distribution of the Wild Orchids of New England, New York, Pennsylvania, and New Jersey

| | Maine | N.H. | Vt. | Mass. | Conn. | R.I. | N.Y. | Pa. | N.J. |
|---|---|---|---|---|---|---|---|---|---|
| *Platanthera orbiculata*, pad-leaved orchis | X | X | X | X | X | X | X | X | X |
| *Platanthera peramoena*, purple fringeless orchis | | | | | | | | X | X |
| *Platanthera pallida*, pale fringed orchis | | | | | | | X | | |
| *Platanthera psycodes*, small purple fringed orchis | X | X | X | X | X | X | X | X | X |
| *Pogonia ophioglossoides*, rose pogonia | X | X | X | X | X | X | X | X | X |
| *Spiranthes casei*, Case's ladies'-tresses | X | X | X | | | | X | X | |
| *Spiranthes cernua*, nodding ladies'-tresses | X | X | X | X | X | X | X | X | X |
| *Spiranthes lacera* var. *lacera*, northern slender ladies'-tresses | X | X | X | X | X | X | X | X | X |
| *Spiranthes lacera* var. *gracilis*, southern slender ladies'-tresses | X | X | X | X | X | X | X | X | X |
| *Spiranthes laciniata*, lace-lipped ladies'-tresses | | | | | | | | | X |
| *Spiranthes lucida*, shining ladies'-tresses | X | X | X | X | X | Xh | X | X | |
| *Spiranthes magnicamporum*, Great Plains ladies'-tresses | | | | | | | | Xh | |
| *Spiranthes ochroleuca*, yellow ladies'-tresses | X | X | X | X | X | X | X | X | X |
| *Spiranthes odorata*, fragrant ladies'-tresses | | | | | | | | | ? |
| *Spiranthes praecox*, giant ladies'-tresses | | | | | | | | | ? |
| *Spiranthes ovalis* var. *erostellata*, northern oval ladies'-tresses | | | | | | | | X | |
| *Spiranthes romanzoffiana*, hooded ladies'-tresses | X | X | X | X | Xh | | X | X | |
| *Spiranthes tuberosa*, little ladies'-tresses | | | | X | X | X | X | X | X |
| *Spiranthes vernalis*, grass-leaved ladies'-tresses | | Xh | | X | X | X | X | X | X |
| *Tipularia discolor*, crane-fly orchis | | | | X | | | X | X | X |
| *Triphora trianthophora*, three birds orchid | X | X | X | X | X | | X | X | X |

# *Appendix 2. Flowering Times for the Orchids of New England, New York, Pennsylvania, New Jersey*

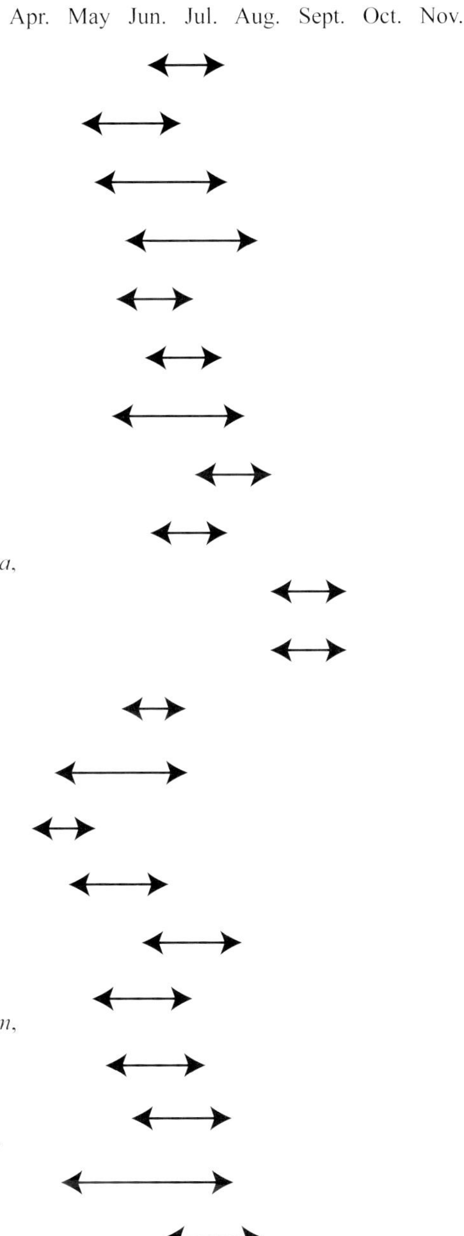


*Amerorchis rotundifolia*,
small round-leaf orchis

*Aplectrum hyemale*,
putty-root, Adam-and-Eve

*Arethusa bulbosa*,
dragon's-mouth

*Calopogon tuberosus*,
common grass-pink

*Calypso bulbosa* var. *americana*,
eastern fairy slipper

*Cleistes divaricata*,
large spreading pogonia

*Coeloglossum viride* var. *virescens*,
long-bracted green orchis

*Corallorhiza maculata* var. *maculata*,
spotted coralroot

*Corallorhiza maculata* var. *occidentalis*,
western spotted coralroot

*Corallorhiza odontorhiza* var. *odontorhiza*,
autumn coralroot

*Corallorhiza odontorhiza* var. *pringlei*,
Pringle's autumn coralroot

*Corallorhiza striata*,
striped coralroot

*Corallorhiza trifida*,
early coralroot

*Corallorhiza wisteriana*,
Wister's coralroot

*Cypripedium acaule*,
pink lady's-slipper

*Cypripedium arietinum*,
ram's-head lady's-slipper

*Cypripedium candidum*,
small white lady's-slipper

*Cypripedium parviflorum* var. *parviflorum*,
southern small yellow lady's-slipper

*Cypripedium parviflorum* var. *makasin*,
northern small yellow lady's-slipper

*Cypripedium parviflorum* var. *pubescens*,
large yellow lady's-slipper

*Cypripedium reginae*,
showy lady's-slipper

*Continued*

*Continued*—Appendix 2. Flowering Times for the Orchids of New England, New York, Pennsylvania, New Jersey

Apr. May Jun. Jul. Aug. Sept. Oct. Nov.

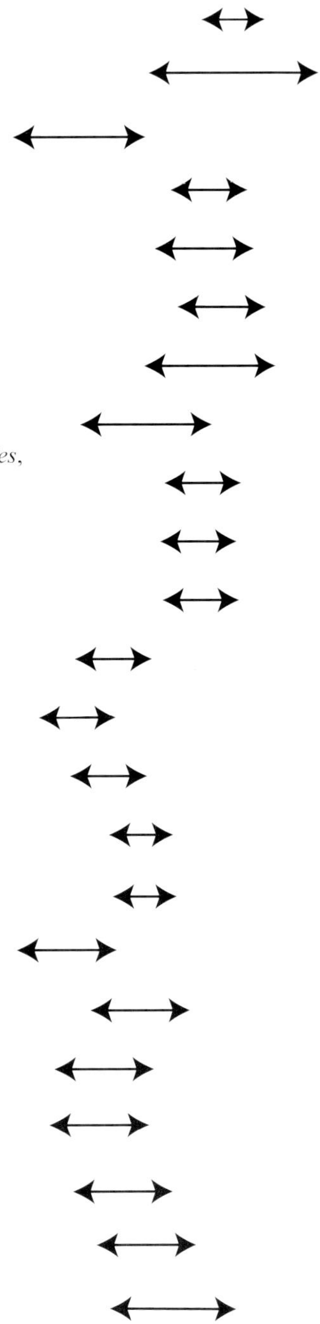

*Epipactis atrorubens*,
red helleborine*

*Epipactis helleborine*,
broad-leaved helleborine*

*Galearis spectabilis*,
showy orchis

*Goodyera oblongifolia*,
giant rattlesnake orchis

*Goodyera pubescens*,
downy rattlesnake orchis

*Goodyera repens*,
lesser rattlesnake orchis

*Goodyera tesselata*,
checkered rattlesnake orchis

*Gymnadeniopsis clavellata* var. *clavellata*,
little club-spur orchis

*Gymnadeniopsis clavellata* var. *ophioglossoides*,
northern club-spur orchis

*Gymnadeniopsis integra*,
yellow fringeless orchis

*Gymnadeniopsis nivea*,
snowy orchis

*Isotria medeoloides*,
small whorled pogonia

*Isotria verticillata*,
large whorled pogonia

*Liparis liliifolia*,
lily-leaved twayblade

*Liparis loeselii*,
Loesel's twayblade

*Listera auriculata*,
auricled twayblade

*Listera australis*,
southern twayblade

*Listera convallarioides*,
broad-lipped twayblade

*Listera cordata*,
heart-leaved twayblade

*Listera smallii*,
Small's twayblade

*Malaxis bayardii*,
Bayard's adder's-mouth

*Malaxis brachypoda*,
white adder's-mouth

*Malaxis unifolia*,
green adder's-mouth

*Continued*

*Continued*—Appendix 2. Flowering Times for the Orchids of New England, New York, Pennsylvania, New Jersey

Apr. May Jun. Jul. Aug. Sept. Oct. Nov.

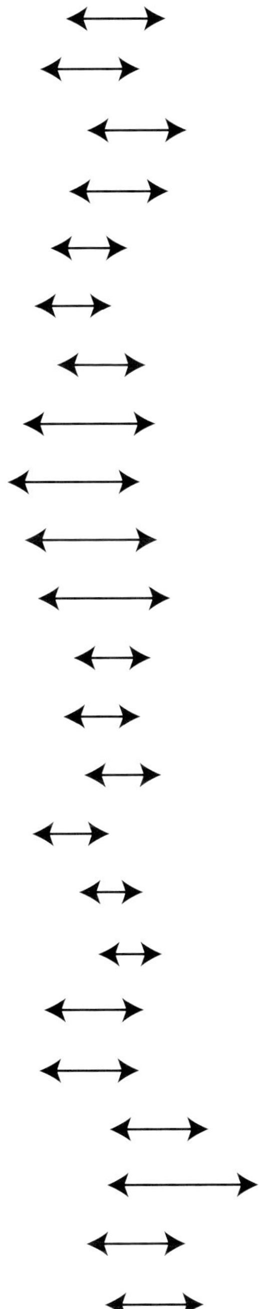

*Platanthera aquilonis*, northern green bog orchis

*Platanthera blephariglottis*, northern white fringed orchis

*Platanthera ciliaris*, orange fringed orchis

*Platanthera cristata*, orange crested orchis

*Platanthera dilatata*, white bog orchis; bog candles

*Platanthera flava* var. *flava*, southern tubercled orchis

*Platanthera flava* var. *herbiola*, northern tubercled orchis

*Platanthera grandiflora*, large purple fringed orchis

*Platanthera hookeri*, Hooker's orchis

*Platanthera huronensis*, green bog orchis

*Platanthera lacera*, green fringed orchis; ragged orchis

*Platanthera leucophaea*, eastern prairie fringed orchis

*Platanthera macrophylla*, Goldie's pad-leaved orchis

*Platanthera obtusata*, blunt-leafed rein orchis

*Platanthera orbiculata*, pad-leaved orchis

*Platanthera peramoena*, purple fringeless orchis

*Platanthera pallida*, pale fringed orchis

*Platanthera psycodes*, small purple fringed orchis

*Pogonia ophioglossoides*, rose pogonia

*Spiranthes casei*, Case's ladies'-tresses

*Spiranthes cernua*, nodding ladies'-tresses

*Spiranthes lacera* var. *lacera*, northern slender ladies'-tresses

*Spiranthes lacera* var. *gracilis*, southern slender ladies'-tresses

*Continued*

*Continued*—Appendix 2. Flowering Times for the Orchids of New England, New York, Pennsylvania, New Jersey

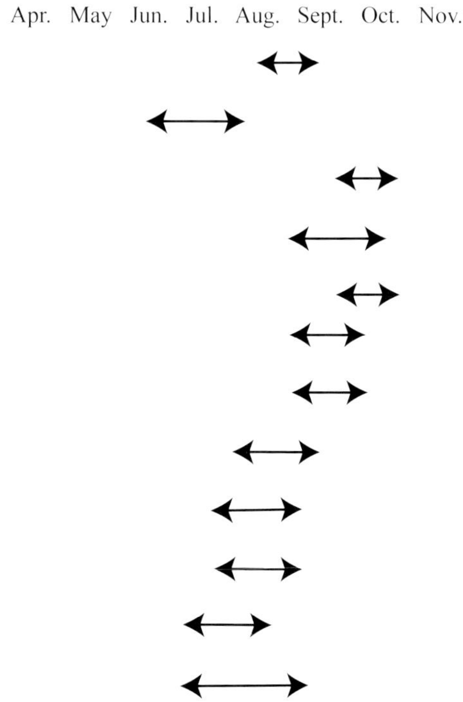


*Spiranthes laciniata*,
lace-lipped ladies'-tresses

*Spiranthes lucida*,
shining ladies'-tresses

*Spiranthes magnicamporum*,
Great Plains ladies'-tresses

*Spiranthes ochroleuca*,
yellow ladies'-tresses

*Spiranthes odorata*,
fragrant ladies'-tresses

*Spiranthes praecox*,
giant ladies'-tresses

*Spiranthes ovalis* var. *erostellata*,
northern oval ladies'-tresses

*Spiranthes romanzoffiana*,
hooded ladies'-tresses

*Spiranthes tuberosa*,
little ladies'-tresses

*Spiranthes vernalis*,
grass-leaved ladies'-tresses

*Tipularia discolor*,
crane-fly orchis

*Triphora trianthophora*,
three birds orchid

# *Appendix 3. The Orchid Publications of Philip E. Keenan*

Philip E. Keenan with *Platanthera* ×*keenanii*; Newfoundland, 1997

Philip E. Keenan (1928–2001) was one of the most dedicated students and photographers of North American native orchids. The majority of his publications pertained to the Northeast. Below is a complete listing of his prolifically illustrated orchid articles.

1986. *Field Guide to the Orchids of Maine*. Freeport, Maine: DeLorme.

1986. New stations for *Platanthera flava* and *Triphora trianthophora* and other observations. *Rhodora* 88: 409–12.

1986. Wild orchids in New England. *American Orchid Society Bulletin* 55(7): 696–99.

1987. The bloom sequence of wild orchids in New England. *American Orchid Society Bulletin* 56(10): 1059–61.

1988. *Calypso bulbosa*: hider of the north. *American Orchid Society Bulletin* 57(4): 375–77.

1988. Progress report on *Isotria medeoloides*. *American Orchid Society Bulletin* 57(6): 624–26.

1989. Butterflies of the orchid world. *American Orchid Society Bulletin* 58(8): 767–71.

1989. The wonderful world of *Cypripedium. American Orchid Society Bulletin* 58(5): 450–55.
1990. Documentation of the longevity of *Goodyera pubescens* leaves and update on *Triphora trianthophora* in New Hampshire. *Rhodora* 92: 126–28.
1990. The big little green orchids. *American Orchid Society Bulletin* 59(3): 228–33.
1990. The pigtails of the orchid world. *American Orchid Society Bulletin* 59(7): 683–87.
1991. The American orchises. *American Orchid Society Bulletin* 60(6): 536–38.
1991. The mighty pogonias. *American Orchid Society Bulletin* 60(4): 338–41.
1992. A new form of *Triphora trianthophora* (Swartz) Rydberg and part three of observations on the ecology of *Triphora trianthophora* (Orchidaceae) in New Hampshire. *Rhodora* 94: 38–42.
1992. Grass-pinks. *American Orchid Society Bulletin* 61(4): 343–47.
1993. Thoreau's orchids. *American Orchid Society Bulletin* 62(4): 363–71.
1994. Pretty in pink. *American Orchid Society Bulletin* 63(3): 250–55.
1994. The coral-roots. *American Orchid Society Bulletin* 63(5): 512–17.
1995. California ladies. *American Orchid Society Bulletin* 64(3): 234–39.
1995. Diversity in *Cypripedium acaule. North American Native Orchid Journal* 1(3): 201–10.
1996. Further observations on *Triphora trianthophora*: part 4. *North American Native Orchid Journal* 2(3): 196–209.
1997. The L & M's. *North American Native Orchid Journal* 3(4): 368–76.
1998. Orchids in Alaska. *Orchids* 67(6): 600–5.
1998. 3rd Annual North American Native Orchid Conference field trips, July 10 & 11, 1998. *North American Native Orchid Journal* 4(3): 285–88.
1998. *Wild Orchids Across North America: a botanical travelogue.* Portland, Ore.: Timber Press.
1999. Home on the prairie. *Orchids.* 68(4): 358–61.
2000. A short history of the genus *Cypripedium. North American Native Orchid Journal* 5(1): 29–42.

# *Glossary*

adventive: non-native
alvar: expanses of horizontal limestone pavement with thin soils, few trees, and grasses
anterior: front or upper
anthesis: time of flowering
apomictic: fertilized within the embryo without pollination; an asexual means of reproduction
appressed: placed tightly against; opposite of divergent
approximate: pertaining to flowers, lying close by but not overlapping
auricle: ear-like appendage
autogamous: one of several means of self-pollination
axillary: on the side
basal rosette: a cluster of leaves all arising at the base of the plant
bract: a modified leaf
calcareous: derived from limestone, limey
calciphile: a lime lover
callus: a thickened area, usually at the base of the lip
capitate: like a head; "with capitate hairs" refers to hairs with ball-like tips
carnivorous: insect eating
cauline: on the stem
chasmogamous: with fully opened, usually sexual, flowers
chlorophyll: a green pigment manufactured by the plant and essential for photosynthesis
ciliate: with short, slender hairs
circumneutral: a pH of about 6.5
clavate: club-shaped
cleistogamous: with closed flowers that are usually self-pollinating
cline: a gradual change in a character or feature across the distributional range of a species or population, usually correlated with an environmental or geographic transition
column: the structure in an orchid that has both the anthers and the pistil
conduplicate: folded lengthwise
coralloid: coral-like
cordate: heart-shaped

coriaceous: leathery
corymb: a determinate inflorescence with all of the branches the same length and the outer flowers opening first
crenulate: with a short, wavy margin
crest: a series of ridges or a group of hairs; usually yellow or a color contrasting with the lip
cyme: a determinate inflorescence with the central flowers opening first
dentate: toothed
determinate: with a specific ending, not continuing to grow indefinitely
dilated: broadened
disjunct: occurring apart from the normal range of the species
distal: away from the center or main body, or pertaining to the underside
divergent: spreading or widely separated
dorsal sepal: the sepal opposite the lip, usually uppermost in most orchids
emarginate: with a short projection at the tip
endemic: native to a specific area
ephemeral: appearing for a brief time, often a few weeks each season
epiphyte, epiphytic: living in the air
erose: with an irregular margin
extant: still in existence
extirpated: no longer in existence
extralimital: occurring on the very edge of the species' normal range
falcate: sickle-shaped
filiform: slender and thread-like
foliaceous: leaf-like, as in foliaceous bracts (bracts that are leaf-like in appearance)
forma: a taxonomic rank that indicates a recognizable variation from the norm usually in either color or form of growth, e.g., white-flowered forms
glabrous: smooth
glaucous: with a whitish cast
habit: form or mode of growth; e.g., upright, or sprawling
habitat: the particular environment of a plant
hemi-epiphyte: usually growing on the base of trees or on logs
hybrid: the result of a sexual crossing of two different parents; indicated with a multiplication sign (×) either before the species name or between the names of the two parents
hydric: pertaining to perennially wet habitat
isthmus: a narrowed portion, often at the base of the lip
keel: a ridge
lacerate: slashed
lateral sepals: the sepals positioned on the side of the flower

lax: (flowers) loosely arranged
lip: the modified third petal of an orchid
lithophytic: growing on rocks
madder: dusky-purple color
marcescent: withering but not falling off
marl: a calcareous or limey wetland
mentum: a short, rounded, thickened projection formed by the base of the petals; similar to a spur but not tapered to a point
mesic: moisture condition intermediate between wet and dry
monotypic (genus): a genus having only one species
mucronate: a short, sharp point
mycotrophic: obtaining food through mycorrhizal fungi, which are attached to roots
naturalized: a non-native species reproducing in its adopted habitat
Neotropical: New World tropics
nominate, nominate variety: the pure species or variety, exclusive of subspecies, variety, or form
non-resupinate: with only a single twist so the lip is at the top
oblanceolate: narrowly oblong
obovate: broadly oblong
orbicular: rounded
orifice: opening
ovary: the female structure that produces the seed
panicle: a branching inflorescence similar to a raceme, with stalked flowers
pedicellate flowers: those flowers held on pedicels or stalks
pedicellate ovary. with ovary and flower stalk merged into one structure, typical of orchids
peduncle: stalk of a flower
perianth: combined petals and sepals of the flower
petiole: stem portion of the leaf
plicate: soft and with many longitudinal ribs, often folded
pollinia: the structure in orchids that contains the pollen
posterior: lower or rear
pseudobulb: a swollen storage organ prominent in many epiphytic orchids and occasionally in a few genera of terrestrial orchids
puberulent: with a fine dusting of very short, soft hairs
pubescent, pubescence: downy with short, soft hairs
putative: assumed, but not scientifically proven, in reference to hybrid parentage
raceme: unbranched, indeterminate inflorescence with stalked flowers; branched racemes are technically panicles
rank: arrangement of flowers in lines or vertical rows, especially in *Spiranthes*

reflexed: bent backward
reniform: kidney-shaped
resupinate: twisted around so that the lip is lowermost
rhizome: an elongated basal stem, typically underground in terrestrials and along the strata (tree trunks, branches, rocks, etc.) in epiphytes
rhombic: with parallel sides but tapered on both ends
rostellum: the part of the column, usually beak-shaped, that contains the stigmatic surface and to which the pollen adheres
saccate: sack-shaped
saprophytic, saprophyte: living off decaying vegetable matter
scape: a leafless stem that arises from the base of the plant
secund: all to one side
segregate genus (species): a genus or species that has been separated from another genus or species
senesces: withers
sepals: outer floral envelope
sessile: without a stem or stalk
spatulate: oblong with a narrowed base
sphagnous: of or pertaining to sphagnum moss
spike: an unbranched inflorescence with sessile or unstalked flowers
spiranthoid: a *Spiranthes* or member of a genus closely allied to *Spiranthes*
spur: a slender, tubular or sac-like structure usually formed at the base of the lip, and often containing nectar
striate, striations: with stripes
subtend: beneath the flower at the point of attachment to the stem
sympatric: growing together in the same habitat
taxon, *pl.* taxa: particular taxonomic classification; i.e., subspecies, variety, species, form
tepal: sepals and petals of similar morphology
terete: rounded
terminal: at the end
transverse: growing horizontally (as opposed to parallel) to the axis (or stem)
tubercle: a thickened projection
umbel: an inflorescence with flower stems all arising from the same point like the spokes of an umbrella
undulate: wavy
waif: a random individual occurrence
whorl: arranged in a circle around the same point on the stem
xeric: perennially dry habitat

# Bibliography


Ames, O. 1906. *Habenaria orbiculata* and *Habenaria macrophylla. Rhodora* 8: 1–5.

———. 1924. *An Enumeration of the Orchids of the United States and Canada.* Boston: American Orchid Society.

Andrew, L. 1924. *Flora of Springfield, Massachusetts.* Springfield: Museum of Natural History.

Angelo, R., and D. E. Bufford. 2000. Atlas of the Flora of New England: Monocots part 3. *Rhodora* 102(909): 1–119.

———. 2005. *Atlas of the Flora of New England: Monocots.* http://neatlas.huh.harvard.edu/Neatlas2/MonoFam-L-O.html

Baldwin, H. 1884. *The Orchids of New England.* New York: John Wiley and Sons.

Bateman, R. M., A. Pridgeon, and M. W. Chase. 1997. Phylogenetics of subtribe Orchidinae based on nuclear ITS sequences. 2. Intergeneric relationships and taxonomic revision to achieve monophyly of *Orchis* sensu stricto. *Lindleyana* 12: 113–41.

Bigelow, J. 1824. *Florula Bostoniensis.* Boston: Cummings, Hillard and Co.

Blewitt, A. E. 1926. *Flora of Waterbury, Conn., and Vicinity.* Lancaster, Pa.: Science Press Printing.

Brackley, F. E. 1985. The orchids of New Hampshire. *Rhodora* 87(849): 1–117.

Blake, S. F. 1963. *The Flora of Stoughton, Massachusetts.* Cambridge: New England Botanical Club.

Brainerd, E., L. R. Jones, and W. W. Eggleston. 1900. *Flora of Vermont*: a list of the fern and seed plants growing without cultivation. Vermont Botanical Club. Burlington: Free Press Association.

Brown, P. M. 1978. Hidden jewels. *Yankee* 39(5): 50–55.

———. 1988. Stalking the wild orchids. *Wild Flower Notes* 3(1): 4–29.

———. 1992. *Platanthera pallida* (Orchidaceae), a new species of fringed orchis from Long Island, New York, USA. *Novon* 2(4): 308–11.

———. 1993a. *A Field and Study Guide to the Orchids of New England and New York.* Jamaica Plain, Mass.: Orchis Press.

———. 1993b. An annotated checklist of the orchids of the Northeastern United States—New England and New York. *Schlecteriana* 4: 174–92.

———. 1997. Taxonomy and distribution of *Spiranthes casei* Catling & Cruise in northern New England. Master's thesis, University of Massachusetts-Dartmouth.

———. 2002. Resurrection of the genus *Gymnadeniopsis* Rydberg. *North American Native Orchid Journal* 8: 32–40.

———. 2002. Revalidation of *Platanthera conspicua. North American Native Orchid Journal* 8: 3–14.

Brown, P. M., and S. N. Folsom. 1997. *Wild Orchids of the Northeastern United States.* Ithaca, N.Y.: Cornell University Press.

———. 2002. *Wild Orchids of Florida.* Gainesville: University Press of Florida.

———. 2003. *The Wild Orchids of North America, North of Mexico.* Gainesville: University Press of Florida.

———. 2004. *Wild Orchids of the Southeastern United States, North of Peninsular Florida.* Gainesville: University Press of Florida.

———. 2005. Additions and emendations to *The Wild Orchids of North America, North of Mexico. Sida* 21(4): 2297–319.

———. 2006. *Wild Orchids of the Canadian Maritimes and Northern Great Lakes Region.* Gainesville: University Press of Florida.

Burrage, A. 1921. *Notes on Native New England Orchids.* Privately published.

Cameron, J. W. 1976. *The Orchids of Maine.* Orono: University of Maine.

Campbell, C. S., and L. M. Eastman. 1980. *Flora of Oxford County, Maine.* Technical Bulletin 99. Orono: Life Sciences and Agricultural Experiment Station, University of Maine.

Campbell, C. S., H. P. Adams, P. Adams, A. C. Dibble, L. M. Eastman, S. C. Gawler, L. L. Gregory, B. A. Grunden, A. D. Haines, K. Jonson, S. C. Rooney, T. F. Vining, J. E. Weber, and W. A. Wright. 1995. Checklist of the Vascular Plants of Maine, 3rd rev. Bulletin 844. Orono: Maine Agricultural and Forest Experiment Station, University of Maine.

Case, F. W. 1964. A hybrid twayblade and its rarer parent, *Listera auriculata*, in northern Michigan. *Michigan Botanist* 3: 67–70.

———. 1983. *Platanthera ×vossii*, A new natural hybrid orchid from northern lower Michigan. *Michigan Botanist* 22: 141–44.

Catling, P. M. 1976. On the geographical distribution, ecology and distinctive features of *Listera ×veltmanii* Case. *Rhodora* 78(814): 261–69.

———. 1978. Taxonomic notes on *Spiranthes casei* Catling & Cruise and *S. ×intermedia* Ames. *Rhodora* 80: 377–89.

———. 1981. Taxonomy of autumn-flowering *Spiranthes* species of southern Nova Scotia. *Canadian Journal of Botany* 59: 1253–70.

———. 1989. Biology of North American representatives of the subfamily Spiranthoideae. In *North American Native Terrestrial Orchid Propagation and Production.* Chadds Ford, Pa.: Brandywine Conservancy.

———. 1991. Systematics of *Malaxis bayardii* and *M. unifolia. Lindleyana* 6: 3–23.

Catling, P. M., and V. Catling. 1994. Identification of *Platanthera lacera* hybrids from New Brunswick and Nova Scotia. *Lindleyana* 9: 19–32.

Catling, P. M., and J. E. Cruise. 1974. *Spiranthes casei*, a new species from northeastern North America. *Rhodora* 76(808): 526–36.

Catling, P. M., and Z. Lucas. 1987. The status of *Calopogon tuberosus* var. *latifolius* with comments on the application of varietal rank. *Rhodora* 89: 401–13.

Catling, P. M., and V. Brownell. 1999. *Platanthera lacera × leucophaea*, a new cryptic natural hybrid, and a key to northeastern North American fringed-orchids. *Canadian Journal of Botany* 77(8): 1144–49.

Catling, P. M., V. Brownell, and G. Allen. 1999. A new natural hybrid fringed-orchid from Ontario. *Lindleyana* 14(2): 77–86.

Catling, P. M., and C. J. Sheviak. 1993. Taxonomic notes on some North American orchids. *Lindleyana* 8(2): 80–81.

Chapman, W. K. 1997. *Orchids of the Northeast*. Syracuse: Syracuse University Press.

Church, G. L., and R. L. Champlin. 1978. *Rare and Endangered Vascular Plant Species in Rhode Island*. Newton Corner, Mass.: New England Botanical Club in cooperation with U.S. Fish and Wildlife Service.

Cobb, N. A. 1887. *A List of Plants Found Growing Wild within Thirty Miles of Amherst*. Northhampton, Mass.: S. E. Bridgman.

Coddington, J., and K. G. Field. 1978. *Rare and Endangered Vascular Plant Species in Massachusetts*. Newton Corner, Mass.: New England Botanical Club in cooperation with U.S. Fish and Wildlife Service.

Correll, D. S. 1950. *Native Orchids of North America*. Waltham, Mass.: Chronica Botanica.

Countryman, W. D. 1978. *Rare and Endangered Vascular Plant Species in Vermont*. Newton Corner, Mass.: New England Botanical Club in cooperation with U.S. Fish and Wildlife Service.

Crow, G. E. 1982. *New England's Rare, Threatened, and Endangered Plants*. Washington, D.C.: U.S. Department of the Interior, Fish and Wildlife Service, in cooperation with the New Hampshire Agricultural Experiment Station, University of New Hampshire.

Cutter, V. M., Jr. ca. 1940. New Hampshire Orchids. Unpublished manuscript.

Dame, L. L. 1888. *Flora of Middlesex County, Massachusetts*. Malden, Mass.: Middlesex Institute.

Dole, E. J., ed. 1937. *The Flora of Vermont*, 3d rev. ed. Burlington, Vt.: Free Press Printing.

Deane, W. 1891. The native orchids of New England. *The American Gardener* 12: 152–57.

———. 1896. *Flora of the Blue Hills, Middlesex Fells, Stony Brook and Beaver Brook Reservations of the Metropolitan District Commission, Mass*. Boston: C. M. Barrows.

Dowhan, J. J. 1979. *Preliminary Checklist of the Vascular Flora of Connecticut*. Report of Investigations no. 8. Hartford: State Geological and Natural History Survey of Connecticut.

Eastman, L. M. 1978. *Rare and Endangered Vascular Plant Species in Maine*. Newton Corner, Mass.: New England Botanical Club in cooperation with U.S. Fish and Wildlife Service.

———. 1988. *Calopogon tuberosus* var. *latifolius* (Saint-John) Boivin (Orchidaceae) new to the United States. *Rhodora* 90(861): 101.

Eastman, L., R. L. Hinkle, and D. M. Dumond. 1982. A new station for *Goodyera oblongifolia* Raf. in northern Maine. *Rhodora* 84(838): 311–13.

Eaton, R. J. 1974. *A Flora of Concord*. Cambridge: Harvard University, Museum of Comparative Zoology.

Eckel, P. M. 2001. A revised checklist of the vascular plants of the Niagara Frontier region. Flora of the Niagara Frontier Region, third supplement. *Bulletin of the Buffalo*

*Society of Natural Science* 16, suppl. 3. http://www.mobot.org/plantscience/ResBot/flor/WNY-Niag/WNYCheck.htm

Effron, M., and E. C. Briggs. 1986. Rediscovery of *Isotria verticillata* (Willdenow) Rafinesque (Orchidaceae) in Vermont. *Rhodora* 88(855): 407–8.

Fernald, M. L. 1950. *Gray's Manual of Botany*, 8th ed. New York: American Book Co.

[FNA] Flora of North America Editorial Committee, eds. 1993. *Flora of North America, North of Mexico*. Vol. 26, *Orchidaceae*. New York: Oxford University Press.

Flynn, N. 1935. *Flora of Burlington and vicinity : a list of the fern and seed plants growing without cultivation*, 2nd ed. Burlington, Vt.: Free Press Printing.

Freudenstein, J. V. 1986. A preliminary study of *Corallorhiza maculata* (Orchidaceae) in eastern North America. *Contributions from the University of Michigan Herbarium* 16: 145–53.

———. 1997. A monograph of *Corallorhiza* (Orchidaceae). *Harvard Papers in Botany* 10: 5–51.

Garay, L. A. 1982. A generic revision of the Spiranthinae. *Botanical Museum Leaflet of Harvard University* 28(4): 277–425.

Gibson, W. H. 1905. *Our Native Orchids*. New York: Doubleday, Page and Co.

Gleason, H. A. 1952. *The New Britton and Brown Illustrated Flora of the Northeastern United States and Adjacent Canada*. Bronx: New York Botanical Garden.

Gleason, H. A., and A. Cronquist. 1963. *Manual of Vascular Plants of Northeastern United States and Adjacent Canada*. New York: D. Van Nostrand.

———. 1991. *Manual of Vascular Plants of Northeastern United States and Adjacent Canada*, 2nd ed. Bronx: New York Botanical Garden.

Gould, L. A., R. W. Enser, R. L. Champlin, and I. H. Stuckey. 1998. *Vascular Flora of Rhode Island: A List of Native and Naturalized Plants*. Kingston: Rhode Island Natural History Survey.

Graves, C. B. 1910. *Catalogue of the flowering plants and ferns of Connecticut growing without cultivation*. Committee of the Connecticut Botanical Society. Hartford: State Geological and Natural History Survey.

*International Code of Botanical Nomenclature* (St. Louis Code). Prepared and edited by W. Greuter, J. McNeill, F. R. Barrie, H.-M. Burdet, V. DeMoulin, T. S. Filgueiras, D. H. Nicolson, P. C. Silva, J. E. Skog, P. Trehane, N. J. Turland, and D. L. Hawksworth. 2000. *Regnum Vegetabile* 138. http://www.bgbm.fu-berlin.de/iapt/nomenclature/code/SaintLouis/0000St.Luistitle.htm.

Haines, A., and T. F. Vining. 1998. *Flora of Maine: A Manual for Identification of Native and Naturalized Vascular Plants of Maine*. Bar Harbor: V. F. Thomas.

Harris, S. K. 1975. *The Flora of Essex County, Massachusetts*. Salem, Mass.: Peabody Museum.

Henry, L. K., and W. E. Buker. 1855. Orchids of Western Pennsylvania. *Annals of the Carnegie Museum* 33: 299–346.

Henry, L. K., W. E. Buker, and D. L. Pearth. 1975. Western Pennsylvania orchids. *Castanea* 40: 93–178.

Hervey, E. W. 1860. *A Catalogue of the Plants found in New Bedford and its vicinity; arranged according to the season of their flowering*. New Bedford, Mass.: E. Anthony.

———. 1891. *Flora of New Bedford, and the Shores of Buzzard's Bay, with a Procession of the Flowers*. New Bedford, Mass.: E. Anthony and Sons.
———. 1911. *Flora of New Bedford, and the Shores of Buzzard's Bay, with a Procession of the Flowers*. New Bedford, Mass.: E. Anthony and Sons.
Heshka, L. 2003. Field identification of the *Platanthera hyperborea* complex in Manitoba. *Native Orchid News* 5(4): 00.
Hoffman, R. 1922. Flora of Berkshire County, Massachusetts. *Proceedings of the Boston Society of Natural History* 36(5): 171–382.
[IPNI] International Plant Names Index. 2004. http://www.ipni.org/index.html
Johnson, L. P. 1995. A new color form of *Amerorchis rotundifolia* from the Sibley Peninsula of Lake Superior. *Lindleyana* 10(1): 1.
Kallunki, J. A. 1976. Population studies in *Goodyera* (Orchidaceae) with emphasis on the hybrid origin of *G. tesselata*. *Brittonia* 28: 53–75.
Kartesz, J. T. 1994. *A synonymized checklist of the vascular flora of United States, Canada and Greenland*, 3rd ed. Chapel Hill: North Carolina Botanical Garden.
Kartesz, J. T., and C. A. Meacham, eds. 1999. *Synthesis of the North American Flora*, ver. 1.0. Chapel Hill: North Carolina Botanical Garden.
Keenan, P. E. 1983. *A Complete Guide to Maine's Orchids*. Freeport: DeLorme.
———. 1992. A new form of *Triphora trianthophora* (Orchidacaeae). *Rhodora* 94: 38–39.
———. 1999. *Wild Orchids across North America*. Portland, Ore.: Timber Press.
Lamont, E. E. 1996. Atlas of the orchids of Long Island, New York. *Bulletin of the Torrey Botanical Club* 123: 157–66.
Lamont, E. E., I. M. Beitel, and R. E. Zaremba. 1988. Current status of orchids on Long Island. *Torreya* 115(2): 113–21.
Livingston, R. B. 1963. *Flora of Western New England*. Amherst: University of Massachusetts.
Loomis, M. L. 1917. *The Ferns and Flowering Plants of Sherborne, Massachusetts, Growing Without Cultivation*. Sherborne: M. L. Loomis.
Luer, C. A. 1975. *The Native Orchids of the United States and Canada excluding Florida*. Bronx: New York Botanical Garden.
MacKeever, F. C. 1968. *Native and Naturalized Plants of Nantucket*. Amherst: University of Massachusetts Press.
Magee, D. W., and H. E. Ahles. 1999. *Flora of the Northeast: A Manual of the Vascular Flora of New England and Adjacent New York*. Amherst: University of Massachusetts Press.
Mehrhoff, L. J. 1978. *Rare and Endangered Vascular Plant Species in Connecticut*. Newton Corner, Mass.: New England Botanical Club in cooperation with U.S. Fish and Wildlife Service.
Mitchell, R. S., and G. C. Tucker. 1997. Revised checklist of New York State plants. Bulletin 490. Albany: New York State Museum.
Mitchell, R. S., C. J. Sheviak, and J. K. Dean. 1980. *Rare and endangered vascular plant species in New York State*. Albany: State Botanist's Office, New York State Museum.
Morris, F., and E. Eames. 1929. *Our Wild Orchids*. New York: Charles Scribner's Sons.

Munden, C. 2001. *Native Orchids of Nova Scotia*. Sydney, Nova Scotia: University College of Cape Breton Press.

Muenscher, W. C. 1946. The vegetation of Bergen Swamp. I. The vascular plants. *Proceedings of the Rochester Academy of Science* 9: 64–117.

Niles, G. G. 1904. *Bog Trotting for Orchids*. New York: G. P. Putnam's Sons.

Nylander, O. O. 1935. *Our Northern Orchids*. Presque Isle, Maine: Star-Herald Publishing.

Pease, A. S. 1964. *A Flora of Northern New Hampshire*. Cambridge, Mass.: New England Botanical Club.

Petrie, W. 1981. *Guide to the Orchids of North America*. Blaine, Wash.: Hancock House.

Platt, J. L., E. Yanuck-Platt, and C. J. Sheviak. 1986. A new station for *Listera auriculata* (Orchidacae) in New York State. *Rhodora* 84(840): 547–49.

Pridgeon, A. M., R. M. Bateman, A. V. Cox, J. R. Hapeman, and M. W. Chase. 1997. Phylogenetics of subtribe Orchidinae based on nuclear ITS sequences. 1. Intergeneric relationships and polyphyly of *Orchis* sensu latu. *Lindleyana* 12(2): 89–109.

Pridgeon, A. M., P. J. Cribb, M. W. Chase, and F. Rasmussen, eds. 2005. *Genera Orchidacearum*. Volume Four: *Epidendroideae*, Part I. New York: Oxford University Press.

Radis, R. 1985. New Jersey orchids: lost and found. *New Jersey Audubon* 11(1): 14–15.

———. 1997. Exalted vegetables. *North American Native Orchid Journal* 3(4): 453–71.

Reddoch, A. H., and J. M. Reddoch. 1993. The species pair *Platanthera orbiculata* and *P. macrophylla* (Orchidaceae): taxonomy, morphology, distributions and habits. *Lindleyana* 8(4): 171–87.

Rydberg, P. A. 1901. *Gymnadeniopsis* Rydberg. In Britton, *Manual of the Flora of the Northeastern United States*, p. 293.

Scoggin, H. J. 1978. *The Flora of Canada*, part 2. Natural Science Publications in Botany 7. Ottawa: National Museum of Canada.

Seymour, F. C. 1969. *The Flora of Vermont*. Bulletin 660. Burlington: University of Vermont, Agricultural Experiment Station.

———. 1982. *The Flora of New England*, 2nd ed. Phytologia Memoirs 5. Plainfield, N.J.: Moldenke.

Sheviak, C. J. 1982. Biosystematic Study of the *Spiranthes cernua* Complex. Bulletin 448. Albany: New York State Museum.

———. 1991. Morphological variation in the compilospecies *Spiranthes cernua* (L.) L.C. Rich.: ecologically limited effects of gene flow. *Lindleyana* 6(4): 228–34.

———. 1995. *Cypripedium parviflorum* Salisbury part 2: the larger flowered plants and patterns of variation. *American Orchid Society Bulletin* 64(6): 606–12.

———. 1999. The identities of *Platanthera hyperborea* and *P. huronensis*, with the description of a new species from North America. *Lindleyana* 14: 193–203.

Sheviak, C. S., and P. M. Catling. 1980. The identity and status of *Spiranthes ochroleuca*. *Rhodora* 82: 525–62.

Shute, F. 1981. Orchids of New Jersey. *New Jersey Audubon* 7(2): 24–25.

Sorrie, B. A. 1987. Notes on the rare flora of Massachusetts. *Rhodora* 89(858): 113–96.

Stone, G. E. 1913. *A List of Plants Growing without Cultivation in Franklin, Hampshire and Hampden Counties, Massachusetts*. Amherst, Mass.: Press of Carpenter and Morehouse.

Stone, W. 1910–11. *The Plants of Southern New Jersey*. Reprint, Boston: Quarterman Publications, 1973.

Storks, I. M., and G. E. Crow. 1978. *Rare and Endangered Vascular Plants of New Hampshire*. Newton Corner, Mass.: New England Botanical Club in cooperation with U.S. Fish and Wildlife Service.

Stoutamire, W. P. 1974. Relationships of purple fringed orchids *Platanthera psycodes* and *P. grandiflora*. *Brittonia* 26: 42–58.

Svenson, H. K., and R. W. Pyle. 1979. *The Flora of Cape Cod*. Brewster, Mass.: Cape Cod Museum of Natural History.

Szlachetko, D. L. 1995. Systema Orchidalium. *Fragmenta Floristica Geobotanica* Supplement 3: 121–22.

Vickery, B. 1981. The Rare Flora of Aroostook County, Maine. Unpublished manuscript. Lewiston, Maine: Bates College.

Wallace, J. E. 1951. *The Orchids of Maine*. Orono: University of Maine.

Wallace, L. E. 2002. An evaluation of taxonomic boundaries in *Platanthera dilatata* (Orchidaceae). *Rhodora* 105(924): 322–36.

———. 2003. Molecular evidence for allopolyploid speciation and recurrent origins In *Platanthera huronensis* (Orchidaceae) *International Journal of Plant Science* 164(6): 907–16.

———. 2004. A comparison of genetic variation and structure in the allopolyploid *Platanthera huronensis* and its diploid progenitors, *Platanthera aquilonis* and *Platanthera dilatata* (Orchidaceae). *Canadian Journal of Botany* 82: 244–52.

———. 2006. Spatian genetic structure and frequency of interspecific hybridization in *Platanthera aquilonis* and *P. dilatata* (Orchidaceae) occurring in sympatry. *American Journal of Botany* 93(7): 1001-9.

Whiting, R. E., and P. M. Catling. 1986. *Orchids of Ontario*. Ottawa: CanaColl Foundation.

Weatherbee, P. B. 1990. *Flora of Berkshire County, Massachusetts*. Master's thesis, University of New Hampshire, Durham.

———. 1996. *Flora of Berkshire County, Massachusetts*. Pittsfield, Mass.: Berkshire Museum.

Weldy, T., and D. Werier. 2005. New York Flora Atlas. Albany: New York Flora Association. http://atlas.nyflora.org/

Wherry, E. T., J. M. Fogg Jr., and H. A. Wahl. 1979. *Atlas of the Flora of Pennsylvania*. Philadelphia: Morris Arboretum of the University of Pennsylvania.

Williams, J. G., A. E. Williams, and N. Arlott. 1983. *A Field Guide to Orchids of North America*. New York: Universe Books.

Young, S. M. 1998. *New York Natural Heritage Program Rare Plant Status List*. Latham: New York Natural Heritage Program.

Zander, R. H., and G. J. Pierce. 1979. Flora of the Niagara Frontier Region: second supplement and checklist. *Bulletin of the Buffalo Society of Natural Science* 16, suppl. 2.

Zenkert, C. A. 1934. Flora of the Niagara Frontier Region. *Bulletin of the Buffalo Society of Natural Science* 16.

Zenkert, C. A., and R. H. Zander. 1975. Flora of the Niagara Frontier Region, supplement. *Bulletin of the Buffalo Society of Natural Science* 16, suppl. 1.

# *Photo Credits*

All photographs were taken by Paul Martin Brown, except for the following, which were generously loaned by those credited.

Heinz Baum, *Amerorchis rotundifolia* forma *beckettiae*
Shirley Curtis, *Amerorchis rotundifolia* forma *immaculata*, forma *lineata*
Lorne Heshka, *Amerorchis rotundifolia* forma *rosea*
Chelsea Kieffer, *Platanthera aquilonis* forma *alba*
Larry Magrath, *Cypripedium parviflorum* var. *parviflorum* forma *albolabium*
Brian Podlisny, *Malaxis bayardii* forma *kelloggiae*
Bill Summers, *Platanthera peramoena* forma *doddsiae*
Francis Underwood, X*Platanthopsis vossii*
Ian Ward, *Amerorchis rotundifolia* forma *wardii*

# Index

Primary entries for taxa are in **bold**.
Photographs are in *italics*

Paul Martin Brown is a research associate at the University of Florida Herbarium at the Florida Museum of Natural History in Gainesville and the Botanical Research Institute of Texas. He is the founder of the North American Native Orchid Alliance and the *North American Native Orchid Journal.* Brown and his partner, Stan Folsom, have published *Wild Orchids of the Northeastern United States* (1997), *Wild Orchids of Florida* (UPF, 2002), *The Wild Orchids of North America, north of Mexico* (UPF, 2003), *Wild Orchids of the Southeastern United States North of Peninsular Florida* (UPF, 2004), *Wild Orchids of Florida*, revised and expanded edition (UPF, 2005), *Wild Orchids of the Canadian Maritimes and Northern Great Lakes Region* (UPF, 2006), *Wild Orchids of the Pacific Northwest and Canadian Rockies* (UPF, 2006), and *Wild Orchids of the Prairies and Great Plains Region* (UPF, 2006).

Stan Folsom is a retired art teacher and botanical illustrator. His primary medium is watercolor, and his work is represented in several permanent collections, including that of the Federal Reserve Bank of Boston.

Related-interest titles from University Press of Florida

*The Bottlenose Dolphin: Biology and Conservation*
John E. Reynolds, III, Randall S. Wells, and Samantha D. Eide

*Entanglements: The Intertwined Fates of Whales and Fishermen*
Tora Johnson

*Florida Wildflowers in Their Natural Communities*
Walter Kingsley Taylor

*Guide and Reference to the Amphibians of Eastern and Central North America (North of Mexico)*
Richard D. Bartlett and Patricia Bartlett

*Guide and Reference to the Crocodilians, Turtles, and Lizards of Eastern and Central North America (North of Mexico)*
Richard D. Bartlett and Patricia Bartlett

*Guide and Reference to the Snakes of Eastern and Central North America (North of Mexico)*
Richard D. Bartlett and Patricia Bartlett

*Journeys Through Paradise: Pioneering Naturalists in the Southeast*
Gail Fishman

*Some Kind of Paradise: A Chronicle of Man and the Land in Florida*
Mark Derr

*Visions for the Next Millennium: Clyde Butcher Wilderness Photography—Focus on Preservation*
Clyde Butcher

*Wild Orchids of Florida, with References to the Atlantic and Gulf Coastal Plains*
Paul Martin Brown

*The Wild Orchids of North America, North of Mexico*
Paul Martin Brown

*Wild Orchids of the Southeastern United States, North of Peninsular Florida*
Paul Martin Brown with drawings by Stan Folsom

*Wild Orchids of the Canadian Maritimes and Northern Great Lakes Region*
Paul Martin Brown with drawings by Stan Folsom

*Wild Orchids of the Pacific Northwest and Canadian Rockies*
Paul Martin Brown with drawings by Stan Folsom

*Wild Orchids of the Prairies and Great Plains Region of North America*
Paul Martin Brown with original artwork by Stan Folsom

For more information on these and other books, visit our website at www.upf.com.